RETIRING IN TURBULENT TIMES

Nine Middle-American Stories of Life, Money, and Challenges in Pursuit of a Satisfying Retirement

With Commentary and
Common Sense Advice from

SCOTT WARDELL, CFP®

with journalist **BRIAN LAMBERT**

ISBN: 978-0-9899982-3-9 (print)
        978-0-9899982-4-6 (ebook)

Library of Congress Control Number: 2013950882

Published by Orchard Press
Minneapolis, MN

Table of Contents

Introduction

Contrary to so much of what you hear, it is still possible to retire and retire well in modern America. What I hope to get across in this book is that while our turbulent modern world has thrown up some serious obstacles in recent years, a person of average means can still live out their retirement happily and without constant financial anxiety. But ... and this is the twist ... you may very well retire *differently* than you imagined through your working years.

The Great Recession has reshuffled the deck for even the most well-prepared. More to the point, after 30 years in the business of financial planning, which is all about dealing with and adjusting to uncertainty, the one thing I can tell you – with absolute certainty – is that most people are not well-prepared for retirement.

Most people, at least those who come to me and other financial advisors, have tried to prepare themselves. They want to be prepared. And I commend them for that. But they're not where they need to be.

One of the great, sad ironies in my business is that so often the people who most need my services are too embarrassed to seek them out. It's an ego thing. They are afraid they'll be embarrassed at having saved and planned so little, or fear they'll be talked down to, or the adviser jargon will fly over their heads and they'll feel stupid.

Many, even otherwise savvy businessmen and women, worry that a candid conversation with a professional about their financial decisions will tear back some kind of curtain, revealing for all the world to see, their bumbling mismanagement of an important facet of their lives.

Fear not, good reader.

Just like there are doctors with abominable bedside manners, there are financial advisors lacking in basic human empathy. I've known a few, believe me. Most of them are now selling cars or lawn treatments. To sustain yourself in my business you have to both understand, and *like* people, at least as much as you understand mutual funds, stocks and annuities and enjoy the challenges of money management.

If your clients think you're talking down to them, you're not succeeding.

My late father wasn't a big rules and order guy. But one thing he taught us kids was the value of a pleasant and relaxed personality. Whether in family, business or social life, being relaxed, informal, and friendly is a vital virtue in getting to genuinely *know* people. That attitude will set a tone for this book. I'll do everything I can to avoid the bewildering jargon and let the stories illuminate issues you've probably thought of. I suspect you'll see yourself in some if not all of the people interviewed here.

I'm in business to help people achieve their financial goals. I get very real, personal, emotional satisfaction out of helping people develop strategies that help to make the most of what they have, no matter where they are in their lives.

So this isn't a book where I go off the deep end and inflate myself as some kind of guru hero. The point of the format is to let you relate to financial situations not unlike yours.

I decided to write this book because I've been talking to so many people whose lives have been jumbled by The Great Recession. Some watched as pensions disappeared. Others as investments tanked, or as jobs evaporated late in their careers.

Even being well-prepared doesn't cover something as profound and disorienting as the financial meltdown we experienced. The picture is improving. But – in my humble opinion, given the competition from economies like China and India, the cost of energy and a heightened vigilance to sustainable budgets on the part of almost everyone from families to corporations to every level of government – it'll be *many* years before the consumer feels anything like the "irrational exuberance" of the bubble years of the early 2000s.

Times have changed. Maybe for the better when all is said and done if you consider the debt so many of us lugged around.

If you need proof that you are not alone in worrying about what has happened since September 2008, here are some stark statistics: According to an NORC Center for Public Affairs Research survey, one-third of the respondents stopped putting money into 401(k) s, IRAs, or any other retirement account. One-third. Perhaps worse, 20% drew money out of their accounts to the point that a quarter of the people surveyed say they have postponed retirement. Fully 14% said they expect to work into their 70s, if they are able[1].

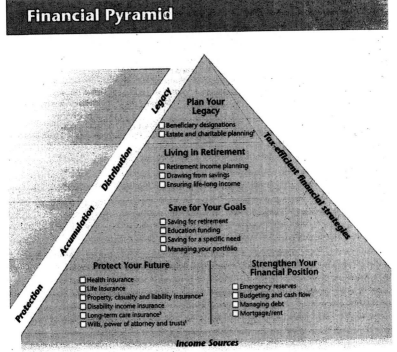

Financial Pyramid

Legacy
Plan Your Legacy
☐ Beneficiary designations
☐ Estate and charitable planning

Living in Retirement
☐ Retirement income planning
☐ Drawing from savings
☐ Ensuring life-long income

Save for Your Goals
☐ Saving for retirement
☐ Education funding
☐ Saving for a specific need
☐ Managing your portfolio

Protect Your Future
☐ Health insurance
☐ Life insurance
☐ Property, casualty and liability insurance
☐ Disability income insurance
☐ Long-term care insurance
☐ Wills, power of attorney and trusts

Strengthen Your Financial Position
☐ Emergency reserves
☐ Budgeting and cash flow
☐ Managing debt
☐ Mortgage/rent

Distribution
Accumulation
Protection
Tax-efficient financial strategies
Income Sources

Source: Thrivent Financial, last modified 2015,
https://www.thrivent.com

With that in mind, I will be hammering pretty hard a few basic themes that are simply vital to helping you achieve what you want in your retirement. One of these points is the importance of considering long-term care insurance as a large aspect of risk management in your retirement; this topic is addressed several times in the book and can't be understated.

Far too few people calculate accurately the cost of caring for a disabled love one in the way they want to care for them. Likewise, they fail to fully imagine the impact of caring for that person will have on their life and the lives of their children.

So bear with me while I re-re-visit the long-term care issue.

A concept you'll be hearing plenty about is "financial imprinting". What I mean by this is the creation of the habit of thinking about the resources you have and how you want to handle them. The earlier you accept "financial imprinting" as a vital habit to acquire and hone, the better you'll be. By reading this book you're demonstrating a desire to educate yourself on better ways to handle your money.

So, congratulations. Your imprinting education is off to a good start.

You will also hear me talk about "The Five Ss," a concept developed at Thrivent Financial[2]. Books like this have a way of drowning in their own jargon, but I really am trying to make this easy to understand.

You have to be honest with yourself about where you're at, not just where you'd like to be or where you want others to think you are. Everyone would like to be rich. Most people aren't. But if they deny the reality of their current situation, it is almost impossible to create a plan to move them toward a comfortable, secure retirement.

So, "The Five Ss" are as follows:

1. **Surviving.** This is not a good situation. It means your time horizon for financial stability is basically – today. You're asking yourself, "How do I get through this day?" Your situation is dire. But you need to accept that and do the necessary work to improve.

2. **Struggling.** The Great Recession of 2008 found too many people living paycheck to paycheck. Their time horizon is maybe two weeks, providing there are no catastrophic events. Again, the situation is tense and stressful. But a candid

conversation, with yourself and, hopefully, a professional, can mean a plan to minimize the worst of the moment.

3. **Stable.** This is most people. You're not going to go under. You have some resources. A job. A home. Savings. Some investments. Maybe a pension. Your time horizon probably extends out into the next year.

4. **Secure.** This is a good place to be and a reasonable goal for most Americans finishing their primary working career. You are beyond stable. You have assets to cover the basic bills and can do at least some of the things you've always wanted to do. No one will confuse you with Bill Gates, but you're in a good position.

5. **Surplus and Sharing.** Pretty much self-explanatory. You've done well enough financially that you have more than you need to live out the rest of your life. You can consider not just the things you've always wanted to do – travel and new experiences – but you're in a position to be a philanthropist, should that be your preference. Nice going.

My experiences have led me to believe most people with a plan have the resources to get to "Stable." My experiences have also led me to believe that getting "Stable" serves as a reasonable baseline goal for opening the door to financial success.

"The Five Ss" lead directly into another key notion. And that is the concept of "threshold". What I mean by this is the point where you make key financial decisions. It is different for everyone. But I've been struck over the years by how many people misjudge their threshold because they don't fully understand their financial situation.

Some people are very conservative, and think they never have enough money to buy a new car or take a trip to Hawaii, when they probably do if they gave themselves an honest evaluation and fully understood their finances.

Others ... well there are plenty of people who believe their threshold for free-spending is a lot lower than it really is. Believe me, I've had to put on my best paternal voice in those cases.

But the point is for you to know where your threshold is based on real world knowledge of your financial situation, instead of guesswork, wishful thinking, or hunches.

Another concept discussed in this book is that of "buckets" i.e., the distinction between different reservoirs of assets – cash reserves, investments with rate/investment guarantees (safer, low-risk, lower gain investments), growth (higher risk, potentially higher gain) and income (part-time work, pensions, dividend paying investments, etc.). It's important to have a properly balanced mix of buckets and know when to move assets from one bucket into another.

We will probably live in a volatile financial world for some time to come.

I won't lay all this out right here. But the concept of these interactive "buckets" can be boiled down to this: You need three. A cash reserve bucket, an income bucket, and a growth bucket. Everyone's circumstances are different, so these three "buckets" will be adjusted. But the framework remains the same.

I am not an expert on the macro-economics of government. But this on-going volatility has us in a chronic situation where our markets go into regular panic/feeding frenzies with everyone running to the same side of the ship to buy and to sell. This sort of herd mentality is what flips ships over on their keel. You want to be smarter than the frenzied stampede.

Throughout the book you'll hear about the essential and emotional facet of managing your money: keep cool. The ability to keep calm and stay rational – when so many others are racing back and forth like headless chickens – is an invaluable virtue.

When all is said and done, you want your retirement planning to have placed you in a livable, stable position at the very worst. When one of my clients tells me they're unhappy with their outcomes, I ask them to give their unhappiness a grade on a 1-to-10 scale, with 10 being the worst possible outcome, like losing your home, for example.

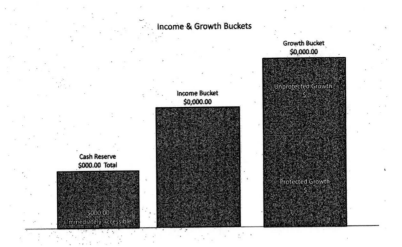

Income & Growth Buckets

If the plan we created didn't reap a windfall bonanza like they dreamed of, but they are comfortable, their unhappiness index is maybe only a "1" or a "2." If they are at a point where they want to retire and can't because the markets are completely backwards and the plan wasn't designed for that, they are very unhappy campers, in the range of a "9," and I can't blame them.

I believe you will recognize yourself in one or more of the people you'll meet in this book. Their situations, predicaments, and adjustments to the "new normal" we're living in today are as familiar to me as my next-door neighbors

There is another interesting facet of the Baby Boom-era retirement. It may be completely separate from the turbulence of 2008.

As I talk with my clients about the nuts and bolts, the decimal points, and percentages in their portfolios, I also find myself talking with them about their dreams and desires, about the things they want to do while they are young and healthy enough to do them. What I hear back often surprises me.

A facet of being too embarrassed to "reveal yourself" to a financial adviser is the matter of never revealing how you want to spend your retirement. If you're wracked with anxiety over finances, convinced you'll be destitute, it's not likely you've let yourself dream, imagining life after the office. But you need to verbalize the dream.

We've all seen the commercial with the guy scoffing at being told he'll retire to his own vineyard, right? Well, I've been struck by how few solid, diligent professionals ever stop and think about *exactly what* they'll do when they stop punching in every day. And by "exactly" I mean "realistically". What is within your grasp? Travelling the country by RV with your spouse and friends? A condo in Tucson? A lavish, four-star Grand Tour of the French Riviera? Being actively involved with a charity or community organization?

The point is to stop and think about what you're building this financial plan for, beyond just paying bills. The assets and the dream go together. Getting real about one helps the design and execution of the other.

Too many people have stunted their own imagination. They distrust their own planning or are overwhelmed by the chaos of The Great Recession. They don't allow themselves to take what should be a pleasant day-dream walk.

That's a shame. Because a good day-dream can lead to a real-world plan, and realistic planning is easier than ever to do in today's interconnected world. Every hobby, avocation, destination, like-minded interest group, community and charitable organization is accessible at the click of a mouse. Access to those kinds of networks and opportunities simply didn't exist even 15 years ago when most of us were hip-deep in our jobs.

There's a very poignant scene in the Jack Nicholson movie, *About Schmidt*. Nicholson's character, Warren Schmidt, is retiring as an actuary from a big insurance company in Omaha. His wife soon dies. He isn't as close as he would like to be to his adult daughter. He's a diligent, orderly man. His work has been his life. As a dependable bureaucrat he's extraordinarily proud of his files. To him they're a trove. A couple days after his perfunctory going away party, he's walking by his company's loading dock, where he sees his files ... *his files!* ... boxed up and set out for recycling/trash. He's heartsick[3].

I've had clients, and I've met people – too many – who were way too much like Nicholson's suddenly at-a-loss-of-purpose Warren Schmidt. They gave everything to their work. They had successful careers. But they never really stopped and thought about what they were going to do when the job ended.

The conversations that make up this book were chosen to offer a balance of corporate climbers and executives, aggressive entrepreneurs, frugal (and spend-thrifty) school teachers, do-it-yourself blue collar workers, self-taught inventors and such. They are as I say, "average"

Americans dealing with the same pressures of economic turbulence, misinformation, luck, bad luck, procrastination and time as you and me.

As I say, I've been in the financial business for 30 years. But talking again with the people you're about to meet, some clients, some old friends, some family, surprised me by how it clarified facets of my own thinking and connected others.

My hope is it does as much for you.

Enjoy, and relax. With a little information, imagination and adjustment, you'll be fine.

–Scott Wardell CFP[4]

Notes

1. NORC at the University of Chicago, last modified
July 2, 2015, http://www.norc.org/Pages/default.aspx

2. Thrivent Financial, last modified 2015, https://www.thrivent.com

3. *About Schmidt*, directed by Alexander Payne (New York, NY: New Line Cinema, 2002).

4. Certified Financial Planner Board of Standards Inc. owns the certification marks CFP, CERTIFIED FINANCIAL PLANNER CFP (with plaque design) and CFP (with flame design) in the U.S., which it awards to individuals who successfully complete CFP Board's initial and ongoing certification requirements.

Chapter 1

Irrational Exuberance

My old friend's real name is not "Tim." In fact, unlike all the other stories here, Tim is not even a client of mine. What he is, however, is someone I've known since we were kids and whose business savvy I continue to admire, despite the story you are about to read.

As a mortgage broker, Tim was pretty much at Ground Zero for the real estate collapse of the late 2000s. In many ways he was a classic front-line character of the whole disaster. His experience, up close and very personal, is both illuminating and instructive for people who find themselves consumed by a seemingly successful career, people who feel in control and fully capable of dealing with whatever may come. Success often breeds false security.

Snapshot

- **Age:** 57
- **Marital Status:** Second marriage. Blended family. Four children.
- **Primary career:** Mortgage broker, with law degree.
- **Asset description:** Excluding home formerly multi-million, now a tenth of what they used to be.
- **Specific dilemma:** Had all financial eggs (including career) in one general investment category of real estate as housing market crashed. Spent heavily on lifestyle.
- **Financial Stability Level:** Stable.

I could sense that Tim was a bit apprehensive when we sat down one afternoon to talk through his story. No one enjoys being embarrassed, and even though I promised to hide his identity and even pixilate any images he gave me, he was a bit edgy. "I appreciate the cover," he laughed. "My butt is kind of hanging out here."

For most of his life, Tim's "butt" was in a pretty good place. He's pretty close to the picture of what most people imagine when they think, "Master of the Universe"; a self-assured, good-looking dude with plenty of resources of intelligence, charm, and ambition. It's safe to say that he'd make a success out of anything he did.

He's fifty-seven today, a kid who grew up in suburban Minnesota, southwest of the Twin Cities. His dad knew his way around business and a balance sheet thanks to his career with Green Giant, the big vegetable company. "He wasn't Warren Buffett, but he understood sales and cash flow."

He moved to Kansas City, went to work for a law firm there, got married for the first time, and began sniffing out the action in the mortgage brokerage business. Tim moved back to Minneapolis, content for the moment being an in-house attorney for a large commercial bank. But soon he and his boss at the time decided to bet that a singularly-focused shop they set up could move loans quicker than the big, bank-affiliated chains. And for a long, fat decade and more they were proven right.

After six years in business, in the mid-'90s, Tim's mortgage brokerage was one of the largest of its kind in the Twin Cities.

"It was good enough that I bought out my partner and, well, 2001-2-3-4, that was party time. It was going really well. The game was super-charged. You couldn't get [mortgages] going fast enough."

He kept expanding, ratcheting both the volume of work and the speed of the transactions, moving hundreds of thousands of dollars a day and reaping the rewards for being the guy in the middle of a frenzied action.

But then the trend changed.

Tim's story from that point on is sadly familiar to anyone who follows business news. Law suits began flying, and with the government slowly accepting that a bubble was close to bursting, belated attempts at regulation began rolling over Tim's go-go enterprise. The easy money evaporated. Ironically, says Tim, "There was a large push to move everything back to the banks. The feeling was they were more stable, safer..."

I know what you're thinking. "Big banks. Mortgages. What could go wrong?"

Within the blink of an eye, the business on which Tim had built an enviable lifestyle, complete with a beautiful home, boats, and nice cars crumbled beneath him. In a desperate move to avoid complete financial disaster, he engineered a "sale" to a big bank, for, as he says, "zero."

"Essentially," he says, "it was, 'We'll take over your leases. We'll hire your people, and we'll buy some furniture'. They didn't want to buy the company, because by doing so they would have been buying the liabilities, the legacy exposure that we had. That probably would have been in the $4-$5 million range. So basically a business that I would have valued at $2.5 to $3 million a couple months earlier pretty much dropped down to nothing."

(Scott Wardell) How much of the company did you own when you sold it?

(Tim) Seventy percent.

(Scott Wardell) And what was your situation on a personal level?

(Tim) As a homeowner, I got nailed because we had started building the dream home, a project that went from $1.2 million in construction costs to a valuation of $730,000 when we finally sold it in 2011. And we felt lucky to sell it for that.

///

Hindsight is always 20/20, but as you'll see, so much of the issue with Tim is his inability to slow down enough to evaluate what his real investment was. He, like so many others in his business at that moment, was deep into a very seductive, incredibly fast-paced, highly remunerative game. To slow down in any way was to lose money. To be "traditional," meaning careful and conservative, was to miss out on how the hottest game in town, in the country, was being played.

Tim was really moving fast. He was surrounded in his business culture by a very powerful group-think mentality. Everyone was focused on playing the same game, and everyone had the fruits of their labor, or the spoils of victory right there for everyone to see.

\\

(Tim) Then of course, knowing more than anyone else, I had my stock portfolio in Citicorp, American Home Mortgage, Bank of America. Buy what you know, right?!

///

Someone like Tim, a smart, aggressive guy with this feeling that he's the Master of the Universe, because he's making so much money so fast, is almost beyond reach of a financial advisor, at least someone like me who is there to preach the virtues of building a traditional foundation. He knows now he should have diversified out from his seriously over-weighted financials-based portfolio. But all he could see was how fast the cash was piling up.

\\

(Tim) It was kind of like the perfect storm for me. Between the three—the business, the house and my investments—I told people, "If I used to have a thousand-acre farm, I'm down to a hundred-acre farm today ... with a lame mule."

So right now we're kind of starting over. And that's fine. A lot of people ask, "How are you doing?" And I say, "I'm fine." Because luckily my happiness, my self-worth, my real joy in life is not tied up in the show of big money. It wasn't like I'm any different as a person. I always say, "My wife still loves me and my kids are healthy. What could be wrong?" I can still smell the roses.

(Scott Wardell) But to that point, how much more important does family and a solid emotional footing become when the cash vanishes? When all of a sudden you've got to take stock?

(Tim) My wife and I have always been really close, and strong in our faith. As far as things that really matter, it's kind of like, "That's what I do, not what I am." When you go through something like we have, you don't have much choice but to take stock of what you had then and what you don't have now. The bottom line is there are things they can't ever take away from you.

I never committed a crime. So they can't put me away or anything. It's just a matter of what I've got, what my basic assets are, and what I'm able to do with them. You reload and rebuild.

(Scott Wardell) Did your father ever have a sophisticated talk with you about money?

(Tim) We'd talk about things. The stock market. It was informal. Things one or the other of us observed; how he'd handled situations. I'd seen him in tense arguments with people, negotiations with vendors. Afterwards, when he saw that this ten- or eleven-year-old boy had been watching, he would kind of explain it. That was valuable.

One thing he always said was, "When someone's very angry with you, let him talk it out. Don't try to cut him off. Don't try to say he's wrong. Let him get all the steam out, and *then* you can deal with the issues, once they've played themselves out." Another thing he said was, "Don't take the wind out of anyone's sails. If they're proud about something, and they feel they've achieved something, don't diminish it."

Those are two things off the top of my head that I remember best. Little things about how to lead people, work with people, talk with them, communicate with them, in a way that encourages them and gets them to their goals.

(Scott Wardell) You went to Carleton College and studied history, is that right?

(Tim) Yeah. Dad didn't have a problem with that as long as I was going to law school. I got a Bachelor's from Carleton, then went to law school at the University of Minnesota. My interests at that time were estate planning, but the first job I got was more in corporate litigation.

(Scott Wardell) Looking back, would you say you were you financially adroit?

(Tim) I thought I was more adroit than I was. I started buying stocks in college and law school if I had money saved up.

(Scott Wardell) How did you pick stocks?

(Tim) Just on my own hunches, or a tip from my dad, or a neighbor, or just things that I thought would make sense. But if you look back on it, I either bought too late or sold too soon. There was no professional advice there.

///

Here's the dilemma: Sometimes well-educated, market-watchers fall prey to the "insider trap," thinking that because they're smart and they're talking to other smart, money-wise people they have some kind of exclusive, foolproof line on investments. The irony is that if you get them alone and get their bravado down, they'll admit the modern market is so sophisticated that the average small investor has very little chance of

grabbing a position better than–or before–the major players.

More to the point, the real trap is overvaluing what you know about the industries and markets you are most familiar with. A financial professional like Tim puts himself in a highly precarious position when he pours virtually every nickel he has into the same industry he's drawing his salary from. It is similar to doctors investing in medicine, or computer people pouring too much into the tech industry.

One of the basic guidelines is ... diversification. (even that will not completely protect you from a volatile market.) There's a reason professional advisors have pounded on this concept since the dawn of time. Spread out–which means seeking advice and guidance– and give yourself the possibility of avoiding getting flattened by a mortgage finance bubble, a new medical gizmo from China, or cloud storage that reduces your hard drive stock to half its previous value.

(Scott Wardell) Had either you or your wife set up any automatic savings or investments?

(Tim) No.

I'm struck here that Tim, while working in a banking-related industry behaved so little like a banker, or at least not the classic small-town bankers many of us grew up with. Those people, a little stiff, a little stodgy, and anything but exciting, might have peeled off even a modest percentage of their income for retirement and rainy-day funding.

(Scott Wardell) What were you making when you gave up the job in Duluth and headed back down to Kansas City in the mid-eighties?

(Tim) $13,000! I was rolling in it!

(Scott Wardell) Did you buy a house?

(Tim) We looked, right before we moved [to Minneapolis]. And we found one. A nice little place. $45,000. But the offer didn't get accepted, which was kind of a blessing. So we rented up here [Minneapolis], then bought a house a couple years later.

(Scott Wardell) So you started your own business with the guy you worked with. From scratch. Was there any capital involved?

(Tim) I borrowed $50,000 from my dad.

(Scott Wardell) Did he give you a good interest rate?

(Tim) Ten percent! And he was worried sometimes! Dad's not an idiot! He felt better when I started making principal payments. The $50,000 was to set up shop and start making payroll. The FHA had a $25,000 net worth minimum at that time, before you could do any FHA loans. Our first financial audit, when we needed that $25,000 minimum, came in at $25,400! Yeah, baby!

We struggled for a while in the first couple of years. But then, like I said, things took off and each year we doubled our production.

Finally we brought in another partner who brought in a whole new level of clients and things really started taking off.

///

Borrowing money from relatives, even parents, is very common. But I have to tell you, it can destroy relationships. For that reason, my advice to clients is to examine the situation with a very high level of caution. The trick is how these types of loans are defined. Everyone has to understand the terms. Treat it just as though you were dealing with a bank.

Unless you intend it to be a gift, it's important that you have a shared written document.

I'll tell you a quick personal story. My dad was in his later years when he came to me and told me he had

loaned $50,000 to my brother to build a pole shed. I asked him, "So why are you telling me this?"

"Because you're the executor of the estate and if he doesn't pay me back you need to know that and take it out of his share." This was Dad doing math. I was going to have to deal with it and I needed to know. But I have to confess: Dad did *not* have written documentation. That was the way he did things, but it opened him up to significant risk. It turned out fine and my brother paid him back, but the situation was unnecessarily risky without the common understanding a shared document provides.

Intra-family loans don't have to be complicated. Write up the terms and make copies for everyone involved. It's a peace-of-mind thing for all concerned. You may even want a lawyer to look it over for you.

The other comment I hear a lot is some father saying, "Well, I loaned him the money, but I doubt I'll ever see it again." Well then for God's sake, just give them the money and forget about it! Don't play some game. If it's a gift, it's a gift. If it's a loan, it has terms. Make sure everyone understands them.

And, by the way, there are online templates for precisely this kind of intra-family loan. You can just download it, print it, fill it out, and copy it. Presto.

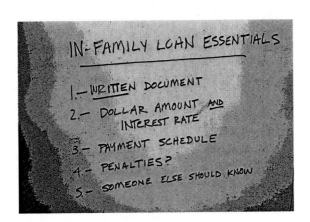

IN-FAMILY LOAN ESSENTIALS

1. — WRITTEN DOCUMENT
2. — DOLLAR AMOUNT AND INTEREST RATE
3. — PAYMENT SCHEDULE
4. — PENALTIES?
5. — SOMEONE ELSE SHOULD KNOW

(Scott Wardell) When the new partner bought in, did that zero out any credit issues you had at the time?

(Tim) No, it just kind of carried us for the next couple of months. But we needed it. It was almost that you could see us getting there; he was the bridge that we needed.

//

Tim was in a pretty high-risk situation here. His was an entirely revenue-based business. When the revenue stopped ... they were out of the game.

But at the point Tim brought in this partner, things were actually looking pretty good. The company was on an upward trajectory. They'd done their math. Their core assumptions–the actual value of the business at that point–were pretty good.

People who find themselves in Tim's situation actually benefit from the no-fun uncle Mr. Stodgy type who asks questions like "Can you build this slower and with less risk?" Such questions, however, are not what people in that fevered business were interested in hearing at that moment in time.

Tim and his team were essentially in the business of paying off one vendor with proceeds from the last. As he described it, they had no choice other than to play the high energy/high turnaround game if they wanted to be competitive and ride the bucking bull as long as they could.

The broader question here is sustainability. Whether you're a farmer, a dentist, or a mortgage broker, ask yourself and methodically assess how much speed and friction your business can take before it blows up.

Cash reserves depend a lot on your cash flow situation. But a basic rule of thumb in terms of personal finances is to have six months' worth of mortgage expenses available to you somewhere – without penalty – should a catastrophe hit.

\\\

(Scott Wardell) I'm curious, how have your business partners fared?

(Tim) The original partner that we started the mortgage business with, after I bought him out, went into a couple of wild ventures. He got into major trouble with the FCC. They didn't really do anything to him except ban him from ever doing anything like it again.

Last time I saw him he was selling cars. But he's not there anymore either. So I don't know where he is. My other partner, the one that came in later and bought in, I eventually bought him out. He had a major personal problem and pretty much lost everything.

He was applying to be a dealer at a casino and anything else he could do. He had one of the most brilliant minds I've ever met. A very charismatic guy.

(Scott Wardell) Personally, what were you doing at the point the partner bought in? Had you bought an insurance policy?

(Tim) I have to think. Probably, but the very minimum.

(Scott Wardell) A life policy to pay off the house?

(Tim) I don't think so. I think we were counting on me living right then. Let me describe the scenario. The first couple years I was literally making piles in my living room. "Here's the appraisers. Here's the rent. Which one is screaming the loudest? Which one can I push off the longest?" It was constant juggling. Dozens of spinning plates. It's a hard lesson in cash- flow management.

(Scott Wardell) At this point you're about thirty?

(Tim) Thirty-three, maybe. Our first son was born in '86. He was born before we started the company. I had no pension, no IRAs. We were just thinking about each day, each month. Retirement wasn't on our minds. It was all about growing the business.

//

Just so we're clear here. Tim was in the classic situation, as the sole earner/high earner. The families of sole earners/high earners are put at significant risk in the event of a death or disability if the insurance is not established because when that high earner is gone, the money is gone, and the spouse and family are on their own.

The touch point for guys like Tim is asking them, "How much do you love your wife?" For healthy individuals, it can be pennies on the dollar to get a million-dollar policy in place. All they really have to do is slow down long enough to sign it.

Is that what I call "core insurance architecture"? No. But it covers a very basic need for people in Tim's situation. A million, two million, even four million can be relatively inexpensive in term life insurance. Other factors advisors talk to people in Tim's situation about are the certainty of cash flow, cash reserves, level of debt and so on.

But that's another casualty of moving so fast that you blow right by some of this *very* important, basic stuff.

\\

(Tim) But the funny thing is, for the twenty years that I had this company, I would say that I lost maybe five nights of sleep.

(Scott Wardell) Is that like saying you basically exhausted yourself during the day to the point you collapsed?

(Tim) Well, not that I was so tired all I could do was fall asleep. It was more like I did what I could do. There wasn't anything more to worry about, to keep you up at night. The biggest worries were like, "We've got $5 million of loans to fund tomorrow, and only $3 million on the credit line. Where am I going get another $2 million so people can move in?"

(Scott Wardell) Two million dollars? That sounds like something I might lose sleep over.

(Tim) It was really a matter of keeping the machinery moving quickly. Everyone was counting on it.

We had a credit line with [a big national bank], and we would sell the loans to [another]. So we'd use the credit line and then send the loan to [the other one]. They'd look at it, make sure it met their standards, would agree to buy it, and they'd wire money to our credit line to pay off the loan. So the faster you could get that process going, the quicker those funds would become available.

///

Money in the U.S. moves very quickly. Much of that is due to our brokering system.

The speed that money was traveling in the U.S. helped to build both the economy of the last decades of the twentieth century and the house of cards that collapsed in '08.

At the micro-level, here's Tim making a lot of money largely because money was moving so fast. Tim was a conduit for the craziness of that era.

\\\\\\\\\\\\\\\\\\\\\\\\\\\\\\\\\\\\\\\

(Tim) We would literally be calling [the second bank] every morning asking, "Who are you gonna pay off today? What about the Adams' loan? Can you pay off that one?" [The lending bank] was a tremendous partner. Their turn time was three or four days. Again, this is back pre-crash.

///

People who are deeply invested in a particular industry benefit from considering that the economy— any economy—has its own planned obsolescence. Businesses, hardware, and services come and go. So if you're in business you have to—*have to*—be asking yourself, "How soon before I'm obsolete?" That is just good business planning. (I remind myself of this frequently.)

> There wasn't much of that kind of thinking in Tim's mind, or the minds of others in his industry. The concept of obsolescence never seemed to have crossed anyone's mind. The money was simply too good. And shelter, i.e. housing, seemed as if it wouldn't be obsolete any time soon.

(Scott Wardell) The big boys had enough confidence in you, in the bubble years before 2000?

(Tim) That was a time when you could see the people socially and it wasn't a conflict of interest. Heck, some of our people were dating some of their people. It was very close. I was good friends with the main guy over at [Tim's major bank]. He kind of built the system up locally and he had a lot of authority. So we had a really good, high-trust relationship.

If they made a mistake and we caught it, we'd let them know, "Hey, you missed this, we're gonna send it back to you." We'd watch each other's back that way. It's changed now. That two- or three-day period is now up to three to four weeks, and there aren't as many lenders out there giving lines of credit.

(Scott Wardell) So you personally were making some good money at this point. You had to be thinking about getting into some long-term investments.

(Tim) Well, that's when we put in a 401(k) plan for the company. It applied to me as well. One of the challenges there was getting enough people buying into it so we weren't top heavy. Other things were, well, not so well planned out. You really start to think you can rule the world because things are going so well. You truly do think you're smarter than you really are.

As for other investments, people would come up and say, "Hey Tim, I got this company over here in Brooklyn Park," or "I got this thing over here in Eden Prairie," [suburbs of Minneapolis] and they were at stage two or three and the Initial Public Offering was coming up around the next corner. You look at it and like the idea, or you trust the guy, so you start putting money in things like that. I did maybe six of those over the years.

(Scott Wardell) What kind of investments were they, exactly?

(Tim) One was a company that built software. You know how with a school computer you can pick sites and block them? This software reversed it and only had allowable sites.

This is actually a good Steve Jobs story.

They went to Microsoft, who wanted to meet with them. But Microsoft then said, "No". So next up was their meeting with Apple. Apple really wanted them. Or so they thought. My guys were thinking, "They're going to come in and offer $10 a share."

The attitude, from these savvy big-leaguers was, "We'll *complain* about it, but, 'Okay, we'll take it.'"

So they went into a meeting, in the boardroom at Cupertino, at Apple, and Jobs had all his attorneys and all the advisors, and he walked into the room and said, "Everyone out," except for the principals of Net-----, I think it was called. So all his minions gathered up their briefcases and left.

When the door closed he turned to our guys and said, "Here's the deal. I know where you're sitting and I know what problems you're having. You're getting fifty cents a share. And that offer is good for ten minutes. I'll step out and you can let my people know when they come back in."

And that was it. End of negotiation. Net----- folded like a cheap card table. Investors like me were out there yelling, "What'd you do that for?" But what choice did they have? I think Apple eventually buried it.

///

The idea of creating a product to sell to some Big Fish company at a fat profit is a pretty familiar dream. But Tim's Steve Jobs story is a great one for illuminating how such dreams often play out.

The lesson here is pretty basic: You have to plan for the worst-case scenario and have a Plan B when the fantasy doesn't bear fruit.

(Scott Wardell) On a more pedestrian level, you did have a 401(k) in place. But what about the rest? It all seems pretty scattershot, sort of whatever grabbed you at the moment?

(Tim) It was pretty much, yeah.

//

There is one component here that Tim understood really well. And that was cash flow with lenders, or maybe a better description would be "leverage". For a time at least, he was a master of managing the ebb and flow of revenue.

\\\

(Scott Wardell) You told me that about this time, back in the early '90s, you did start making a monthly mutual fund contribution.

(Tim) Yeah, I started working with a financial advisor. I got into the thing of dropping $2,000 a month into this mutual fund. That went fine till I had to quit sending them $2,000 a month. Once you stop, it's hard to get back on that again.

(Scott Wardell) And, again, the insurance architecture?

(Tim) There were other people who came around selling some type of investment strategy. But I have to tell you, sometimes I just said, "If it's over my head, or if I think you're talking circles around me, like, we're done."

//

What I think happened here is Tim, a smart guy, probably looked at a ledger statement somewhere along the way that told him he didn't have a break-even point until six or seven years into the policy he was being pitched. In his world, with the kind of money he was turning every couple weeks, six or seven years was glacial and self-hobbling and a tough argument to make.

In the context of basic life insurance architecture, people like Tim avoid these problems by considering a few core items. Namely, how much of their income they

want or need to replace, how much debt they would like to have paid off, and their expenses if they were to die.

(Tim) Quite honestly, I wanted to have fun. I bought a boat slip on the St Croix River and bought a series of boats. I sold the boats, bought a cabin. I sold the cabin and bought a house. I bought another cabin. I bought all sorts of things. I'd buy a car, and if I really didn't like it after a couple a months I'd sell it and get another one.

Obviously, these are terrible consumer choices. But there was always a Band-Aid. The money was always there. At some point, I think I looked at my wife and said, "Really, I don't think that there's anything that we would want, that we could not get." I mean, I don't want a two hundred-foot boat, but if I wanted a forty-footer or a fifty-footer, yeah. If we wanted a brand-new Sea Ray fifty-foot boat, we could have afforded it.

Ok. That is not exactly a textbook example of good cash flow management. But remember, Tim saw an endless stream of fresh revenue.

Back in 2002, right after the tech bubble, I was training some Generation-X planners, and they kept asking me, "Why are you recommending these fixed accounts for people?" They'd tell me, "My clients are

objecting to these 3% to 4% fixed accounts," and I'd say, "No. *They're* not. *You* are the ones objecting. Not your clients."

It was the "investment professional" who was objecting.

Because the way it actually worked was this: If your client was in an investment and it paid off at 8 to 10% you were a hero. They loved you. But if it didn't return near that or even lost money, they were upset and were demanding to know why you had made the recommendation you did. They're calling you a fool and demanding to know why you pushed them into that.

On the other hand, if your client was in a product with a fixed rate but a lower return, they'd say, "I didn't like it at first. But it saved my butt."

Right now some annuity contracts that were issued in the early 200s and before have a 3% to 4% floor, which is higher than a lot of interest you can get in most everything else.

The point here is that the insurance and investment architecture comes first. Make certain it is set up in a reasonable way – that you can afford – and that, in terms of insurance, guarantees that you are protected no matter what kind of calamity strikes, personal or market-shaking. Gaudy but volatile performance matters less than guaranteeing you have what you need.

Keep in mind that guarantees are backed by the strength and claims-paying ability of the issuing insurance company.

(Scott Wardell) Somewhere in all this you divorced and remarried. Is that right?

(Tim) Yes.

(Scott Wardell) If I do my math, that means five years of wild and crazy bachelorhood?

(Tim) Exactly. A lot of money went down that river.

You get into that lifestyle a little bit and it kind of sucks you in deeper. We built a house in [affluent] Lake Elmo, sold it, then built another house in Lake Elmo, right next door. Through it all you lose a little money. Well, more than a little.

(Scott Wardell) So your current wife, how's her financial literacy?

(Tim) She's really sharp, very conservative. Her dad earns a dollar and puts a dollar in the bank. And that's where it still is. I don't think her dad has ever bought a stock or a mutual fund. I don't know if he's got a 401(k), I really don't know. He's *very* conservative. So she's always nervous on any kind of spending. But I'm saying, "Hey, let's buy this alien technology. We heard about this and couldn't stand the thought of not doing it and then having it succeed." Soon though she's saying, "I told you Tim!"

(Scott Wardell) What's that called, pride? So we're into the late '90s now, it's basically all growth, and then we enter the real go-go years.

(Tim) Right.

(Scott Wardell) How much dramatically different was the cash flow for you after 2000?

(Tim) Sad as it was, what really kicked off the go-go years for the mortgage industry was the drop in interest rates, and the drop in rates started when the economy stopped, really stopped, on 9-11. People weren't buying homes and weren't buying cars and stereo equipment, and people just kind of went into a kind of spending coma. Interest rates from then on just went down, down, down.

We also had a huge influx of people from other countries moving to Minnesota who had a strong desire for homeownership. It was a tremendous growth area. So, well, everyone knows the story, first-time homebuyers could afford to go buy their second home and so on.

With each little notch down, interest rates brought customers back in to refinance again, and it just kept going.

As I've said, the cash flow for us was amazing. Especially at year-end when we were giving out the bonuses. There were six-figure checks. Over a year it was a seven-figure income.

> It's like the old adage about power and absolute power. When the money starts rolling in it is so seductive, logic just goes out the window.

(Scott Wardell) So at least were you still paying the $2,000 a month into the mutual fund through to [your advisor's bank]?

(Tim) During that time, no. What was I doing? Some investing with [a big European bank], maxing out the 401(k), and enjoying the lifestyle. [The Europeans] had me mostly into individual stocks, and some mutual funds.

(Scott Wardell) You said earlier that you ended up with lots of financial stocks.

(Tim) Yes. At my direction. My guy, would often say, "Tim, you're over-weighted here," and then he'd make some recommendations. But I just never made a change. It wasn't his fault at all.

(Scott Wardell) Did they run you through a risk calculation process? To determine where you were at and what level of risk you could take?

(Tim) I don't remember it by that name. My guy would take the annual analysis and put me through their program, but I don't know if it was a risk assessment.

///

Tim is an interesting variation on the "Five S's" concept introduced earlier, in that he was moving so fast he blew by all of them–Surviving, Struggling, Stable, Successful, Surplus/Sharing – in record time, and so fast almost none of the realities of those levels sunk in. There was certainly no sense of appreciation for "Stable."

The opposite of Tim is the following chapter on my friend Loren, the southern Minnesota farmer. For years he was in the "Survival" and "Struggling." range. He now has a deep appreciation of "Stable." The experience of "Survival" and "Struggling" put a profound, valuable imprint on Loren. He learned how not to get crazy, and how to protect himself from falling backwards.

As a species, we're not built to handle meteoric changes in our basic standards of living. And that failing may be more acute when our quality of life improves too fast.

\\\

(Scott Wardell) But the worst your brokerage guy said to you was that you were "over- weighted" in financial stocks.

(Tim) Well, financial and high tech, and emerging growth. He said, "You should put some over here in international." But I resisted. What I had was working. Hell, everything was working.

///

I have doctor clients who do the same thing. They read their literature and believe they see a rising star in some device or medicine and pour in money.

Medical/Health industry investments strike a lot of smart people as safer investments. Working for an industry or having an intimate knowledge of an industry doesn't necessarily make that industry an obvious investment opportunity for individual investors.

And it's not just go-go financial and professional guys like Tim. I had another client, a blue-collar guy, working his whole career for Andersen Windows. Terrific product. Great company. With an Employee Stock Ownership Plan. This guy had everything in Andersen stock, because he loved and trusted the company so much. He couldn't imagine anything diluting the value. But then, like Tim and so many others, he couldn't imagine the home-building industry going nearly bust over the course of just a few months.

(Scott Wardell) Where was the main source of your financial information? The Wall Street Journal? Barron's? Knowledgeable buddies?

(Tim) Knowledgeable buddies, things I'd read, CNN, things that just sounded good. We were doing a lot of business with Citicorp. We were growing and things were doing well. My brother is very savvy, very intelligent. But there was very little he could tell me. You know, because he's my brother and because there were things he wasn't legally able to give me any heads-up on ahead of time.

Tim was getting cocktail advice. By that I mean, Tim meets people, who probably have a certain level of respect for him and his business acumen. They exchange ideas and tips, which is really to say they try and impress each other with how in-the-know they are and how clever they are. It's The Smartest Guy in the Room Syndrome.

But what's going on is that they are acting on cleverness. They are not talking foundation, with solid financial architecture protecting them if a gamble goes bad. Foundation planning is dull. It has no cachet with the crowd moving as fast as Tim was.

In their world, and I know it, they tend to think, "If only two out of a hundred of these ideas pans out, I'm ahead of the boring 'Foundation Game.'" What's more, they believe they're clever enough to winnow out ninety of those bad ideas, so they're really only dealing with two winners out of ten.

It doesn't work like that. But it's virtually impossible to convince guys like Tim of the inevitable failures of this system ... until they've experienced a serious crash.

I'm a fan of Dave Ramsey's system[1], or I should say "systems," since he's got one for just about everything you can imagine. But they are practical and rooted in common sense.

(Scott Wardell) Did your father say anything to you about how you were handling money, or the high-flying lifestyle?

(Tim) No, he was proud of me. There was no fatherly scolding. I was King of the World; it really felt that way!

(Scott Wardell) So did all this continue right up to the crash?

(Tim) There were some slimmer years in '05 and '06. But it was still profitable. The notices on the defaults and the requests for loan repurchases started coming in late '06 early '07.

//

Too many people, even today, look at their businesses in the standard expansion model, with modest uphill growth, followed by accelerated uphill growth, then a plateau, maybe a modest setback or two then a recovery and a return to the sweet cycle. Almost no one considers, "What if this all crashes and burns?" That sort of thinking is too gloomy, it suggests to others you're not "positive."

With twenty-first-century technology, there are so many business models that bear little resemblance to the experiences of companies even twenty years ago. Most innovation, which is to say preparation for the worst-case scenario, or what comes next, only comes at the onset of dire urgency. That's like the guy who has to jump out of an airplane and starts designing his parachute on the way down.

Foundation planning, the dull-but-vital cement block work of adequate insurance and systematic monthly investments or savings, with balance and diversification, all personalized to your situation means you've asked yourself, "How am I situated for long-term, sustainable growth?" and "How am I protected if something goes really wrong."

\\

(Scott Wardell) Some people at age forty-five to fifty start thinking about "how's this gonna look at age seventy?"

(Tim) Yeah, I know. But I thought I'd be all done at fifty-five. My exit strategy was to get the top people in the company together and allow them to come up with a plan to buy me out over a period of time.

(Scott Wardell) Because ... you anticipated that the company would be so solid that all they could see was the upside?

(Tim) Of course, and up till '06 or '07, they were waiting for me to give them that signal. I had employees that were almost demanding to become shareholders or larger shareholders. We just never agreed on a price.

(Scott Wardell) So you did have the conversation? The subject of them buying you out was broached?

(Tim) Right, but in a very general way. There was nothing like, "We're sitting down at lunch today and we're talking about what we're all thinking about." The actual deal was still probably two years off when everything fell apart.

(Scott Wardell) But if you were thinking to get out at fifty-five, what were you going to do after that?

Rev up the boat! Waikiki! Or just consult. Everyone else does! I always said when I retire, "I'm going to sell real estate. They don't do anything!" [He laughs.]

///

Tim's reality is now a lot different. But hardly miserable. Instead of retiring at fifty-five, he may retire at sixty-five, with probably some part-time work as long as he can. Social Security, which wasn't even a factor to him fifteen years ago, will now be a significant part of his retirement income.

It's a bit embarrassing I suppose, but not what anyone would call fatal. As you emerge from one of these crash-and-burn scenarios, you simply scale down the grand lifestyle expectations and the "when" of retirement. It's survivable, on an ego level, if only because so many other people have gone through a similar re-boot.

The new model is "semi-retired." It could be worse.

\\\

(Scott Wardell) Had you and your wife planned on traveling? What are your hobbies?

(Tim) It was simple. We're not big travelers, we've never been overseas. What we like is Arizona, Palm Springs, a winter home, spend time down there, continue to raise the kids and just be quiet about it. There weren't any grand plans. Right now if you asked me, "Tim, what would be your dream retirement job?" I'd ask you if you were familiar with Nelson's ice cream shack, off of Greeley Street in Stillwater? It's just high school kids and tubs of ice cream. I just want an ice cream shop.

(Scott Wardell) Give us a picture of your life, post-Apocalypse. How do you handle what must be a pretty dramatic shift in lifestyle and all?

(Tim) Like I said at the beginning, it's where our lives' focus truly was. Running around, playing king of the world, that was fun. But even at that time, it wasn't where we were grounded.

(Scott Wardell) You were thoroughly enjoying it though.

(Tim) Oh yeah. Of course. But we also enjoy where we are now. We're raising our kids, we live in [a small town]. We went from the million-dollar house to the $200,000 house. It still has a pool.

(Scott Wardell) You haven't joined the Third World.

(Tim) No. We still have our friends. We still have our faith. Nothing out there is going to take that away. You get kicked. You get knocked down. What choice do you really have? You pick yourself back up again and keep going.

(Scott Wardell) Whatever happened to what you had saved or put away?

(Tim) Well, there still was money saved, a lot of it. But when the income drops and you're still paying on the mortgage on the big old house, you dip into the savings to keep it going. Until you can sell it.

(Scott Wardell) What about long-term care insurance? Was that ever one of the bills?

(Tim) My wife is sixteen years younger than me. That's my long-term care.

Do you really want your wife, or your husband to have no other choice but to take over full or even nearly full-time care for you if you're incapacitated?

No one does. But that is what happens.

I have a relative who was a 24/7 caregiver to her husband. She couldn't even leave the house once a week to play cards with her friends. It was a terrible situation.

I also had a client with pretty much the same situation. The husband has Parkinson's Disease. Needed full-time care. They had no long-term care. The advice of her attorney, for her to avoid financial ruin was, "Divorce him." The poor woman was weeping in my office.

Having a long-term care policy that would allow someone else to come in for a few hours each day would be huge. Tim's situation here is very similar.

I hate to sound monotonous about this, but long-term care planning is integral to a well thought out retirement but is often ignored in many informal financial conversations.

The basic rationale for long-term care insurance never changes.

1. So as not to impoverish the spouse.
2. To protect something for the heirs for all your hard work and savings, i.e. To help protect your remaining assets and saving from being depleted to pay for long-term care.
3. To provide respite for a family caregiver.

(Scott Wardell) In the scaled-down mode now, what are you doing with what was in your 401(k) or monthly retirement investment?

(Tim) Well, the 401(k) has now been rolled over to an IRA, and that's being managed by a good, trusted conservative friend I have, a professional advisor. It's just not something I'm going to watch day-to-day. So I couldn't tell you offhand where it's weighted.

(Scott Wardell) But you're not playing day-trader, buying your own stock?

(Tim) No. I learned that lesson. I am not astute.

(Scott Wardell) But, very ironically, that's exactly what people would say about someone like you. "He's running with bankers and brokers and serious money people. He's gotta know the ins and outs and everything. He's astute."

(Tim) I suppose they would, or did. What I know about what I'm good at is leading people, encouraging them, putting together a good team, helping them reach their goals. That doesn't necessarily transfer over to Mitt Romney's style of business. But when I started to think that it did, that's where I got into trouble.

(Scott Wardell) The Arizona dream, did you ever consider buying property there?

(Tim) We made an offer on a townhome in Arizona. I think the price was $385,000 or something like that. But we had a cabin on a lake [in Wisconsin], and we made the offer contingent on the sale of that cabin. They weren't taking contingent offers [in Arizona]. It was either you buy it, or you don't buy it. If you don't buy it, the next person out in the lobby will. So luckily, we didn't buy it. Because I'm sure that $385,000 is now less than $80,000. I'm sure it's just wiped out. The scary thing is, you buy it for $80,000 and you think you've got a good deal, but the association is in such trouble, you're going to have to be supporting the association. It was pretty ugly down there.

//

If you are itching for a vacation home, do a very careful cash-flow plan, one that looks at the worst-case scenarios, and whether your assumptions, like renting it out for several months a year, are based in reality. Can you afford it if no renters appear? If your plan is to own something you only use three months out of the year, there's rarely an equation you can come up with that argues in favor of owning as opposed to renting.

\\

(Scott Wardell) So the ice cream shop is the current dream?

(Tim) It shows my age! Hell, the dream started out as a disco.

(Scott Wardell) How old are the kids now?

(Tim) I have a son from my first marriage and we have two kids in college and a fourteen-year-old daughter.

(Scott Wardell) How are you handling all the college stuff?

(Tim) Stafford loans. We'll probably use a home equity line of credit, and they're [the children] gonna have to work for it too.

(Scott Wardell) Have you had that conversation?

(Tim) Oh, yeah. They almost like it that way. They're very good well-balanced kids.

Good for Tim for having these serious financial conversations with his kids. He appears to have taken a sober and adult assessment of his experience and applied that attitude toward his children. If the kids are ready for college, they're ready for a Big Boy-Big Girl talk about how the money is going to happen.

He has a First World Problem here. The kids may have to work while they go to college. As I've said before, this isn't fatal. It could be much, much worse.

(Scott Wardell) You've got several kids so you'll likely have to pay for at least one wedding! I ask that because we've had a couple people already straining at their budgets who pretty well blew what was left to finance lavish weddings ... as well as schools that they should have told the kids they couldn't afford.

(Tim) The boys are going to state schools, so they're reasonable. They weren't academically gifted enough to even think about an Ivy League school or a high-end private school. We'll see how we're doing when it's time for a wedding.

(Scott Wardell) When everything cratered for you, was there a struggle dealing with debt and re-arranging finances?

(Tim) Not really. Well, a bit. But it wasn't critical. I don't like debt, so over the years whenever I did build some up, I paid it off. I'd build it up and pay it off, build it up and pay it off. At one point I qualified for a large credit line. I'm not sure what we're good for now. Selling the boat slip alone brought in a lot of cash.

What I really admire about Tim is that he took ownership of his situation: he isn't finger-pointing, blaming someone else for what happened. He isn't wallowing in self-pity. He's accepting reality and has made a concerted–and very healthy–effort to reevaluate his priorities, the things he needs and wants most, and is moving on.

(Scott Wardell) Are you philosophical about everything? Some people will at least take the attitude that life is short, you go around once, and in this case you had the experience.

(Tim) My wife says we have a lot of great memories. We've done things that thirty years ago I never thought I'd do. We're not big travelers, but things we wanted to do. You know, rent a limo, take the neighborhood to the Fleetwood Mac concert. Play King of the World ... for a while.

Summary

A couple things that are notable, maybe thuddingly obvious in Tim's story: There are people out there who make one-third, one-fifth of what Tim made in his go-go years who are now more financially secure. So again we have the issue that it isn't how much you make, it's how much you save.

It is important to believe that no matter how successful you are, there's always going to be a rainy day, and you better pack for it.

Finding success through a few clever choices has inherent risk.

Some people have the mentality that they don't have to go for the classic dividend-paying stock. Instead they're going after the hot thing that makes up the difference in one move. At that point, you've turned investing into gambling. This method often leads to disappointment.

I personally don't know a single middle-class retiree who pulled it off with a "shoot the moon" strategy.

Another fateful component to his story is that he invested almost entirely in things he associated with his line of business. In his case, financials. Superficially, this sounds smart. But in investing you're creating too much exposure in an associated industry, where one systemic mishap can take the entire sector down.

If you put your income and investments in one category, such a move magnifies risk.

What happened to Tim is that with the crash of '08 he lost both his income and his assets at the same time. Both were in the same industry.

The upside for Tim is that he rarely makes the same mistake twice. But as history teaches us, there's always another generation who looks at fast money and thinks, "This time it'll be different."

It's human nature that guys like Tim are bored with the mundane stuff. They see big money moving very quickly and fat fortunes piling up all around them. Realistically, all an advisor can do is make suitable recommendations and hope the client will make choices to cement the foundation.

By the way, did you catch the part where Tim was a history major, right? You can't make that stuff up.

Things to consider:

1. Do not over-invest in what you think you know best. While even diversification carries risk, over-loading in one sector magnifies risk.

2. No matter how well you're doing at any given point in your career, be absolutely certain you understand and have established a basic foundation of insurance and savings, and consider establishing a systemic monthly investment strategy.

3. Without falling into a gloom and doom psychology, stop and imagine a worst-case scenario from time to time and assure yourself that you and your loved ones can survive it.

Notes

1. Dave Ramsey, Lamp Licensing, last modified 2015, http://www. daveramsey.com/home/

Chapter 2

Integrity Pays Off

The description, "salt of the earth" has gotten a little overused in recent years. It's to the point that all you need to qualify as "salt of the earth" is a shotgun, a dog, a truck and a Toby Keith CD.

When I was growing up someone had to be unimpeachably honest, hard-working, patient and humble to qualify. Or be a lot like Loren Brekke. Loren is all that and resilient to boot. The USA is a great country because of all the diverse people that make it up, but I think we'd survive and prosper pretty well if a couple hundred million more of us had Loren's virtues.

His story would be fascinating if we never went beyond how he and his three brothers survived the deaths of their parents when they were all just young men, and how they carried on the family farm. But in Loren's case, I have been amazed and impressed with the way his values, the pride he took in doing a job well, and his calm, thoughtful manner not only saved his farm and family, but inspired others in his community to follow his lead, to everyone's benefit.

It was a bright, unseasonably warm January day when I drove out to the Brekke farmstead and sat down in the kitchen with Loren and his wife, Joan.

Snapshot

- **Age:** 74
- **Marital status:** Married, three adult daughters.
- **Primary career:** Farmer, civic activist.
- **Asset description:** Owns farm without debt. Estimated value over one million. Rents acreage for additional income. A variety of investments, mostly focused in mutual funds. Social Security.
- **Specific dilemma:** Life-long recovery from loss of both parents before high school graduation.
- **Financial stability level:** Surplus.

Loren and his three brothers, two older, one younger, lost both parents in four years. Their father died when Loren was 16. The two older boys knew just enough about farming that they resisted advice to sell and decided to stay together and work the land as best they could.

But wanting to do something and getting the credit to do it from banks and co-ops are two completely different matters. Loren's mother had a gall bladder attack on Christmas Eve 1952 and died within days. "She lived to serve Christmas Eve dinner," Loren remembers.
In those days, tradition was that the deceased was returned home for viewing in the family living room. "Everybody was coming and looking at her for visitation, and I went outside and I pinched myself. I thought, 'This has got to be a dream (nightmare). But I didn't wake up. It wasn't a dream.' Four years later Dad was gone, too."

Among the lesser challenges was Parents Night at the high school football games. Loren was a pretty good player, but the announcers, not knowing how to handle such a delicate situation, simply ignored him when they read off the roster. "That was a tough deal. All the parents would come out and stand next to us players and the announcer read off the names. But when he came to me, he didn't even read my name. There you are, kind of a loner. You really grew up young. You didn't have a choice."

He recalls, "With something like that, losing both parents, you could have gone goofy. But we had a really good pastor at the time who stopped in almost every day for a while to talk to us kids." There was also a cousin who offered good advice as weeks turned to months.

Led by his oldest brother, Duane, the boys decided to stay together rather than shuffle Loren and his youngest brother off to foster homes. "The decision was that Howard and I would finish high school and help Duane run the farm. When I graduated, I would start farming this land that Dad had, along with Duane's land that he owned and grandpa's farm over east of here. It was a lot of work, but to tell you the truth we were pretty much destitute."

Expenses didn't help. But on top of medical expenses from dad's illness was the bad deal he struck with his second wife.

"After he lost my mom, Dad hired a lady to come take care of us, cooking and so on. He had livestock to care for and that really takes up your time. Well, as these things go, Dad got interested in her and married her. But when he died, she got half the farm and we got half of nothing. We got the bills. So really, we never got a thing from Dad. It was all gone. There was 160 acres that we owned, but the new wife got 80, so it would have been 20 acres for each of us, and that was all in debt because of the hospital bills and so on."

Deeply in debt, with no real credit standing, the boys were at the mercy of strangers, or at least local bankers and businesspeople. What they had going for them was a work ethic and a good name. Their local community knew the parents, knew the boys, and knew the story. But money talks and as we'll see charity is a sometimes thing with certain types of people.

(Scott Wardell) So after your dad died and you settled things with his second wife, you boys were in a situation where the value of everything you owned pretty much equaled your debt? Is that right?

(Loren) Well, we didn't have any land, really. We got it, but it was all mortgaged. The lawyer told the bank, 'If those kids make it, it'll be a miracle.' But we did make it.

What likely happened in the estate settlement was that all debt was assigned to those operating the land, namely the boys, while the second wife just collected her winnings and departed. It goes without saying that was astonishingly bad planning on his dad's part. Even Loren isn't certain how it happened, but I'm guessing his dad set it up without a second opinion. Any estate issue, especially when you're mixing bloodline heirs with second or third spouses, should be professionally vetted by at least two sets of eyes, probably a lawyer. Families can fight well enough among themselves.

(Scott Wardell) What kind of pressures were the bankers putting on you kids?

(Loren) Well, being 16, I wasn't too aware of all that. Duane, my older brother, did most of the business end of it. What I did was the day-to-day work on the farm.

(Scott Wardell) But you were aware that you could lose the farm at that point?

(Loren) Oh yeah. We knew that. We grew up knowing it was bad and we weren't always pointed in the right direction, you know. Bankers, bless their souls! They could have pointed us to much cheaper interest. But they saw a chance to make a little extra money if they handled us differently. But we adjusted to it.

These are local, hometown bankers taking advantage of four boys that had just lost their parents.

(Loren) Yeah. We ended up paying 1% higher than we would have if we'd gone to a different place. When I grew up a little, I started checking around and found that out. I told Duane that we didn't have to take that. So we switched to a different bank and saved a percent in interest, which is a lot of money over a period of time.

///

You have to be smart enough to shop. Make your banker compete for your business. The boys here relied on a neighbor who was also the family banker. They looked nowhere else.

This sort of thing is much less likely to happen today because of the internet and a generally higher awareness of competing financial products. With Loren and his brothers, their story would have been different today simply by virtue of the fact that International Harvester and other big equipment manufacturers have their own financing systems, although a farm co-op/credit union would likely still have been their best move.

\\

(Scott Wardell) Were you boys getting any kind of professional advice?

(Loren) Well, there were uncles and stuff. They were very nice. They had us out for dinners and stuff. But they didn't have any business savvy, so we didn't get any advice, no.

(Scott Wardell) So what you knew at the time was work and to keep doing it?

(Loren) That's right. To make it, I went out and baled hay for the neighbors, shelled corn for the neighbors, pitched manure and threw fertilizer sacks for the co-ops around here. It was hard work that few wanted to do, and that was in addition to running our farm.

But it wasn't all a grind like I'm making it sound. There's an old motto people use. They say, "We work hard and we play hard." And we Brekke boys did that. We worked hard all week and then we took time to go down to the lake and water ski, and play at the lake over here, running up the ski jumps and really having a terrific time on Sunday afternoons. That was a fun time. I actually remember that more.

(Scott Wardell) To put a point on it, though. There's no investment money left. There's no insurance money. Your balance sheet is zero, or negative?

(Loren) Right. Actually we couldn't even borrow any money, because the bankers were afraid they'd lose it. We really owed almost everything to a local businessman who ran the International [Harvester] dealership. He lent me money so I could buy a baler, to go out and do custom baling. The bank wouldn't give me any money.

(Scott Wardell) So you had a tractor, then you bought the baler so you could do the custom baling, and you paid him back?

(Loren) Right, and I paid him back really quickly. I saved and didn't spend anything. I had to be careful. But I paid it back faster than I would have had to. He said, "You know Loren, forget the interest. Just pay cost." There were some nice guys around here. Guys like him. But the banks ... you have to be careful with them! I found that out pretty young! They claim they are your best friends. But they aren't!

///

The game in this context has changed ... a lot. There might still be a "good guy" who'll extend you credit based on the fact he knows you don't smoke, don't drink, don't carry on, work real hard and are kind to animals. But the fact today is that the giant credit rating agencies, TransUnion and the like, are all about numbers, and these kids had nothing.

The building of credit today is pretty well understood. If Loren and his brothers were starting out today they'd have to apply for a small amount of credit, pledge something – equipment maybe – and pay it back as fast as they could. They'd have to climb the credit

ladder, which would take a few years and might have drowned them.

But a facet here that I like is the decision that one of the boys, Howard, was going to go to college, and there was no complaining that it was him and not anyone else. Loren and the others knew one of them had to go. It's a nice family values twist.

\\

(Scott Wardell) Tell us about the decision to send your youngest brother, Howard, to college.

(Loren) We had an uncle who was pretty brilliant. He went to college forever. He had a doctorate and everything. Economics and agriculture. He wrote several books. He thought one of us at least should get to college.

At first, we thought, "There's no way." We were good football players. I was good. We had invitations from some of the smaller schools around here. Not the University of Minnesota. But places like Brookings and Worthington and Mankato. They wanted me to play fullback. But there was no way. I didn't have the money to do that. There weren't any scholarships, and there was no help at all. Nothing. But after I graduated we got on our feet just a little. So when Howard came along, we helped pay, and this uncle gave some money, too.

(Scott Wardell) So the rest of you said "We're going to help Howard get through college?"

(Loren) Yeah. But he was a pretty smart kid, too.

(Scott Wardell) How did the family councils go? Did the four of you get together, sit around the table and say, "Now you gotta do this. And you, you're going to do that?"

(Loren) No, it came pretty naturally. There were things you liked to do. I was in the field and did the chores a lot. Duane did a lot of the business end of it. And he would plant the corn and so on. We never actually had a meeting. If something had to be done, we did it!

Once I got out of school, when I was 18, then we had a Brekke Brothers checkbook. Then I wrote checks, too. But Duane really did most of the business.

(Scott Wardell) How long was it before you were out from under water?

(Loren) I aimed for getting everything paid for by the time I was 62 1/2, because I wanted to retire then ... and I did! Finally got out of debt when I was 62, and I retired when I was 62 1/2.

(Scott Wardell) But by then you'd acquired more land.

(Loren) Oh yeah. We'd bought extra land, But getting out of debt for the first part, after Dad died, probably took about 30 years. Then we bought more land, or I did anyway.

(Scott Wardell) But during those early years?

(Loren) No. After that. Although I guess in those 30 years we did buy one piece.

(Scott Wardell) So you were doing all this off of the 80 original acres?

(Loren) Yeah. Well, we had the 80. But then we had to buy another 80 from our stepmother. So we had 160, and then Duane ran my grandpa's farm, which was 160 acres, and he rented another 80 from a neighbor. So we had more land that we had rented and so on.

(Scott Wardell) So combined, you were at about 400.

(Loren) Yeah. Then we worked up to 600. Duane and I farmed it. When Duane quit and I ran the whole 600.

(Scott Wardell) Of the 600 you were running at that time, how much did you actually own?

(Loren) I owned 385 at the time I retired.

(Scott Wardell) What's the interaction that you were having with the business people in town? How long did it take before they were treating you like an adult?

(Loren) It didn't take very long. I was in one of the business places and said, "I don't have any money right now," and the man said, "We know you, you're a Brekke boy. You can borrow the money. We trust you." They knew we worked hard and we were accepted very quickly. It was surprising.

After high school, at 18 or 19, they would treat me like a man. Which was nice, I thought. The people were really good. You can't imagine how good they were.

(Scott Wardell) This was the late 1950's. At what point do you guys actually have some cash flow going? At what point was the operation standing up on its own?

(Loren)I suppose it took 15-20 years before we felt like we could go out and buy more land and stuff. It took that long to have something so that you had a solid credit background.

(Scott Wardell) You had credit for equipment though?

(Loren) Like I said, this local businessman just wrote it out on a piece of paper, a contract, and I paid it back. Somehow they just trusted us.

(Scott Wardell) More than once?

(Loren) Yeah, we did it a lot. The bank wouldn't help at all, really. They had this limit, they said. We were trying to raise cattle, and they said, "That's all you can borrow. We can't trust you for more." But the people, the equipment and feed dealers and so on were very good. We wouldn't have made it without them. No question about it. If it would have been only the bank, we wouldn't have made it.

(Scott Wardell) And these are local bankers? Not big corporate banks from Minneapolis.

(Loren) Yeah. Our neighbors across over that way were running the place! It was a home-owned bank. But they wouldn't risk their money!

///

As we'll see, Loren eventually realizes he has to diversify his income a bit. In his early years he's in an "all your eggs in one basket" scenario I caution people against. It happens when business owners have their income dependent on the business they own and their savings and investments dependent on equity in that same business. This is a dicey situation.

If your business is both your income and your

retirement plan, consider what would happen in the event that your market dries up or your business becomes obsolete? I could tell you the story of people I knew who were living the good life with places here in Minnesota, Florida, and Hawaii, all sustained by their own business. Everything they had was dependent on that business maintaining high revenue. It didn't, and many of them now have part-time retail jobs to pay the bills.

Here, as you'll see, Loren buys IRAs instead of new farm equipment. He fixes the old stuff, allowing him to move his savings and investments away from dependency on the farm business.

(Scott Wardell) How old were you and Joan when you met?

(Loren) Early 20's. And, [he turns to his wife] you were teaching school at the time. You came and rescued me off the farm! I was always working. I'd bale hay all day and shell corn all night and might go to bed at 10:00 p.m.

(Scott Wardell) It sounds like it was kind of a boys' world over here.

(Loren) Oh, it was. I didn't know much about girls. I thought they were kind of cute. But until Joan came along I didn't know a lot about 'em.

(Scott Wardell) What's the quick story of how you met?

(Loren) One night I was in bed, and here comes this racket in the house. My brothers are dragging all this commotion in. There's three guys and three women, and they're hollering right below my bedroom. And I heard one say, "I can't get the oven to work." They were going to make pizza. So I got up and went down and fixed it. So they said, "Stay and have some pizza." She [nodding toward Joan] must have thought that was all right, you know, that I could make a stove work. Heck, they just had the timer set wrong.

But that's how we met. Also, I had a '57 Chevy. It was a nice car back then, older car, but it looked really nice. I showed her that, and she liked the car I guess. That's what she tells me now, anyway!

(Scott Wardell) That Chevy is what we call a chick magnet.

(Loren) Right! So we got married. She was 23 and I was 25.

(Scott Wardell) Did the finances improve with marriage?

(Loren) Not really. She'd been teaching for about five years and didn't have enough to buy furniture for herself. We had a kitchen table, a stove, and a refrigerator. In the living room we sat on boxes. After a while we got a davenport and a coffee table, and end tables. All Danish modern. She bought the furniture for the house (from her teaching income). I didn't have money to buy furniture.

(Scott Wardell) So early in your marriage you're sitting on boxes. She was still teaching, right? You had two incomes, though?

(Loren) Well, I made her quit. She taught to the end of the next year. I didn't want her to be running off all the time. We're married. So let's be together.

(Scott Wardell) And now, today, you have three daughters and nine grandchildren. So at some point you had to start planning. Do you remember when you looked at each other and said, "We're not always going to be 30. I want to be able to do some things ... ?"

(Loren) About 1980 or something like that we actually started making some money and thought we should be putting something away for later years, I'd done some reading and we started to buy some IRAs. That was the beginning of it really.

If you're starting your investment portfolio late, my first question is, "What's your cash reserve look like?" The reason I ask is because you don't want someone to start and then come back in six months later and say, "I can't make this. I need more cash for day-to-day stuff," which could mean paying penalties and taxes for early withdrawals and all the other nasty side effects. By the time you're done with that stuff, you could be out as much as 35%.

Next is understanding what your asset allocation and risk tolerance is. In a moment we'll see Loren get in to precious metals among other things. But at the point he does that, he has a solid understanding of what he can afford to risk.

Loren was never a guy who liked bonds. He wanted his money in something that had the potential to show some growth. However, in volatile times like these, most people would like to have some element in their portfolio that potentially softens the ride.

But starting late, the temptation for people is to think, "I gotta really put the pedal to the metal." It's generally not a good strategy. As I often say: Know your risk tolerance and stick with it.

CORPORATE BOND

(Scott Wardell) Any other income at that point?

(Loren) I was in National Guard, and got a check every month. I always sent it back to Joan. We had that put away. Then I got on the REA [Rural Electrification Association] board, and I put the income away.

(Scott Wardell) So you kind of defined money coming in as either operational or extra funds?

(Joan) Also, I subbed for like 15 years after the girls got old enough. They were short of subs in the district here and I really never thought about it. But friends said, "Why don't you try that." It worked. It helped (cash flow).

When Joan and you got married were you supporting four families off this farm?

(Loren) No, eventually it turned out to be only two. Duane and I bought out the middle brother, and then my younger brother, Howard. We had to borrow the money again. But we borrowed from these co-ops, like AgStar. Back then it was Federal and you got a better interest rate from them. Every time we'd buy, we had to borrow the money to do it. The good thing was that by that time, we were getting in a financial shape where we could manage it (debt service).

(Scott Wardell) Then you also started selling seed corn, right?

(Loren) Yeah. We quit the cattle operation in the 80's when interest rates got to 18%. That just didn't work. We'd buy these cattle, borrow when we bought them, borrow again to buy the supplement and the feed, and you just couldn't make it. It just didn't work. We were losing too much on the whole deal. So we quit the cattle business. I decided instead to go into the seed corn business. It was crazy. But it was good for paying taxes. We hadn't paid any income tax for several years we had so much loss. But when we quit the cattle business, boy did we start paying income tax!

(Scott Wardell) Did the seed business help at all?

(Loren) It was helpful. We could do some things that we couldn't do otherwise, like buy a boat or something. I've been a sports guy my whole life. I like to hunt and so forth. And for the family too, there were some things that we could finally get with the seed corn money.

The thing about that business was what I learned and applied to my own operation. It was almost more about the experience and the know-how. You'd go to meetings and they'd fill you in on how seed corn was developed and how they did this and that to make the yield 150 [bushels per acre] rather than 125 or something.

I learned so much that I applied on this farm. All that new information made me a better farmer. I probably made more money improving my own farming than I did from the seed corn business itself.

//

I hear this a lot, the happy consequences of taking on new side businesses, interests and hobbies. In Loren's case, one thing quickly led to another. He's a terrific personality and wonderfully curious. But even someone less out-going benefits just from getting involved with a new group of people. What's the line? "Ninety percent of life is just showing up?" Change "showing up" to "getting involved" and the same thing applies.

Being a good student, Loren brought what I think of as a worst-case scenario mentality to both his own planning and this outside work. That is to say that he prepared his customers and the various boards he ended up on for the worst that could happen, in which case everyone was pleased when things turned out better.

Do not expect only good things to come your way. Be prepared for bad times.

\\\

(Scott Wardell) Some folks, hard workers like you Loren, have a hard time imagining what they'll do when they finally stop working.

(Loren) I quit slowly. I've heard about that, about people who don't know what to do with themselves. It was nothing for me to put in a 16-hour day, because I'd work the farm and run meetings and wouldn't get home until midnight sometimes.

(Joan) Then after he got home he'd have to tell me the whole story!

(Loren) Some of those [board] meetings got a little bit, you know, tightened up! A little tense. So I'd have to come home and tell her the story so I could relax and sleep! But like I was saying, I put in a lot of 16-hour days. That had to stop. But I thought, "I want to retire at 62 1/2, but I'm not going to just quit." I decided to farm just 130 acres, to kind of get slowed down.

I always want to get better. But at the same time, I don't get all worked up about it.

///

The point of Loren's stories about his activities on boards is to underline the value of getting involved, of pushing yourself to try new things and meet new people. Loren may be more of an extrovert than you or me, but new ventures, especially as you move into retirement are invaluable to creating new opportunities and relationships. It's a people world.

On the "slow down" toward retirement, as a landowner and a farmer, Loren is in a unique position to ratchet down from full-time work. He can decide one spring to rent out a big chunk of his land and suddenly all that work is off his back.

Your average corporate middle manager can't make that adjustment unilaterally. But you don't know what is possible until you ask. I'll say this several times throughout this book: There's more negotiating going on now for part-time and consulting work than ever before.

If you've always thought about doing something after retirement, the "slow down" or the "try out" is a great idea. I have an executive buddy who knows I operate an apple orchard. He told me he always thought

it might be something he'd like to do, asked if he could drive down some Saturday and help out.

"Of course," I told him, "have at it." Well, long story short, it was a day we were pounding eight-foot posts, for tree supports. It's grueling work that would wear my 20-year-old kid out. But this guy loved it. Most people would have left at lunch and never eaten another apple for the rest of their lives. But this guy came out and got a first-hand feel for it.

The larger point is that it is worth looking at how you might scale down your primary career and test out what you think you want to do next.

(Loren) I like to golf, and I like to fish, and I like to hunt. I had those things to do, too. When I'd get anxious, I'd go golfing. That can be very relaxing, golfing. I can't understand people who say, "I don't like to golf because I can't hit the ball. For me it's just the getting away from everything else and relaxing. I miss the ball, I say, "Dumb, Brekke," and go hit another one. I'm very competitive, but only with myself.

(Scott Wardell) So at that point, as you begin retirement, you're farming the 130 acres and renting the rest of it out?

(Loren) Right.

(Scott Wardell) And you're putting in your own golf course.

(Loren) I quit farming, partially, in 2001. Or 2002. I wanted to rent out this land down by the lake. But it was really quite low and not exactly favorable for planting. So I farmed the top, the higher ground. One day I mentioned to my brother, Duane, that we should put in a driving range down on the low six acres. So we spread it out, planted the seed, and when we got done we said, "Heck, we should have a green on one end." So we went and bought bent grass for the green, which looked pretty nice. And because it did we said, "We can put a green on the other end" and that was good too.

After that it just kept going. We made another tee box

down on the point and hit back and put in another green in the middle, so we could play nine holes from different tees, coming from different directions to these three greens!

(Scott Wardell) It takes 65 acres or so to make a nine-hole course. But you figured it out on six and a half acres! I thought of you when I was listening to an interview with Steve Jobs the other day. It was the graduation speech they kept playing after he died. One of the things he said was, "You can't really connect all the dots looking forward. But when you look back, you can say, "Yeah. We did this. We did this and we did it and it came together." Did you ever see how things were going to work out before it actually happened?

(Loren) No. You plan as you go. Like with the golf course, we started out with a driving range, and it kind of grew out from there. Like the seed business too, I guess.

(Scott Wardell) So what was different for you? You raised a lovely family. All the work on the land paid off, eventually. You're a prominent person in the community down here. What do you think you did differently than someone else who had big challenges at the start, like you did?

(Loren) Just determination and hard work, I think. Maybe, [he laughs] there's a tiny piece of intelligence in there, too. But we knew how to work.

(Scott Wardell) What kind of financial decisions did you make that made a difference?

(Loren) I think I was very [thrifty]. I never wanted to waste money on anything that wouldn't make money. Other than recreation. Golf and so on. I spent a lot on fishing, but I didn't gamble anything.

(Scott Wardell) And really no bad habits either. You boys didn't drink.

(Loren) We lived in a neighborhood out here with some good people, bless their hearts. But some of them had a problem with drinking. Some lost their farms because of it. They just never made it. They drove old dumpy cars and lived tough lives. So here I was 16 when Dad died, kind of looking around at what the future might be like, and I thought, "Boy, I'm not gonna do that."

I guess you could say I credit a few poor neighbors for their bad example, if you know what I mean. But there are good neighbors who didn't make it, either. The cousin of my Dad's. I mentioned earlier was really an influence. He was a Christian guy. He'd come over and every time had a big smile, "Hello! Hello! Hello!" I'll never forget it. He'd come in and we'd visit with him. Those people meant a lot to us.

(Scott Wardell) And you needed that.

(Loren) Yeah, we really needed that. Some settle their nerves with a cigarette or a bottle of beer. I settle mine with going to church. Or going golfing!

(Scott Wardell) A lot of farmer clients of mine say, "My tax deduction is my equipment." So they buy more and more equipment every year. You boys took a different route.

(Loren) [He nods toward Joan]. We were just talking about that. I have a good friend who is one of these guys constantly buying machinery for the tax deduction. They're making good money these days. But I think they should be going out and buying IRAs, and not paying a tax on it. I know they're getting into the high brackets, because they're buying all this new stuff. $200,000 for a corn planter. Stuff you really don't need. The old one works.

Me, I've got an IRA. You get into a lower tax bracket and if you're about to retire you've got this nest egg in case things fall apart like they did in the '80s. A lot of guys lost their farms then. Some because they got in over their heads on equipment. I didn't do that. I wanted to avoid that.

//

Times right now are pretty good for farmers, and have been, in cycles, throughout the past century. Land near my apple orchard was $3500 an acre six years ago. It's over $7500 now.

The caution I suggest here, which Loren embodies, is not getting carried away when times are good. A lot of his friends, and I'm certain you know friends of yours, thought the milk and honey days of the 1990s would never end. But life doesn't work that way. Everyone knows that, but too many people forget it.

Whenever anyone tells you there's only one way and that's up, that's your cue to run.

\\

(Scott Wardell) Obviously you had some kind of good, basic numbers savvy. It sounds like you were asking the right questions as you went along.

(Loren) Well, I did two budgets every year. I always knew where I was at.

//

Loren always had two budgets, one for standard pretty much year-to-date costs, and another for the worst-case scenario. The worst case never happened. But he had done the math so he knew how close he was getting and had already thought through what he'd have to do to survive some kind of disaster.

Back in the 80's, farms were coming up for sale because of those problems.

\\

(Loren) What I did was sit down and figure what I could pay for at the farm auctions that were going on back then. A lot of times the first bid was higher than the break-even price. I know a guy who bought 80 acres at one auction for way more than I thought reasonable. He lost it in a few years. He didn't do the figuring.

(Scott Wardell) And you're doing this yourself? There's no accountant?

(Loren) No. I just did it myself. That's how we made it. We never bought anything unless I figured there was gonna be a profit in the end.

(Joan) And he stayed away from the casino bars!

(Loren) Right. Never. Well, I take that back. I had to go see the casino when it opened. I gave myself a limit of $5! I lost it in five minutes! That's not the place for me! I've been there since and eaten dinner. We've had meetings there and such. But I stay away from those one-armed bandits. I worked way too hard for my money.

(Scott Wardell) On a scale of 1 to 10, how would you grade your retirement?

(Loren) From what I expected when I was very young, probably a 10. It really went well for me. But if you'd grade it right now, it'd be an 8. But when I look back, the chances of being where I am now were quite slim.

(Scott Wardell) You ended up with a lake place in South Dakota, a place in Arizona, the whole farm, and zero debt.

(Loren) We have a place in Tucson. It's just a double-wide trailer, a co-op thing, and we own a certain percent of the golf course there too. It's an 18-hole course. I wouldn't go unless there's a golf course.

(Scott Wardell) At what point did you buy these places?

(Loren) 2001, I think. 1996 was when we first went down to Tucson. We rented for 5 years. The lake home, we inherited from Joan's dad. That was about 30 years ago. We didn't put any money into it. We inherited it. The old cabin was in pretty bad shape. But we inherited enough to put a new cabin on it. We have to credit her Dad and Mom for that South Dakota place.

(Scott Wardell) The Arizona place, was that yours? A straight cash deal?

(Loren) No. We borrowed money from [a farm lending organization] to buy that. But we paid it back in two years.

///

Vacation property, as I've said before, is a very tempting expense layer a lot of people cannot resist. Whether it's a lake cabin, a condo in Florida, or a time-share, that extra layer can be a killer, if only because you feel you've earned it and need it.

One way to make it work is pretty simple. Finance little or nothing. If you have to take out a loan, consider setting up a payment mechanism that gets it off your books very fast. By "fast" I mean five years, maximum, not thirty. We're talking a luxury here that you do not want to risk becoming a financial albatross.

\\

(Scott Wardell) Joan, it sounds like your dad might have had some money to lend, but it also sounds like you never asked.

(Joan) No, we never asked. He was very secretive about money.

(Scott Wardell) Did you know that there was even money there to ask for?

(Joan) No. We didn't know anything about it. It wasn't my place to ask, I didn't think. If he wanted to offer it to us, well maybe. But with the South Dakota place he said, "You don't want to get stuck with a cabin. All you do is go up there and mow and fix."

(Loren) He tried to sell it before he died, and he wanted

too much for it and didn't get it. So we bought it from her brother. So actually, we inherited half and bought the other half.

(Scott Wardell) So when you see people today who are trying to get their retirement plan figured out, what advice would you give them?

(Loren) I think it's good to be prudent. You've got to make these different buckets. You have to know where you're at, and never overspend. But you know, you also have to keep your eyes and ears open and be aggressive enough to buy too. If there's a farm that comes up for sale and you figure you could make money in a couple years (and get the thing paid for without using the land you already have, which is difficult in this day and age) go ahead and do it.

Then, with the extra money, put it in something else. I didn't go into stocks very much. I had enough bookkeeping just keeping track of the farming end of things. I didn't want to be monkeying with stocks. So we bought into [mutual] funds and let those build up.

(Scott Wardell) The other part of your story, Loren, is you've never been very much for simple guarantees. You're kind of on the risk side of things, which people might not expect. It's an interesting mix!

(Loren) Maybe I'm in a different situation than other people. I think the farm end is kind of conservative. The land is always there. So you've got that. When I want to go into investing, I want a chance to see what it'll do, not just sit there with a bond. I've never had a CD (Certificate of Deposit) in my life. Can't stand them! I can't stand to have a thing just standing there. There's nothing happening. Drawing a couple percent interest. That doesn't interest me at all.

(Scott Wardell) But the risk part of it requires you to do your homework.

(Loren) Oh yeah. But the money that's in it we don't really need. It's just a fun thing now. Back when I put it in there, we needed it for backup. But now when things are kind of together, we're okay to just see what happens.

(Scott Wardell) Give me an example of something you spotted and wanted to get into. Something that looked like a good bet.

(Loren) In stocks, we bought Maytag. We had it for about a year, sold it and made some money on that.

(Scott Wardell) Didn't you do a spell with precious metals?

(Loren) I think so, yeah. We grabbed some of that when precious metals were low. I think there were three or four years there when the precious metals fund went a little nuts.

And then there was the time we took a camper trip down to Oklahoma. That's when we bought oil wells! [He laughs.] The neighbors [invested] with us! We had a friend who got us into that. He was going to sell these oil wells. So we bought in and went down to Oklahoma and looked at, you know, *our oil wells.* Duane and I bought two or three together and I bought one on my own.

(Scott Wardell) Was this speculation? Were the wells pumping?

(Loren) Speculation. They knew there were reserves. But they didn't know if there was going to be oil right there. Some of them didn't turn out. But I had one named Bradstreet that did very well. We broke even and then we sold out.

That was my biggest endeavor. It was fun. And we made a commercial down there that was fun.

(Scott Wardell) A commercial?

(Loren) Well, somebody must have known me a little and

knew I had the gift of gab. So they said, "Hey, how'd you like to do a commercial?" They told me to come on down to Mankato [Minnesota]. So I went down and it was just kind of like what we're doing here, with a guy interviewing me. When it was over he said, "I'll call ya."

A few days later he called and said, "Hey, we selected you!" He told me we were going to Paris ... Tennessee! I got real excited for a second there. But we went and they filmed it and it ran for quite a while. I got royalties for three years. Joan got a couple hundred bucks for being a stand-in.

(Scott Wardell) I'm struck by how open to opportunities you've been. When opportunity came your way, you weren't the one to say, "No, thank you."

(Loren) No. I kind of liked to get into stuff.

(Scott Wardell) Have you ever come up with any rules of risk assessment? You talk about doing your homework, knowing where you're at. That's part of your "financial imprinting." You understand cash-flow. But it sounds like this is something you enjoy. There's a game here that can be played and you like to win. Any rules of thumb? Rules for people about how to handle risk?

(Loren) Like I said, I never went in with big money unless I could see a profit with it within a couple years. I looked for a short win. The oil wells were probably the riskiest thing I ever did. But I always did my math. When I was on the school board, I went through all the numbers. I knew the numbers. And they had to be solid.

We had a gal who wanted to build on to a school and said we'd get a grant. My question was, "Is that guaranteed?" She said, "Oh no. But they usually come through." So I said, "No. We aren't going to take that chance. We've got to educate these kids. It's more important to have good teachers than it is to have this building." Be sure it's a sure thing when it came to something like that. Solid numbers. That would be the biggest thing for me I guess.

> I mentioned Loren's two-budget process. But in his public board work, Loren only used worst-case budgeting. "Best case" was left to other board members.

(Scott Wardell) The other thing that comes to mind is the matter of your own personal reputation. The machinery guy in town knew the family. He knew the Brekkes were a solid crowd, even though you boys were young. Credibility is a tough thing. Once you lose it, it's tough to get back. So I gather you were careful about protecting your reputation.

(Loren) I always told the kids, "If you got something to say that might not be just right, say it to yourself first. If it doesn't fit very well, just forget it. If you blurt it out, you just hurt people. We told the girls if you ruin your name, you ruin my name and your mom's name. We're all connected."

Summary

The model here for Loren Brekke is the one that says, "I'm just not going to put myself that close to the edge of the cliff." Maybe because he had no choice but to become an adult at an early age, working extraordinarily hard to feed himself and keep his parentless family together, Loren developed a vivid understanding of where you don't want to go, of where the limits were financially. When he took what for him were big risks, he did it with money he knew he could afford to lose. He had run the worst-case scenarios.

Loren brings a lot of classic "salt of the earth" virtues to the table – the ability to work, ingenuity, resourcefulness, an engaging personality and solid judgment. He protected the assets he had, established credit through his character, didn't over extend himself, stayed rational in bubbles, pushed himself out into the community and did the math for worst-case scenarios.

He always knew where he was, and who he was.

Questions to Consider

1. Do you look at your household budget and imagine what would have to change if you fell into a worst-case scenario?

2. Do you truly have sufficient assets to "gamble" on speculative investments?

3. If you are approaching retirement age, have you considered expanding your civic involvement?

Chapter 3

The Frugality Trip

It's a nice situation to be in, having all the money you'll ever need. Being rich has great appeal. Conventional wisdom says that then truly, you can live the life you dreamed of. Travel. Vacation homes. Artistic avocations, whatever. Throughout my career though, I've worked primarily with people who never expected to be wealthy, as in hedge fund manager/pop star/corporate tycoon wealthy. Most of my clients chose careers for reasons other than money. Some of them planned for retirement accordingly and entered retirement with many, if not all of the outward manifestations of much greater wealth. They traveled. They vacationed at second homes.

Most never felt deprived. Others didn't plan and lived a far different life after their careers ended.

The story of Becky Wardell – that's right, my very own sister – is very much the former. I knew I wanted a chapter in this book on smart, frugal living and I quickly realized that right there in my own family was as good an example as I could find. Becky's career of choice was as a public school teacher, and no teacher ever expects to be at private boardroom lunches trading financial tips and secrets with Warren Buffett or a Saudi sheik. Becky made several moves over the course of her working career that I'd advise doing differently, but overall, the Great Recession withstanding, she and her husband have reached retirement age by practicing a cardinal virtue that was out of favor in fatter, flusher times ... frugality.

They learned to live within their means. They lived well by any objective standard – owning a second home on the Wisconsin shore of Lake Superior – and in later years they have traveled abroad annually, although not in the kind of first-class accommodations luring you from the pages of glossy travel magazines. But they achieved the life they wanted, which is close to the essence of "wealth."

There are a handful of vital lessons in Becky's story for anyone preparing for or riding out unstable financial times.

Snapshot

- **Age:** 67
- **Marital status:** Married, no children.
- **Primary career:** Public school teacher.
- **Asset description:** Teacher's retirement account. Husband has railroad pension. A paragon of frugality.
- **Specific dilemma:** Married later in life, merged finances. How to satisfy goal of regular international travel on a modest budget.
- **Financial stability level:** Stable.

Becky and I were raised by children of the Depression. Money was something you never wasted. You saved and purchased what you needed and what you really wanted in a sensible way. We both were encouraged to get part-time jobs and start savings accounts as kids. Becky recalls, "My first job was at a drugstore for 75 cents an hour. And I made more money babysitting. Dad used to get mad because I'd make 50 cents an hour babysitting and sometimes come home at two o'clock in the morning. He'd say, '50 cents an hour! That's not fair! At two in the morning, you have to start a sliding scale and charge more'."

She had her missteps of course. Like the department store sales job with the employee discount where she quickly spent more than she was making. Good thing for her Mom taught her how to sew. I remember her making herself a new dress for every Easter. Our Mother was a coupon clipper. Both of us remember going to the store and saving more in coupons than she spent for the groceries.

Both Mom and Dad were good at gardening. We had a big garden full of sweet corn, tomatoes, cucumbers and beans. Every summer night they would walk around the garden, picking vegetables for supper. It was their time together.

Not to make it sound all "Walton" like, but it was a different time. The whole Wardell family, six kids and Mom and Dad, sat down for dinner every night at 6. No cell phones. No texting. Actual chatter about what happened that day.

(Scott Wardell) Becky, paint a quick picture for us of how you and your husband John look at the consumer society we live in.

(Becky) Neither John nor I can figure out why people need so much money to live. Who *needs* $1 million a year? We do everything we want on a much smaller income, and always have. I mean club memberships, cable TV ... we don't have any of that. When people tell me they have to go to the club to work out and it's a beautiful day, I think, "What's the matter with you?! You're missing one of the best things in life, a lovely day!"

We also think TV creates too much stress. I never do e-mail or Twitter or watch the news after 8:30 at night. When I heard about Osama bin Laden, people were telling me they stayed up all night watching. One friend said, "I would have never been able to sleep." I don't get it. That sort of thing just gets your brain going too actively too late at night.

(Scott Wardell) I think it's fair to say that if there is a theme to your life, it's "frugal living," which to me means controlling your life to make the most of your money. Is that fair?

(Becky) I agree with that. If you want to know where it started, the short story is that when I was in elementary school we were taught to save money. Our school had an arrangement with Farmers & Mechanics Bank. We kids had an envelope that we turned in every week with some money in it for deposit in a savings account. It started as a penny. It was part of the actual school curriculum to teach us how to save.

//

This really does sound like something out of *The Waltons*.

I doubt there's anything like it being taught at any public school today. But it used to be a hands-on kind of thing. Schools would tell students, "Not only are we going to teach you the principles, we also will teach the methodology to create a habit."

Saving, good money management, is all about the habit. But the days of kids in school stuffing pennies into envelopes is completely gone. For one thing, it stopped making sense for the banks. Too much handling expense. But it really did teach future customers something valuable. "Financial imprinting," the creation of a habit, and a positive one in this case,

is a critical virtue that everyone should learn at an early age.

Today, this kind of education is entirely up to parents, and today's parents often have no model for good imprinting. Let's face the facts: We've been terrible savers. The habits kids learn – about credit cards for example – usually do more harm than good.

(Scott Wardell) Did Mom and Dad ever sit you down and talk to you about finances?

(Becky) No. But you remember, we did have these values that Dad would actually talk about. "Have a relaxed, friendly attitude, and self-discipline."

Wait! There were four. Now I remember. Number one was health. Two was self-discipline. Three was the friendly, relaxed attitude, and four, which he added later, was intellectual curiosity. I think all of us live by those values. Just as important was that Dad modeled them so well himself. [Dad was an engineer, a supervisor of a materials and testing laboratory].

(Scott Wardell) Remind me, how did you handle your college costs?

(Becky) Mom and Dad said, "You go to the U [of Minnesota] and we'll pay your tuition. You pay for your books and you can live at home." It was a pretty good deal.

Some churches, kind of like Becky's school, handed out savings kits with three different accounts. The point was to teach, or "imprint" three specific things.

One was the sense of contribution: If you make a little money, there were things that needed your help, like your church.

Second, long-term savings.

And third, saving for something nearer-term. Something you wanted.

My wife and I did this with our kids, particularly

on the contribution end. At the end of the year we had a family meeting and said, "Okay, we've all saved and we've been making contributions throughout the course of the year. Our contribution budget still has $1,000 in it. You all have some interest in this. So, it'll be a joint decision on what we'll use this money for. You to come to dinner on Sunday night and try and convince us that this is where $500 or the full contribution should go. Make your pitch for your project."

It was an interesting experiment, because the kids got after it big time. There was a sense of competition between them to see who could make the winning pitch.

The point was financial imprinting. Thinking responsibly about money. The process asks you: "Have I given enough?" "Should I give more?" And, "How should I make this decision?" The whole process was about how to make a financial decision and giving back.

(Scott Wardell) How old were you before you actually thought in terms of a career plan?

(Becky) It took me a couple of years, but I decided to go into elementary education. Mom and Dad always said, "You'll be a great teacher." But I said, "I'll be single my whole life. I'll be an old maid!" I didn't want to do that! But they told me I had to start applying for jobs. Because I had been a student teacher in Bloomington [Minnesota] they sent me a contract for a full-time job. I hadn't even applied! My first job was as a third-grade teacher at Oak Grove Elementary.

(Scott Wardell) So then, with your first adult job, were you thinking more seriously about budgeting, cash flow, savings and all that?

(Becky) Sort of. I mean, I bought a car. The school had a program where I was able to buy a car with no down payment and no payments until fall. Just for teachers. So I bought a blue Camaro that cost $2,200. I loved that car! I think the first year I taught, I made $4,600. It was really a small amount of money.

That same year I taught, I lived at home and saved to go to Europe the following summer. Dad was going to charge me $50 a month to live at home. His rationale was, "Because now you're working." I was so angry. I mean, I was saving to go to Europe! I didn't want to pay that. But in reality I was able to save quite a bit of money. I did pay him the $50. Probably not the first couple of months, but after that I paid him.

This is a bit different than today's "helicopter parent" who can't resist giving their child whatever they want, much less need. But this old school-style taught a lot about financial responsibility.

That year two friends and I went to Europe and we did it for less than $5 a day. It was really frugal. We took the train around. We had a rail pass and we had the Frommer's book. I went with another friend a few years later and we did almost the same thing: $5 a day. So the roots of being able to travel cheap started early.

Remember how Mom and Dad loved to travel? They would take us in the car and we'd go off to Yellowstone, six kids in the back of a Ford station wagon. Dad was one of those people who could not drive past a historical marker. Lord, he was slow in a Civil War park! My husband is a lot like that. It once took us two weeks to get to Salt Lake City [from Minneapolis].

(Scott Wardell) Have you made financial arrangements, special accounts, to ensure that you'll be able to travel?

(Becky) We don't consciously save for travel. So no. I guess we don't need to. The way we operate we usually just have enough money when we're ready to travel. Just because we have an extra $1,000, we don't take the attitude that we have to go out and spend it.

//

As I've said previously, good financial imprinting, knowing what is coming in and what is going out, brings a sense of your personal threshold. In one sense, this means knowing almost instinctively what you can afford at a given moment. Good imprinting gives you this innate sense. This isn't an argument for unstructured budgeting. My point is only that if you develop imprinting, a sense of your personal cash flow, you can operate quite well without hitting the smartphone app to your savings account ten times a day.

Quick story: I was working with a client in a small Midwestern town. The wife had always wanted to go to Hawaii, but the husband was never sure they could afford it. They had a clash of thresholds.

He sees the money over there and says, "We cannot spend it." She sees the money over there and says "You're right, but we can spend part of it." He wants to take the vacation, too. But he thinks the threshold needs to be a little higher. They need more savings before they can go. Otherwise, to him, it looks like they're depleting something. He's anxious and wouldn't enjoy the trip.

So ... we worked through the numbers. We looked up what they had flowing into their cash reserve. Their advantage was they'd had this elongated period of semi-retirement income. We coupled that with their Social Security and found there was more than enough in-flow for a trip to Hawaii.

A year later, I went out to do an account review, and the wife was grinning from ear to ear. I said, "Okay, what's up?" She said, "We're going to Hawaii!" They had the money all along, but only by taking a serious look at their cash threshold had they gained the confidence in the system do something they had always wanted to do.

Their threshold was adequate. But they had spent years in anxiety over whether it was or wasn't. All that anxiety was wasted energy. Good financial imprinting means you're aware of your threshold for expense, and it spares you a lot of fretting and regret.

(Scott Wardell) As you began teaching, what was your pension plan like?

(Becky) I think you had to teach [many years] before you could get into the tax-sheltered plan. The school district had a teacher's retirement that came out of your salary. I remember all of us young teachers trying to figure out how to get our money out of teacher's retirement [to spend]. We didn't make that much money, and here was this pool of a couple thousand dollars that had built up. All of us teachers wanted to get that money out.

Over the years many of my friends figured ways to get at it. But whenever I got serious, something stopped me. It just bothered me. So I never touched it. It helped that I never changed jobs, which meant I didn't have to think about rolling it over somewhere else.

These teacher friends of Becky's were not trying to get out of the plan to reinvest it elsewhere. They were trying to get the money out in order to spend it. They saw a chunk of their money and they wanted to lay their hands on it–for a trip, or furniture, or a car.

Here's my perspective. If someone has attacked their retirement plan – which has a fortress built around it specifically to discourage from pulling money out early

– those people often do poorly in the rest of their cash flow.

People who pay a lot of attention to their money often ask, "I'm in this retirement plan and I've changed jobs, is this old plan really the best plan for me?" It's a good question, as far as it goes.

But the people asking that question often roll the money into an IRA or something else because 1) they want more control of the money, or 2) they want more investment choices, or 3) they want protected growth, which, in my opinion, a lot of retirement plans don't have enough of. All of those are good reasons.

Most people can't afford a self-inflicted backward slide. On the other hand, how people decide how to invest in their own accounts can be detrimental to the plan itself. Unfortunately, the way people select what they think of as "safer" funds is completely backwards in terms of successful investing. Way too often what they do is go through the investment sheet they're shown and say, "Wow, this one did 28% last year! I'm putting my money in there."

That shows a fundamental lack of understanding of how the markets operate. Dropping the bulk of your assets into the account that returned 28% last year and less or nothing into the account that delivered 3% is basically impulse shopping. Often this results in poor investment returns.

Why? Because rarely do investments repeat a stellar year immediately after a year of great performance. Sound asset allocation and diversification is something to consider.

Control your impulses. If you've got an account to rollover or a windfall to invest, continue to diversify.

By the time one category is doing well again and you finally invest in them, you'll probably find the recovery's over. It's the classic "chasing returns syndrome," like rushing out to by $1700 gold.

(Becky) The Teachers Retirement was a forced savings [plan]. And I'm glad for it now. Very few of those people [who pulled their money out] are going to be able to retire easily. Some do volunteer work. But most of them who started teaching with me are still working. A lot have part-time jobs, full-time jobs, or they substitute teach. Out of necessity. They think they need that money to spend. Most of them don't have their houses paid off. They still have mortgages. They have payments on their cars. They just need more money than we do.

//

I must add: One of the key components of successful investing is getting the allocations right. My rule of thumb is that most performance is based on broad asset allocation, and only a small percent is based on the investment itself. Get the allocations right and it is likely the rest will follow. Allocation should be about risk tolerance, not just returns expected. There a plenty of good tools available to help you measure your tolerance. If you can give your advisor a realistic picture of the retirement lifestyle (expenses) that you are likely to bring with you into retirement and give your advisor a sense of your risk tolerance, he/she are usually able to construct an investment plan that fits those together neatly.

\\\

(Scott Wardell) When did you buy your first home?

(Becky) I bought my first house in 1972. I started teaching in 1967. In '72 I had a boyfriend who read a book about buying real estate to become a millionaire. He was from Seattle, and everyone out there was buying these big duplexes. He was a laid-off airline pilot. He had no money. So in 1972 we found this duplex and I decided I was going to buy it. Between us I was the only one who had any money. So there I was, a single woman and a teacher. I made $11,000 a year at this point. I applied for a loan. $32,500. A beautiful duplex.

To get the loan, the bank made me write this long letter saying I was going to teach summer school. It took them a month to decide before they said, "no" And this is the best part: The realtor said, "It's just because you're a woman. I know that." He said, "I have a bank that will give you a loan." He was right.

I got a loan in a day from the other bank and I bought the duplex, lived in half, rented out the upstairs. We fixed it all up, stripped the wallpaper, painted it, and it turned out to be a really good investment. The renters covered over half the mortgage.

But it was scraping bottom financially for me. I was bouncing checks. That was the most over-extended I've been in my life. Sometimes I'd buy groceries and I'd think, "I don't think I have money for this." But after a couple years it worked out.

//

I've seen too many people overplay their hands.

If Becky had bought the whole unit and had *not* lived in half, and then tried to make payments on another homestead property, it could have been a crash-and-burn scenario. That's how close to living beyond her means she was.

Here again is a cash-flow issue.

For the right investor, income-producing rental property can be a good idea. But what we can't count on today that clients and advisors counted on even a decade ago, is significant and sustainable returns. The market has ebbed and flowed as it always will. You have to have a solid, numbers-on-paper understanding of your limits and tolerance for market variations.

Becky also bought the duplex without falling victim to the curse of high credit card debt. She wasn't charging anything. Her straight-cash lifestyle required her to have money on hand every month. It may have been god-awful tight in the early going, but it was survivable because she wasn't paying 15% a month on thousands in consumer credit bills.

Frankly, in today's world, Becky is a great model for middle-class rental property ownership. Her model says, "I'm going to live in half of what I'm going to buy. Also, I will be a 'present owner,' so if the toilet needs fixing, I can take care of it myself."

If you take the attitude that on a modest income you're going to hire a manager to do the sweaty, dirty stuff, it's going to be far more expensive.

You've got to have cash reserve and you've got to have low expenses for managing your properties (and the ability to do so if you're going to take the DIY approach). You've got to be honest with yourself.

(Scott Wardell) How many houses have you bought over the years?

(Becky) My friend went back to Seattle and I wanted to live alone. I didn't care to have people living upstairs. I just wanted to have my own house. So I bought the house that John and I live in now. I sold the duplex on a Contract for Deed. I bought it for $32,000 and I think I sold it for $114,000, twenty years later.

A Contract for Deed (CFD) is when a seller of property provides financing to the purchaser of that property. Essentially, the seller is playing bank. The seller retains the legal title to the property even though the buyer is living in it. The seller takes an initial down payment and the buyer makes loan payments (versus rent payments). Once the full purchase price has been paid, including interest, the seller turns over title to the buyer.

Contracts for Deed are not a bad idea -- if structured right. CFDs are all about structure. If you're considering this, remember, *you are playing bank*, you need to balance your exposure with collateral. The risk with a CFD, is default, deterioration, or lack of maintenance by the new occupant owner.

For example: You agree to sell for $250,000. You take $30,000 down. Then, if the new "owners" don't make the rest of the payments and you get the house back valued at anything less than $220,000, you're taking a loss. So be certain that you get enough cash up front to protect yourself from the other party's misfortune or foolishness. In other words, build in a serious penalty for them walking away from the deal.

In a stable market, CFDs are beneficial. Properly structured, you could probably charge about 5% interest on a CFD today. Done right, they are really more like a bond than a loan, and 5% is not a bad return. In today's market, as a reliable cash flow, I personally would take it. Bottom line: If you have your financial ducks in line to back up a CFD, meaning you have wiggle room in an emergency, they are not a bad idea.

But remember, *structure is critical.* The property is still yours. It has to be properly maintained, and not just "adequately." The underlying investment must be fully protected.

The new "owners" could run it down. Everything has to be spelled out, and the new owners should be thoroughly vetted. Do NOT give a Contract for Deed to just anybody.

(Scott Wardell) Given your income, even with the rental property, tell us how you were able to afford a second home up on the south shore of Lake Superior.

(Becky) I always wanted a lakeshore lot. It is kind of a "Minnesota thing," the lake cabin. I searched all over, and lots were so expensive. But a friend of mine ran into someone who said there were inexpensive lots on Lake Superior. So we went up there and I saw one for $6,000. Just the lot. No house. My friend loaned me some money, which meant I was able to buy the lot for cash. I negotiated the price down to $5,000.

The land belonged to a couple going through a divorce.

They took $5,000 for 200 feet on Lake Superior. It's on a high cliff overlooking the lake. Two hundred feet of shoreline and 600 feet deep. About three acres total. I still think it was really a good move. Almost better than buying the duplex.

When my husband first saw it, he said, "I can't believe you have this. It is so beautiful." He bought a trailer to put on it. He said, "You've got to have a trailer on this or someplace where we can stay." We didn't like the trailer, so we eventually built a house on it.

There are two ways to look at vacation properties for people with a modest income.

If you look at all the people who bought properties at the high point in 2006 in an upscale area, like the popular Whitefish Chain in northern Minnesota, they were in a world of hurt for years after the crash, some still are. Many of those "peak of the bubble" properties are still worth less than what their owners paid.

Vacation property is an expensive proposition. In turbulent financial times, it can be one of the first realty markets to collapse. But Becky's value of frugality, her financial ethos, was such that she only bought when she found a lot for an unbelievably low dollar amount and she bought in fully prepared to develop it herself.

Also, when you find yourself thinking about vacation property, the other key piece to think about is how long you are going to stay in it. Is this a lifelong investment, or a phase you're in for five or six years? You really have to be honest with yourself about this.

(Scott Wardell) Prior to buying the lake lot, did you find you were able to travel much during the early years of owning a house?

(Becky) My boyfriend at that time owned a plane. The pilot, remember? So until about the 1980s most of my travel was more local, flying around with him. Just around the country.

We would go to Seattle, or we would go out skiing in Bozeman. We did fly to Cincinnati one time.

A friend of mine and I went to China in about 1986. About then I met my husband, and we started doing Europe. He hadn't traveled much. When we met he had just been to Scotland. That was his first trip to Europe. I had just been to China. We thought, "Well, we have this in common."

(Scott Wardell) As your teacher's salary increased did you make additional retirement contributions?

(Becky) The one thing that I did do was max out with additional education, which meant salary increases. Every summer I was going to school. I got so that I had my Bachelor of Science plus 60. [Teacher contract jargon for "additional credits"]. Then I started over and got my Masters. So for twenty years, I went to school. I took every class, and my salary went up accordingly. It was a lot of work, but I enjoyed it and I learned a lot.

(Scott Wardell) Had you hired a financial advisor during this period?

(Becky) One thing that you had to do when you got into the tax shelter that I did, a 403(b), was to have [an advisor] set it up. It was kind of like throwing dice to pick someone. The first couple I met were really not very good. They took my money and never called me. I found them by word of mouth. The school district had certain people that you had to use, because they were matching your contribution. They had approved vendors. You had a choice of three or four.

But I wasn't really with a serious financial advisor. I was just putting money into different funds. That is when I had money. Through the district, I was assigned to a financial planner and she called me every six months to come in to talk. She actually took me on. My husband is not into [financial planning] very much. But he knew I had confidence in her. Actually, when it came to retirement, she said, "You're fine. You have enough money. You can retire."

Then of course the stock market sunk. But she's managed our money so that we take so much out of our investments all the time. I didn't understand you could take money out before you were fifty-nine. When I retired at fifty-four, almost fifty-five, she set up a plan that allowed us to begin withdrawals.

The investments are quite conservative. Especially now that we're retired. She knows we don't want high risk. It's all very low risk.

There are at least two phases of retirement. What works for someone like Becky in her first fifteen years of retirement may not work as well in her next twenty.

Becky was lucky to be invested very conservatively when the stock market crashed in 2008. But she is now seventy. If she lives to eighty-five, the stuff we run our lives on–gas and food–will likely continue to increase a lot. Her problem is that these safe investments might not keep up in terms of the new costs of transportation and food.

Unless she finds a way to get some growth in her portfolio, I worry that hers is not the best recipe going forward. You should consider having properly allocated investments in a "growth bucket." That's the flag I raise on a situation like Becky's. One of the biggest keys for people when they take early retirement is that they should have a portfolio that has the potential to keep up with inflation. Investing in extremely conservative investments with low annual return might add up to a weak stew once you get further into retirement.

Becky might consider a combination of her conservative investments with some sort of growth/equity portfolio.

Also, let me add here that what I call "categorical investing" often gets people like Becky into trouble. You shouldn't just buy real estate or stocks without a micro-examination of what you are getting and how it fits your longer-term needs. News flash: Diversification.

(Scott Wardell) So in terms of real estate you have the house in Minneapolis and the lakeshore property. Is that about it?

(Becky) I did buy another lot with our brother in Hawaii. Its value hasn't increased much. He has kind of taken that over. It hasn't been a very good investment. It's a lot of volcanic rocks. I've been there only once to see it. But, like Dad said, "Buy land; they aren't making it anymore."

(Scott Wardell) On a personal level, you got married relatively late in life.

(Becky) John and I were married in 1988. I was forty-two.

(Scott Wardell) Tell us what John is like with money.

(Becky) He is very conservative with his money. He worked for the railroads for many years and often in the winters he was laid off. So he always had a sense of having little or no debt and quickly paying things off. He's really a nut about not paying interest. He bought a house when he was relatively young, out on the West Coast. He went to school out there. He has always bought the houses he lived in. He doesn't believe in paying rent, nor does he believe in paying interest.

(Scott Wardell) Pretty debt-phobic, I gather?

(Becky) We live in the house that I bought. But we used a lot of the money he got from selling his house when we built the lake place, which he just paid off. We had a relative of his build the house, and we pretty much paid it off as it was built.

But I bought the house in the city when interest rates were 12%. That was a fifteen-year mortgage. So it was a big monthly payment in the early years. Eventually, I refinanced that. When John and I got married, his top priority was paying off the Minneapolis house.

(Scott Wardell) Did you use tax-sheltered annuities?

(Becky) Yes, we did. When we were building the lake place, we needed $10,000 to pay for a car. I used that annuity to pay for the car. But it only took us a year to pay that back. Dad always said, "Never borrow money to buy a car. Always pay cash."

(Scott Wardell) So did you make pre-payments on the house, buying down the principal?

(Becky) Oh yes. I can't tell you how much more, but we were paying it off so that we had the fifteen years reduced to probably seven years, if I remember right.

(Scott Wardell) And other purchases, you mentioned a car, things that have to be replaced. Did you save in expectation of these costs?

(Becky) Not really. We kind of buy what we've got money for. We only have one car. That is a big savings. When we were both working we had two. But having just one inexpensive car really makes a difference.

///

That new car smell is one of the most expensive aromas known to man. On the other hand, leasing, in my humble opinion has turned out to be an even worse option. Leasing after all, is just borrowing. It is not owning.

The key here, and Becky's husband has it right, is how you buy. If you borrow for a car, you're borrowing for a depreciating asset. If you get ten years' use out of it, it'll probably come out okay. The risk you run is to owe more on the car than what it's worth.

However, as Becky mentions, transportation costs are reduced substantially if you can get by with one car. Half the purchase price. Half the repair costs. Half the insurance bill. Once you factor that in, every year, you've nearly paid for a nice vacation.

\\\

(Becky) Naturally, our biggest expense in retirement is health care. We were paying $15,000 a year, it went up so much. So we really had to work on health care costs.

Before Medicare we stayed with the school district plan. That was a terrible mistake. It was very expensive. I thought, "We've had such good luck. We are so healthy. Why would we want to switch health insurance?" We should have, but we didn't. But now we have much better cash flow simply because [of Medicare].

//

For someone like Becky who retires early, the bridge to sixty-five is a huge deal. She specifically was looking at a very long bridge. That's ten years post full-time income before getting to Medicare. Her husband is four to five years younger, so his is even longer. The disadvantage of Medicare is that you can't add a spouse to the coverage. It's not like your old company plan. So the shopping piece of the health care dilemma is very important in that bridge period.

A high-deductible plan with a Health Savings Account (HSA) might be an efficient way to manage a case like this with a ten-year bridge phase. Make sure you have an adequate cash reserve to pay the deductible.

Here's what I mean: Lets say you're looking at a $2,000 deductible. You have to begin building that account pretty aggressively at least four years before your retirement. Aim for $10,000 or more sitting in the HSA as you retire. So then if your health fails, or if something catastrophic happens, and you have to pay $2,000 or $2,500 out of pocket, you're covered for several years before Medicare kicks in.

HSAs also have attractive tax benefits. You get a deduction (pre-tax dollars) when you contribute to the account. The earnings while your money is in the account are tax free and when you withdraw for qualified medical expenses that money is also tax free.

Obviously, you've got to look at the details of which plan—an HSA or a regular health plan—serves you best.

(Scott Wardell) Tell us the story of the trouble caused by an oversight in retirement-planning paperwork early in your teaching career.

(Becky) Oh, that. When I was in my late twenties or so, we [teachers] had to fill out a form declaring whether we were choosing to go into a fixed account or a stock market-based account. Some of us didn't take it very seriously. I don't know if I checked anything. Probably because I didn't know what to check.

I can't tell you how many people don't know what to check when they see this box. Most of the other teachers checked this "fixed" thing.

So when the stock market was doing so well in the '90s, and teacher's retirement had all this money, the school district was encouraging people to retire. Some people like me who had been placed in the stock market plan by default because we didn't make a choice years before had a lot more money than the "fixed" people. So the district was giving us more money to retire.

The other teachers, who had chosen the fixed account, kept bringing this up to me. They kept pointing out that I was in the other, better-performing plan. Some called it a "special plan," like it was a conspiracy or something. Well, what could I say? It's an investment. It was purely accidental. I didn't really know what the choice was. I just lucked out. Ignorance is bliss, I guess. I got the full benefit of the '90s stock market.

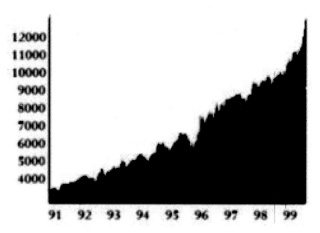

//

Becky ignored her selection but fell into one that worked out okay for her. That's luck.

But retirement is not a luck plan. Honestly, she got lucky because she was in the market in one of the best, most successful periods of time for stocks. I say again, luck. Plain and simple. But don't count on it.

It goes without saying Becky should have sought advice when she didn't fill in that box on the form.

As for the other teachers, the ones who said, "I just don't understand it, so I'm going with the fixed" ... what irks me is that these are educators. Come on, people! When you don't understand something, you have to do your homework. You have to find a partner who will coach you through it. Next to a heart attack, fundamental retirement planning is about as critical as you can get.

\\\

(Scott Wardell) In retirement, do either of you have any continuing income, from side jobs or whatever?

(Becky) Well, John is an author. He has a very small income from royalties of books he's written. And we do work as election judges; that's really our only job.

//

Part-time work in retirement fascinates me. A lot of people, skilled professionals, retire and go off looking for something entirely alien to what they've known. They tell me they want to do "something different."

So I hear a lot of stuff like, "I want to work in a nursery, or a flower shop" or other things. But what I discover as I talk to them is that part of the reason they want to put distance between the thing they're most skilled at is because it owned them. They're exhausted by it.

When they take their primary skill to a part-time position, I tell them it won't own them anymore. It isn't as binding and all-controlling.

So I ask, "If you took your current job, and dropped it down to twenty hours, or even fifteen hours a week, and you make three times the money that you make over here at this florist job that you've romanticized as this beautiful, wonderful thing, does the deal still work?"

If you still can't stomach the thought of a variation on your skill job, then fine, go take the floral job.

But after some rational consideration, you might see this in a new light. You may discover that your career job, or something closely related to it, at only fifteen hours a week, could not only be enjoyable but far more productive. Certainly more than when it consumed 45-50 hours a week.

I say again, have an honest conversation with yourself.

\\

(Scott Wardell) So right now income is primarily pension and interest?

(Becky) I have Social Security. A small amount. But it does make a difference. It means we can take less out of our investments. Thankfully, we do have good health. We take care of ourselves. We always eat healthy. We've never smoked. We don't drink. That, by the way, is another thing people think they need. What some people spend on drinking! We laugh at people who spend so much on wine and stuff. We both have special reasons why we don't drink.

(Scott Wardell) Let's talk about how you manage expenses now that you're retired.

(Becky) As far as costs go, every year we have been married, we have taken an overseas trip. That's our big splurge. The cost obviously depends on where we go. We used to be able to stay in a lot of places for $30-40 a night. You still can in Eastern Europe. There are all sorts of things we do to make this possible. The Internet for researching and booking is great for keeping costs down. And guide books. We used to use *Let's Go*, for example. It's kind of a kids' way to travel. I like *Lonely Planet,* and *Rick Steves'* books. They always give you places to stay, and they always tell you what to do to stay safe.

(Scott Wardell) So this isn't exactly flying first-class and staying at the Ritz?

(Becky) I used to tell people, "We travel like college students, with a pack on our back." We only take what we can carry on our back. I was so happy when the little roller cases came, you know, with the wheels? The first time I got my roller case, we were in Thailand and my husband said, "This doesn't work in these countries. There isn't enough solid ground."

We walk everywhere, or take public transportation. My husband likes trains and he's good at figuring it out. And as far as food, well there are a lot of really good places to eat all over for $30 a night. For two people. We love the food that we get. In Turkey, Bulgaria, Eastern Europe, the food has been fantastic.

(Scott Wardell) So how have you controlled the status issues? You know what I'm talking about. Lots of people think they have to have a house as big as their buddy's, take trips that impress their friends. That sort of thing can be quite an expensive trap.

(Becky) Well, as you know Scott, Mom and Dad were not keep-up-with-the-Joneses people at all. Actually, Dad used to make fun of it. And my husband! If something is popular, he'll go the other way.

Neither of us, though, wants to feel like we're twenty years behind the times, as far as fashion goes. But at the same time, we don't feel the need to have a great big car. It just doesn't meet our values. It doesn't bother us for a Saturday night date to take the bus. Last Saturday night, we took the bus to a coffee shop, we watched a music group, which was great, and we had a snack and tea for $5. We had a lovely night.

Most of our friends who are retired aren't keeping-up-with-the-Joneses types either. Shared values, you know.

(Scott Wardell) And in terms of home maintenance, are you do-it-yourselfers?

(Becky) I would like to pay to have more things done. But my husband tries to do everything. He's pretty good at it. He can figure things out. When he wanted to install our dishwasher ... well, it was so much work. It took us a whole day. That kind of thing I wish we would hire someone to do. But he likes to work with his hands. When we travel, he loves getting all the maps. It's a puzzle. It's a real challenge.

///

Doing things for yourself is an enormous cost saver. Think about The Greatest Generation. They were fix-it-yourself kind of folk, by necessity. Now, simply put, people don't even fertilize their own lawns.

If you relate to Becky's cash-flow situation, stop and think of the economics of this.

A lawn spreader costs maybe $30, if you buy a high-end one. So, if you want a good-looking lawn, you can take care of it for about 1/5th of hiring a service.

Moreover, there are advantages to self-sufficiency beyond saving what might seem like a few paltry dollars. On a modest income, cultivating a garden and planning meals around what you grow gives you the benefit of a substantially smaller food bill, especially if you think in terms of your home-grown dinner substituting for dinner out with a couple glasses of wine.

You're going to have a little more time in retirement. That is one primary point of retirement, right? This should suggest to you that you now have a fresh opportunity to learn new skills. Like DIY "puzzles."

Instead of reaching for the phone and credit card to get a plumber to install your dishwasher, say, "I'm going to figure this out myself." It may take a while. There may be some exasperation and language unbecoming a lady or gentleman, but you're learning new skill. (Plus, there are YouTube videos showing how to do almost every household task imaginable.)

Becky and her husband have turned frugality into

a puzzle, a game they play against goods and services they need. They've done a very good job of paring out the frills and junk people think they need, or can't live without. Everything about their strategy is a winner.

\\\

(Scott Wardell) And what about simple things? Items you don't want to make yourself. Like clothes?

(Becky) Most of my clothes-buying involves travel clothing. Ninety percent of the time I wear my travel clothes. They're comfortable and durable. I buy most of our stuff at REI. My husband is really into USA-made, like I said. He won't buy anything made in China. As you can imagine, that has gotten nearly impossible. Although, I did find a site on-line where I could buy him US-made clothes. So now he's very happy.

(Scott Wardell) You mentioned the savings of good health. You have had a lifelong exercise ethic.

(Becky) Almost lifelong. I started running when I was thirty, I've always stayed active, and I like to hike. John was into track when he was in high school. He started running again when he met me. We kind of play off each other a little bit. I consider myself a lot more active than he is. I walk with friends. He doesn't. He doesn't get as much activity. He works on his computer.

///

I'm often tempted to say, "Balance is everything." If you take the holistic view of retirement you'll say: Body. Soul. Mind. Money.

How does the money play into this? Money doesn't sound very Zen. I've had interesting talks with Becky about the cost efficiency of taking care of oneself.

Do you want to save some money? Go for a walk! Stop eating fried food! Becky and her husband walk down to a little club, listen to a jazz band, and have a cup of tea. They got their evening's entertainment for maybe $15 and some exercise.

Others in her economic position might drive to a fancy restaurant, spend $150 eating (and drinking) stuff that isn't all that good for them. Over the course of a retirement, who is better off?

Of course there's middle ground. Becky's lifestyle is more frugal than a lot of Americans can tolerate. But something middle of the road might work pretty well if you give it a shot.

\\\

(Scott Wardell) Has this "relaxed" attitude helped you in terms of your financial situation?

(Becky) I think so. It's hard to explain. It is not the same as being complacent. In my twenties, I probably was asleep at the switch in terms of making financial decisions. But not today. It just doesn't help to worry about it. My husband and I both think we have good sense about money. But we don't walk around always saying, "Oh, that's too much," and feeling oppressed. By now being frugal is just embedded in the fabric of who we are.

(Scott Wardell) So it is an unconscious competency.

(Becky) Yes. That's a good way of putting it. Unless someone asks, we don't even think of it.

We think more in terms of what's comfortable, not what's cool. Also, I should add, I make point of taking really good care of my stuff. Very good care. That is a value too.

//

There was study several years ago out of Princeton University into the correlation between money and happiness. They put a number on happiness. It was regionalized. The number in Mississippi was very different than the number in San Francisco. But the national average was $48,500[1].

It goes like this: There is a substantial increase in people's happiness in relation to their income ... up to $48,500. From $48,000 up to $96,000 it slows, but for that doubling of income you only get about a 3% growth in happiness. Above $96,000, though, a strange thing starts to happen. Add more income and there is no appreciable increase in happiness. None. What's more, when you get to roughly $500,000, the happiness quotient actually starts to drop, and pretty dramatically.

The explanation, according to this survey, is that peoples' attitude about money changes as their income grows. At a half million dollars, your money is there to buy you happiness. You are not looking forward to something simple as a walk on a pleasant evening. You're not looking forward to time with people you love. You're looking to all the things that you can get, that your money will buy you. Below $96,000 people have the wherewithal for the things they truly need and desire and are experiencing less stress in sustaining the lifestyle of their "class."

Another interesting fact is that basic charitable contributions, as a percent of the total, goes down at higher income levels. Substantially. At greater levels of wealth it becomes "all about me." You can lose a sense of community, or at least a simple one. Relationships have business components instead of just cultural and social affinities.

Summary

The words "frugal" and "exotic" rarely go together. But they do in Becky's story of retirement. The power of her story is the way she and her husband prioritize what is important to them.

To them international travel, the "exotic," is more important than season football tickets or regularly dining at nice restaurants. Theirs is a study of choices. They very consciously said, "Because we want to do this, we're not going to do that." These are choices that happen day-to-day and moment-to-moment. But, and this is important, they don't regard them as hard choices. *They do not feel deprived.*

To live as frugally as Becky requires a special kind of mindset. My point in including this chapter is to emphasize that a modest career income, with modest retirement income does NOT translate to a deprived retirement. Rather, a retirement fulfilling to you is absolutely possible, but ... *but* ... you have to make choices. While Becky talks about being a bit feckless with money in her youth, her financial imprinting established by our parents meant she was always cautious about over-spending her income. She knew her threshold.

The choice function is critical if you relate to Becky's situation. Ironically, that choice function is imperiled as The Great Recession recedes and people feel the ability to release pent-up demand. I listen to people tell me how much they learned during the recession. How they really disciplined themselves to make rational expense/spending choices, and then in the next breath they're telling me how much they need a new car, how good the food is at the hot new restaurant in town, and basically how eager they are to return to their 2007 lifestyle.

What Becky did, and everyone can do, is designed for frugality. Just saying, "We're going to be more watchful" never works. Never. You have to design not only what you're going to stop doing, but also what you are going to do by way of replacement.

Becky and her husband make a night of walking to a neighborhood restaurant and listening to a jazz group. Becky "replaced" the upscale version of a pleasant night out with one that left them with probably $180 still in an account for their next trip to Istanbul.

There is no point ignoring the status/pride-related peer pressure in "replacement" thinking like this. Some of your friends are going to wonder about you. "Are you broke?" Or, to others, "Boy, they must really be hurting." How often have you spent more than you were comfortable spending just to demonstrate that you could?

To make sure these "replacement choices" stay on track, I often recommend that couples take a hard look at their individual, discretionary expenses and each accepts responsibility for trimming 30%. Then I recommend taking their adjusted cash flow and spending choices to a professional advisor and saying, "This is what we want to do. We want to be in Istanbul or Fiji next year at this time. Show us what we're doing wrong and right here."

Opportunities and choices usually come to us one at a time. We rarely sit down and look at the list and say here are *the three possibilities*. Which one am I going to spend my money on? Most people don't get the relationship between the $4 cup of coffee and the ski trip to

Colorado. Those who do get it and make choices accordingly very often get to live their big dreams.

The following pages have a worksheet to help you turn impulsive opportunities into financial choices.

Questions to consider:

1. Do you ever take an inventory of discretionary spending? On clothes? Restaurant dining? Entertainment?

2. How important is it to you to "matchup" well with friends and neighbors? How much extra does it cost you?

3. Are you a savvy shopper? Not just for the occasional item. But everything you buy, including necessities like insurance?

Notes

1. Eric Quiñones, "Link Between Income and Happiness is Mainly an Illusion," Princeton University, last modified August 10, 2006. http://www.princeton.edu/main/news/archive/S15/15/09S18/index.xml?section=topstories

Personal Expense Worksheet

Directions: Please record each expense on either a monthly or annual basis.

Approximate monthly amount available to fund and protect your goals: _____.

Housing and Maintenance	Monthly	Annually
Mortgage/rent/insurance		
Home equity loan/line of credit payments		
Property Taxes		
Homeowner's/renter's insurance		
Utilities (gas, electric, sewer, etc.)		
Maintenance/repair/association fees		
Furniture, decorations, lawn, etc.		
Total Annual Housing and Maintenance: _____		

Transportation	Monthly	Annually
Loan/lease payments		
Auto insurance premiums		
Auto registration/taxes		
Gas/maintenance		
Total Annual Transportation: _____		

Health Care	Monthly	Annually
Medical insurance premiums ☐ Pre-tax		
Health Savings/Flex Spending Acct ☐ Pre-tax		
Co-payment/out of pocket		
Prescriptions		
Total Annual Medical: _____		

Insurance Premiums	Monthly	Annually
Life Insurance		
Disability income insurance ☐ Pre-tax		
Long-term care insurance ☐ Pre-tax		
Total Annual Insurance: _____		

Food and Clothing Expenses	Monthly	Annually
Food		
Clothing		
Total Annual Food and Clothing: _____		

Other Expenses	Monthly	Annually
Church and charitable contributions		
Credit card payments		
Phone/television/internet		
Children (e.g. support, daycare, etc.)		
Education		
Employment (parking, dues, etc.)		
Financial managing/legal/tax accounting fees		
Pets		
Total Annual Other: _____		

Discretionary Expenses	Monthly	Annually
Recreation/fitness memberships		
Travel/vacation/gifts/holidays		
Personal care		
Entertainment/dining out		
Total Annual Personal Expenses: _____		

Chapter 4

The Control Tower

Once in awhile you meet someone who on first impression seems as normal, as completely routine as any next-door neighbor. Another guy doing his job, living his life. But then you start peeling the onion and you discover something really quite remarkable. My first take on John Shanks was that here was an air traffic controller of modest means with a very conscientious perspective on his personal finances. But as I got to know him, the guy's ingenuity pretty much blew me away. We won't have time in this chapter to discuss his work building sets for the well-known Children's Theater Company in Minneapolis. Ask yourself, though, if you know anyone who could design and assemble a full scale, down-to-the-last-detail-perfect replica of the flying car from "Chitty Chitty Bang Bang" – without blueprints?

John had a career that was going to allow him to retire quite early. But he had children to put through college and an elderly parent who was going to need either expensive care, or some plan for allowing him to stay in his home years beyond what others of his father's age and condition could do.

Snapshot

- **Age:** 52
- **Marital status:** Married. Two college age children.
- **Primary career:** Air traffic controller.
- **Asset description:** Government pension. Modest but adequate investments. Continues to work to get kids through college.
- **Specific dilemma:** Building retirement while caring for elderly, increasingly more dependent father who insists on staying in his own home. No long-term care planning for parent. Mandatory government retirement.
- **Financial Stability level:** Secure.

Five kids plus Mom and Dad in a two bedroom house breeds a lot of "close-ness," and John's family always had that going for it. For 37 years John's dad was a mechanic for Northwest Airlines, a mainstay of the Minneapolis-St. Paul economy until it merged with Delta a decade ago. Their suburban home was in the flight path of planes coming and going from MSP International and Dad imparted a love of flying in each and every one of his children.

Hand in hand with the thrill of controlling your own plane in flight was the groundwork of maintenance, of figuring things out and solving problems. John's dad was good at it, and so are John and his siblings. Something broken is a challenge for them.

John's mom was a homemaker who kept that side of the family operation running, and John's dad's free hours were spent in his fully-equipped garage where he repaired engines of all kinds for friends and neighbors. "Watching and talking to Dad in that environment, a curious kid couldn't help but pick a lot of tips on what screw comes before what bolt on what gasket."

Despite the cost of flight school, all the kids scraped together cash to take lessons while they were in high school. "We ran Christmas tree lots, put on air shows, and threw all kinds of fund-raisers," says John.

A determined character, as you'll see, he soloed at 16 and was a flight instructor at age 18. One of his sisters was the first girl allowed into the local flying club, largely due to John's dad putting the squeeze on his buddies to wake up and get with the 20th century.

"Dad had all his great aviation stories. He told us about barnstorming around to different places. He wanted us to be out in the garage helping him and learning. Kids don't do that today. They don't get hands-on, not even my own kids. My wife and I were talking about that the other day. As kids, we made stuff. I remember finding a set of wheels and a board, and making a scooter. Then I put a motor on it. My brother and I put a motor on his ten-speed bicycle. I'd block the street, and he'd come whizzing down the road at forty miles an hour."

The flying gene kept a hold over the Shanks family. John's eyesight wasn't quite good enough to make commercial pilot, but he's still a flight instructor. Like his older brother, his primary career was air traffic control, an extremely demanding job for both the boredom in down time and the adrenaline at rush hour. Again, like John's dad in his garage, traffic control is a lot about keeping everything in its proper sequence and position.

"There are moments of stark terror," John says with a smile. " People ask about the stress. But you're trained for that stress level. It's like McDonalds at a lunch run. You're trained at that level."

(Scott Wardell) What is the general aptitude the FAA looks for in air traffic controllers?

(John) A lot of thinking outside the box, and math you can do in your head. Not anything sophisticated. Rate times time. Distance stuff like that. Spatial memorization, that's what the tests are now. When it was all paper, there were timed tests. Now the kids are taking tests on the computer and they're running video games. Kids with video game knowledge can do pretty well.

(Scott Wardell) At the point you went full-time with the FAA, which is a government job, were you planning financially for the future? The FAA comes with a pension.

(John) Yeah, I had talked to my older brother about that. Controllers can retire after twenty-five years at any age, or over age fifty, and you *have to retire* at age fifty-five. When I started, I always thought that I would go back to flying. I thought, "I'm gonna do this, because it pays really well, and I'll get a pension, and I'll be young enough to do something else, like fly, after I'm done."

//

Government jobs, with their traditional government pensions are under a lot of political pressure these days. But they are one of the last safe havens in terms of secure pensions left out there. People like John accepted salaries less than what they might – *might* – have made in the private sector in large part because of their retirement contract and the security of those government jobs.

If you are fortunate enough to have two financial layers, like John has, with his government pension and Social Security, you're likely to have a pretty secure retirement. Nothing lavish, but secure, assuming you can live within your means. Then of course you factor in your own investments.

With his part-time work giving flying lessons, and a consulting gig, John set up a very solid situation. The essential point here is that John planned it from early on of his career.

(John) When I was hired, the FAA was just starting the 401(k). Before it used to be all pension. I was first in the Federal Employee Retirement System (FERS). Before that it was the Civil Servant Retirement System. FERS was not as big as the Civil Servant Retirement pension. With mine, the other half was a 401(k) in which the government matched up to 6%. So the idea was to put in as much as you could as soon as you could.

But like a lot of people, I had bills to pay, cars to pay for, apartment rent, things like that. So I didn't start out putting in the max. But I put something in right from the get-go.

It was a no-brainer. I started putting away what they were gonna match.

//

In case you're wondering, John is correct about all those numbers. More importantly, John left nothing on the table. Rule Number One, which I harp on frequently, is, "Never leave anything on the table." If you have an opportunity for matching funds in a 401(k), take everything you can. Period.

Rule Number Two is, "Add whatever you can" to hit the number you need to retire in the manner you choose. It's different for everyone, but the math can be done quite easily ... if you stop to do it or ask your financial advisor to do it for you.

If you don't have the opportunity to contribute to a 401(k) through your work, check to see if your employer allows you to contribute to a 403(b). Don't let that get away from you (A 403(b) is an account set up for tax-exempt entities, school teachers, church employees, ministers and, like John, public employees. There are a number of tax benefits, if you are eligible.).

\\\

(Scott Wardell) So you began making your contributions right out of the gate?

(John) Right. Then, little by little I got stuff paid off, cars and other bills, and I upped it to 10%. Eventually I started putting in the max, which I think was $15,000 a year, something like that. It was all in a 401(k).

I was in the common stock fund. But you could pull [money] in and out and put it wherever you wanted: Government funds, bond funds, and common stock.

(Scott Wardell) Were you talking to anyone at that time, a professional, about making those decisions?

(John) Back then I wasn't. I did see a financial advisor for a little bit and he said to just keep doing what I was doing.

I knew I wanted to retire at my minimum age and that I wanted to go back to flying.

Clearly John's awareness that he had to retire at fifty-five catalyzed his retirement thinking. As I've said before, the question, "What am I going to do after retirement?" is vital to so many of the retirement decisions you make. For one thing, it is a huge factor in figuring out what you need and absolutely have to save. If your plan is to retire early and travel the globe staying at swank resorts, that's one set of numbers. A condo in Tucson? Another set. Gardening at the home you live in now? Another, again.

(Scott Wardell) Today you're retired and working part-time. What percentage of your present income do you say comes from your part-time work?

(John) I work for Raytheon, who contracts training out to the government. I was at thirty-two hours, but now they've cut me back to twenty-seven hours. When I was at thirty-two, I was pretty much bringing home what I was as a controller. I still haven't touched my TSP [Thrift Savings Plan] . . . my 401(k). I always knew I had to do some part-time work.

We have a whole generation of people today who have no idea how money works, mainly because they were never brought into those kinds of conversations by their parents. John had some parental direction, but not a lot. He pretty much acquired his own financial intelligence. He is a rare bird.

I can't tell you how much I wish every family had an open conversation about money. My mom walked me through how to balance a checkbook when I got my first paper route. I hope in John's case he is imprinting his knowledge on his kids, because he has learned a lot of valuable stuff.

(Scott Wardell) Back to your early financial decisions. What choices did you make about insurance when you started with the FAA?

(John) Well, the nice part is the government offered great insurance. I started out with the basic life insurance the government had. They also had great medical insurance. They paid for 75% of it. I got everything through them.

I did see a financial advisor back in my late twenties when we started thinking about having kids. At that point, it seemed a separate policy would be better than the government's policy because theirs' would only give me a certain amount (capped at their annual earnings).

I decided to go with a term life policy because I figured I wouldn't need insurance when the kids were out of school and on their own. I felt I could be self-insured with my 401(k). Right now I just keep up with my term. I think it takes me to sixty-five. I hope the kids will be on their own by then.

//

Oftentimes people like John who watch their cash flow closely also tend – on the downside– to be Do-It-Yourselfers when it comes to investments. What is unusual here is that John sought advice. And sought it early.

This might be another aspect of the air traffic controller mentality, where you are part of a large, interactive system designed to produce the safest result. John understood that there are other people out there at least as smart as he is willing and prepared to help.

On the specific insurance question here, John could do better on the "insurance architecture" as I like to call it.

Like most people, John bought cheaper insurance – term – because, well, no one likes paying insurance premiums. His critical question, as I see it, was, "Does my income need to be replaced?"

But if John dies early in retirement, the decrease in income to the family could be substantial (not to mention the fact that he is the money manager for

this family) because of the loss of Social Security and potentially part of his pension.

The plan he has is somewhat dependent on John surviving.

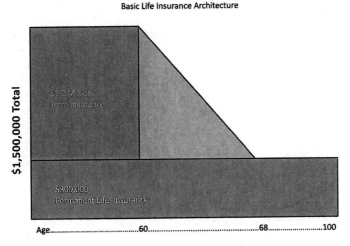

Scott's simplified view of Life Insurance architecture model[1]

For some, term can be a good short-term answer. But term is priced the way it is because only a small percentage of term policies ever pay a death benefit.

In John's case specifically, he still has a spouse. She might need some kind of bridge of cash to replace the possible reduction in his pension, and the loss of his part-time income should he die.

John is the sort of guy who is going to putter around making money of some sort until his last breath. He needs to be asking himself, "How do I replace that?"

Term insurance is about cost. Permanent insurance is about long term coverage. Often it is prudent to consider a combination of each of these.

(Scott Wardell) So you made all these decisions yourself?

(John) Pretty much, with a little affirmation from the financial advisor. I watched what other people were doing in the field, and what older people at the FAA were doing. They're a great knowledge base, the other controllers. Some of them have side jobs and things like that. It's a great knowledge base to tap into.

(Scott Wardell) So you were looking at this and thinking, "This will be twenty-five years. I have to get out at fifty-five." Unlike a lot of people, your road map was right there in front of you.

(John) Right. You had to start retirement planning early. You had to start thinking about it. I was thinking about it when I was twenty-five years old.

(Scott Wardell) That's unusual. Tell us a little how you handled consumer debt and your mortgage?

(John) Well, the job paid really well. But I figured that if I did want to retire in my mid-Fifties, I didn't want a house payment. So I refinanced because mortgage rates had dropped so low. I figured out how much extra I would have to add to my mortgage principal a month so my loan would be paid off in the year and month I retired.

I just started paying $500 more a month. Automatically. The idea was once the mortgage was gone, I could use the cash flow for the kids' college. I planned that out at least eight years before I retired.

///

> There are two parts to make this very smart strategy work. Begin by buying a house you can afford and pre-pay on any mortgage you have.
>
> I have a couple with a combined income of $300,000 a year. No doubt they've been told "they're good" for a house worth a lot more than the $250,000 one they live in. But by keeping their mortgage down in a reasonable line, they have so much extra cash left over to save and invest.

\\

(Scott Wardell) Was there another, additional plan for the kids' college?

(John) I did set other money aside. I didn't want to do the 529 [college fund], because at that time it looked like the fees were too high.

So I did go in for some brokerage accounts for their college. I still have those accounts and one of them will pretty much pay for my son's school.

///

> Before his father died, John was the classic "sandwich guy" who needed time and money for his kids and time and money for his aged parent.
>
> In terms of the 529 college fund, (a tax-exempt savings plan for designated beneficiaries), he's right that he should check to see if his income would make him ineligible for financial aid. There are many 529 plans available, so it's possible for him and others to find a plan with lower fees. So it makes sense for him to have a plan with or without a 529 college fund.

The downside to a 529 is that it has to be used for education. 529s come with a 10% penalty for withdrawal for anything other than education, *and* you'll have to pay tax on the gain.

On the other hand, a Roth IRA doesn't count against you (FAFSA) and can be used for college tuition with some stipulation.

\\

(Scott Wardell) What was your philosophy regarding credit cards?

(John) I learned that from my dad. He said, "You never buy something if you don't have the money to pay for it." I learned by watching him. When he bought a car, he saved the money first. I rarely ever saw his credit card. I don't even know if he had one. I never carry over any credit card debt. I pay it off at the end of each month.

That said, there were some months when I had to say, "Okay, I'm gonna pay it off in three months." When you're buying furniture and stuff, when you build a house there were times like that. But 90+% of the time I pay the complete balance.

(Scott Wardell) You seem to have your financial literacy down. How's your wife? Is she pretty good with budgeting?

She's pretty good. When we had a kid, she stopped working. She wanted to do that. She's done some work out of the house, medical transcriptions and stuff like that. But mostly here lately, she's been doing a lot of volunteer work with schools and the church, and Habitat for Humanity. She's actually been swinging a hammer.

She likes it. It gives her gratification. And so long as she can do what she likes, that's great. But with Michael going to school, and Sara coming up and going to school, she might go back to work and do something else for a while. Or even do medical transcription out of the house again.

But she doesn't like to carry debt either. We buy what we need to buy. Other than that if we don't really need it, we think about it and weigh it out.

(Scott Wardell) So you say the air traffic job pays well. The benefits were good. A lot of the people we've talked to got into the go-go Nineties and went off on a spending spiral. They treated their homes like ATMs. How did you manage the feeling of greater wealth?

(John) It helped I was established in my job before we got married. We planned when to have kids, and that was after I got to [Minneapolis-St. Paul International Airport] and I was able to double my pay.

We built a house for $87,000 when we got married in 1987. We had to live in an apartment for three months while it was under construction. We lived in it for seven years and made $20,000 - $25,000 when we moved. It just never occurred to us to get into anything bigger than we needed or to tap the equity for stuff we probably could do without.

(Scott Wardell) So you didn't go buy a boat?

(John) No, I've got a boat. But I saved for the boat. *Then* I bought it.

(Scott Wardell) What are you saying to yourself and your wife about what you're not going to do, or buy?

(John) Well, like I say, we're not super materialistic. We aren't going to go out and refinance and take the difference and spend it. If we refinanced, we put it back down in the house. We wanted to get the house paid for. Back then you didn't hear much about foreclosures. At the end of the 2000s, you did. We're thankful we did it the way we did.

That was the goal for us. We didn't like any debt hanging over our head.

///

Easy credit was not tempting to John. To him it was foolish and frivolous. Credit offers weren't even a conversation between John and his wife. It was simply, "Throw it away."

Put another way "Don't buy stuff you don't need." Or, as I've drilled into my kids, "Never borrow money on a depreciable asset." Or, put even another way, *talk* about money. That is one way to achieve positive financial imprinting.

\\

(Scott Wardell) Did you ever have anybody advising you not to pay the house off, because you'd lose the tax deduction?

(John) I did. It was the financial advisor I was seeing at the time. But I thought, "Well, I've got extra money. I'm going to pay off the house." He wanted [me] to put [money] into mutual funds. The idea was that when I retired, I would have an option. I could take the mutual fund money and pay off the house, or I might decide to keep the mutual fund cash and refinance.

But in 2008 the stock market crashed, and suddenly that idea didn't look so good. I did put a little money into mutual funds. But I kind of half and halved it: Some in mutual funds, for kid's college and stuff down the way, but still some to pay the house off early.

Back in the Eighties leverage was king and it was considered foolish to pay off your house because of the interest (tax) deduction. Never mind that the government was only helping you with one-third of that cost. But the market was going up well beyond interest rates, so it all worked out for a while. But remember, hindsight is 20/20.

For most people it would be a mistake to say, "I'm not going to save a dime until my house is paid off." On the other hand, this advice to not pay your house off early and instead invest in mutual funds should be taken with a grain of salt.

When you consider the market crash of 2008, the vulnerability of investing in mutual funds instead of paying off your mortgage is immediately apparent.

(Scott Wardell) You describe yourself as "not materialistic." There were no lavish vacations. But there are some families that think of these as bonding experiences that are important to a family, whether it's road-tripping to Yellowstone or whatever. How did you balance that out?

(John) It was tough when other people were going on cruises and stuff. When the kids were younger, we would go up to Lake Vermillion [in far northern Minnesota], and rent a cabin there. We did things like that as a family.

Flying was always a big part of our life. My son and I, we'd fly together to play golf or go for a hamburger and my daughter would come with. We do a vacation every once in awhile. I think it's more special than if we did it every year. Every three years we might do something bigger.

(Scott Wardell) You mentioned long-term care insurance. What do you have today, for yourselves?

(John) I've had LTC for about a year now. But the real story there was trying to care for my dad, who did not have anything like it and wanted to stay in his house.

(Scott Wardell) Okay. Tell us about your dad's situation. It could have been very expensive for someone.

(John) He made me promise him that we wouldn't send him anywhere other than his house. I told him, "Dad, I'll do the best I can." He was in his mid-eighties when this was happening and losing his memory. He definitely had need for 24/7 care.

Our financial fix for him was a reverse mortgage. It was the best thing in the world for Dad at the time we got it.

I knew I never wanted to be in that situation, because I saw how much it cost to care for somebody. Everything I've read in *Long-Term Care Insurance for Dummies* – there is such a thing – says to start shopping when you're fifty-nine and a half, because at sixty you want to purchase the thing.

I started weighing that and talking with my Thrivent guy. There were some new products that my wife and I could share. So we figured, "Why not?" We don't know if we're going to be able to get it later, and it's not going to cover the works. But it will supplement our care, so the kids don't have to worry about us.

There are three reasons to consider long-term care insurance.

They are:

1. **So you don't impoverish the spouse. Or reduce their standard of living substantially.**
2. **So you do have some reserves and something to pass on to your heirs.**
3. **To provide respite for the caregiver. And that is absolutely huge.**

In the case of his father, John and his siblings were scrambling to figure out where the money was going to come from to care for him in his home as they promised. The only thing they could think of was a reverse mortgage. But John was quickly becoming the long term care provider for his father.

(John) In my dad's case, he had just a money market account. The way it eventually worked out, if we hadn't done the reverse mortgage, that account would have been exactly the amount needed to take care of him. Had he lived longer he'd have been left with nothing, and we'd have been left with a house that wasn't worth much and needed a lot of fixing.

By going the reverse mortgage route, his house took care of him until he passed away. But it was a gamble. He could have been one of those guys who lived to one hundred. What did we know? I was always afraid once the house was tapped out we'd be in a tough situation. We didn't really have a plan for additional money beyond the house to take care of him. So it was good that as he began needing full-time care we had the house plus his [money market] account.

///

Had John's dad had a long-term care (LTC) policy, most of what John went through from this point of the story on probably would have been handled. Coordinated care. Dollars coming in. Home modification. Almost all paid for with an LTC policy.

Please note however that you have to examine policies to make sure they cover home modifications.

For those who need long-term care and don't have LTC insurance, the county will take control if you're out of money. In the case of John's dad, that would have meant leaving his home and going to a nursing home. The county would then put a lien on the house and, on the death of John's dad, the county repays itself for his expenses in the nursing home.

John took back control of that situation by using the reverse mortgage. The financial outcome is the same. The house is gone. But it's a matter of who is in control, and they did get to keep their dad in his house.

In the right situation, reverse mortgages can be one way to go, but be extremely cautious. What is going on now, post-2008 and in a real estate upswing, is banks are offering much lower assessments of the houses they're appraising for reverse mortgages. Also, interest rates are still comparatively low, so the imputed interest you're going to get on that reverse mortgage pay-out is also going to be low.

Generally speaking, a reverse mortgage is usually a last resort.

\\

(Scott Wardell) How much did in-home care cost per month?

(John) Initially we tried commercial care agencies, but it was *way* too expensive. It was like $200 a day.

(Scott Wardell) How many times did you have to go in and check on your dad before you had that commercial care?

(John) Dad needed some kind of care for the last nine years of his life. The last three it was 24/7. The six years before that he needed only part-time care.

He was forgetting things. His memory was bad. He couldn't drive anymore, even though he thought he could or wanted to. He needed some form of regular care.

(Scott Wardell) This meant you and your siblings?

(John) Right. It started with me going over there every day, every other day, and setting up meals. Frozen stuff with labels on it. There were five kids, but I drove by his place on the way to the airport.

Dad also had heart arrhythmia and stuff like that. He needed to take medication. But he wasn't taking it. So we got an electric pill dispenser and left notes all over the place. We left notes on how to do a microwave dinner.

He loved his dog, so we hired a neighbor girl to walk it and an older lady to come by and check on Dad and call if something didn't look right. Well, she did and there'd be pills all over the place. It wasn't good.

He'd say he was taking them, but he wasn't.

(Scott Wardell) So what did you do? This is the kind of stuff you pay big money for an in-home care provider to handle.

(John) My brothers are pretty bright on computer stuff, so we hooked the wire from the pill dispenser back to Dad's computer. He had a basic computer that he kept stuff on file, his Popular Mechanics or machinist magazines and things like that, steam engine magazines. He built steam engines out in the garage.

We ran a wire back to the computer so the computer would dispense dad's pills automatically. He could push the button on the pill dispenser as many times as he wanted, but it wouldn't do anything. The computer would dispense it only at a certain time.

Then we rigged it so we could go online into his computer via the Internet and actually dispense them ourselves. We also put an alarm clock on the computer screen, it would go off and the pills would dispense, and then we'd follow it up with a phone call. "Hi Dad, are you taking the pills?"

(Scott Wardell) Was he stable on his feet?

(John) It got to where he started to fall or he'd go outside and we couldn't find him. So we told him it was time that he came to live with one of us. Either that or go to an assisted living. Or ... we could try putting cameras all over the house. He said he to wanted to try that. He did not want to leave his house.

So we installed seven cameras. In his bedroom, in the living room, in the bathroom downstairs, and outside. We were able to go online anytime of the day and watch him.

(Scott Wardell) All of you kids were watching in?

(John) We were able to take turns. We still had the pill call to make sure he took his meds. Otherwise, we'd just go on the Internet throughout the day and check. One morning my sister in Eau Claire went on and saw Dad had fallen the night before. She called me at work and I went over and set him back up. He was okay, thank God, but she saw him on the camera lying on his bedroom floor and couldn't get up.

I went and played back the cameras and he had fallen the night before. He'd been there all night. I had been there the day before and wasn't going to go until the day after. Without the camera system, he could have been on the ground for two days.

We also put a phone-off-the-hook alarm, so if the phone was off the hook for a certain period of time, an alarm would beep and say loudly "PHONE OFF THE HOOK," so he'd hear that. Sometimes that would work, sometimes not. But with the cameras, if I couldn't get a hold of him, I'd call him and watch him pick up the phone and talk to him.

(Scott Wardell) The whole plan sounds like a good business idea.

(John) We had to do more. With his memory going we ended up purchasing the rights to this talking clock program. You put speakers throughout the house to remind him through the day to do stuff. "It's time for Meals on Wheels," the speaker said. Or, "Dad, it's time to feed the dog and let the dog out." Or, "Dad, make sure the doors are locked."

We put speakers throughout the living room and his bedroom. They'd wake him up in the morning and tell him it was time to get up and get some breakfast.

(Scott Wardell) This was all via the Internet?

(John) This product wasn't Internet driven. You put it on the computer and programmed the times. This wasn't Internet, but switching other things was. Web cams and all that were via the Internet.

Since he was unsteady, we made the living room like this park. We took pipe flanges and screwed them to the floor and took 1 1/2" pipe up and over and down everywhere he walked so he had something to hang onto. We put in rails at the door, and things like that so he could hang onto something the whole way.

(Scott Wardell) What did the neighbors or other people think of this?

(John) People were saying, "You don't want your father with dementia living there." We had a social worker out one time to see what we were doing. He had fallen at the doctor's office so automatically they sent a nurse to the home. The social worker looked everything over and said, "Normally we wouldn't let your dad live here. But with everything you've got going, he'll be fine."

She then said, "What you've got going here, is there anyway we can get some info on this for other clients?" So I made up a little brochure that we could provide.

We also had an emergency response system we purchased for him and our own account, so we worked directly with the communications system.

But yes, we made a brochure to provide the county with stuff, and we got phone calls from people asking how to do that kind of thing, to help others like we helped Dad and ourselves. Eventually I made a website, to get this info to people.

(Scott Wardell) And Dad's dog died at one point.

(John) He was very depressed. He needed a dog. So we replaced his dog with another, similar to the first. He even gave it the same name. But this dog wanted to run. So we put in an electric fence. I had to come over every day to train the dog and finally got it to stay in the yard.

But Dad would let it out at night and it would bark, which meant I had the neighbors calling me and saying, "Your dad's dog is barking!" Eventually I had to put these dog-barking things on the side of the house, so when the dog barked they would squeal and scare the dog into stop barking.

Also, I didn't know if the dog was being fed or not, so I got automatic feeders that automatically fed the dog at certain times of the day. The food came down and the water was refreshed throughout the day through a recycler.

Then, Dad would let the dog out in the middle of the night. So we put up motion sensors that could sense movement at 10:00 or 11:00 at night. If Dad walked out in the kitchen at 11:00 or midnight, a big red light would come in his eyes and a voice – my voice on a recording– would say, "Dad, it's the middle of the night. Do not let Holly out. Go back to bed."

Dad's doctor loved what we were doing. He actually endorsed our products.

(Scott Wardell) Are you selling this stuff?

(John) We were. We had a website. We had tons of calls and tons of people wanted information. We gave it to them freely.

(Scott Wardell) How much longer did your dad stay home than doctors originally predicted?

(John) This went on for six years. It was that long before we needed any in-home care. Then it was three more years before he died.

(Scott Wardell) How much did the modifications to the house cost?

(John) The computer, we built it up ourselves. We made a DVR computer ourselves. The cameras were inexpensive, $100 apiece. All of it was done for less than one month's stay in a facility.

(Scott Wardell) For the cost of one month's stay in a care facility, your dad remained at home for an extra nine years?

(John) Well, the last three. But I set up the reverse mortgage for that. It worked out really well. I read up on it a lot.

(Scott Wardell) And tell me again, what would you have done if he'd outlived the reverse mortgage? Was it set up for his lifetime?

(John) No, it wasn't set up for a lifetime. It was $2000 a month. And that was not one third of what it would have cost to keep him in the house with a care attendant. With the reverse mortgage, he also had $200,000 in savings. We would have gone into that. But without the mortgage, we would have gone through that savings [and] we would have been stuck with the State (taking care of him).

(Scott Wardell) You think the State would have left him in his home?

(John) Probably not. He would have had to go somewhere. We knew it was going to be expensive, so we looked at some private care options. But they were very expensive. Eventually we found a person that had left an agency and wanted to start a company on his own. We hired him, but that didn't work out either.

(Scott Wardell) You found, through your cameras, that this person wasn't working.

(John) Right, we found that the care provider wasn't paying attention to Dad. You know, they were working on something and Dad was in the bathroom for forty-five minutes, or Dad was trying to get his socks on for an hour, and this person was smoking in the back room, which they weren't supposed to do.

They knew the cameras were there. We said, "We're gonna keep the cameras here, are you okay with that?"

When we started with in-home care, we thought it was a great deal. The agencies were more like $160, but the individual person was $120-130 a day.

((Scott Wardell) So almost $4000 a month.

(John) Yes, plus utilities, plus food. It was about $6000 a month.

//

My recommendation for most healthy people in their fifties is to think about a LTC policy and determine if it's something that's right for them and their situation. Don't take out the fully upholstered, dripping-in-chrome Cadillac policy. Look also at the keys and heater Chevrolet policy. A policy that basically says, "If you become uninsurable in the future, you've got this baby."

Long-term care policies generally overcharge in the early years. I'm sixty-one. I've had my policy since I was fifty-one. I know the risk is essentially nil to the company of me collecting on that policy up to the age of seventy- five. So they are sitting on this premium for which they expect to pay zero.

But when I get to sixty-two or sixty-three and if I'm still healthy, I can take out another layer (policy). The savings is the difference between the thin policy in the first ten to twelve years and the fuller policy after 63 is worth significant consideration understanding that if

I become uninsurable at the age that I apply for more insurance, that my strategy won't be fully implemented.

(Scott Wardell) At the end of your career, had you been thinking all along that you'd be moving into a consultancy phase?

(John) There's always air traffic controller jobs available. Either as a consultant, or advisor. There are a lot of contractors to the government, but you can't just take somebody off the street, or from another facility to do our training. So I knew I would do something like that or go back to flying.

I knew I had to do something. Go into flight instructing, or work as a charter pilot. Now I work for the contractor [Raytheon] who works for the FAA.

(Scott Wardell) How much longer do you want to do this?

(John) My plan is to do it until both kids are through college. Then we'll see.

(Scott Wardell) What was your understanding with the kids about how college finances were going to be handled?

(John) It's funny. When the kids first heard I was retiring, they were still in high school, and they blew a top! They were upset that I was actually going to stop working. They were worried about how it was going to affect them, what their friends would think. There were tears!

I had to assure them that I was going to supplement my pension, and that I was going to do some other work, but that we wouldn't be making as much as I was making as an air traffic controller. Still, we'd be fine and their college would be paid for, and things like that. But they didn't like the idea at all.

I assured them that we had a plan, and that I did have money put away. Not enough to put them both through school, but some. In the end, they would have to go to community college for two years, like I did, and if they proved themselves they could go wherever they wanted.

My son did that, and now he's going go away to school for a couple years. We'll see if it suits him.

(Scott Wardell) So you said they had to start at a community college?

(John) Right, and live at home for two years. Prove it to me and themselves. Rather than go somewhere because their friends were going there.

John's building financial independence in his kids. That's a good parental goal. John has set good rules for his kids contributing to their own well-being.

(Scott Wardell) So you want to maintain your current work pace until the kids are through college.

(John) My idea is not to tap into my 401(k). I transferred my TSPs [Thrift Savings Plan, essentially a 401(k) by another name] into the government handling of it, [to] a private 401(k). People think I'm nuts for doing that, because the fees in the government were the least that you'll ever pay anywhere. However, I didn't think they were as proactive as they should be. I thought they could be getting a better return than they were. But the government's investment procedures are meant to be pretty conservative.

I've seen some charts side by side, with the [government] TSP managing vs. a managed account, and across the board it was at least a percentage point better with the managed account, which pays for the fees. So I took a chance, I think. A lot of the controllers left theirs in the government account.

But mine has been doing very well. I was worried about that, and I think I might have jumped in too soon. But I never knew what we were paying the government. They didn't expose that.

(Scott Wardell) With the government was there a person at the end of the phone?

(John) No, there wasn't a person. You went in and did your own stuff. You could go in and change allotments. I did that right before I retired. The government came in with these 2010 programs and I did go into them at the very end. I mimicked them. It's what I'm doing now, so I'm feeling good about it.

When the kids are out of school, I'm still going to have to be doing something. I'm going to be working with my hands. I've got to be building something, maybe an airplane. My wife and I will travel some.

But I want to wait till fifty-nine and a half. That's nine more years [before I] draw on my 401, to supplement my income. If I do that, I'll be in good shape. I can do something called a 72T to draw on it right now without a penalty. Some people are doing that. But the problem with that is you can't change it. You can stop it. But you can't start it again. And once you have an allotment, you can't up it if you need money later.

A "72T" is this: A lot of people who want to retire before fifty-nine and a half want to be able to draw from a qualified retirement account without the 10% penalty. In the previous chapter, Becky, a school teacher, ran into the same issue.

With a 72T you can avoid the 10% penalty if you take equal and periodic payments. The payments have to be consistent and last for five years or more. These are IRS rules.

So, then, it is possible to retire early and draw out the money without a penalty.

(John) The idea for me is to wait [five years] to start some kind of allotment, if I need money to help with the kids' college. But I'm thinking we could probably go for another nine years before I touch it.

(Scott Wardell) Are the kids expected to work during college?

(John)My son did. He's been working as a fueler for Delta. They don't pay as well as you think. It's a $10-11/hour job. The responsibility he has is unbelievable. The stuff they do could affect safety. It's amazing that they don't get more compensation for it. But he seems to enjoy it. And they like him. So even when he goes to school, they're going to give him a leave of absence.

(Scott Wardell) You seem to always have looked at the consequences of decisions before you made them. When it came to actually signing up for retirement from the FAA, how much analysis and calculation went into that?

(John) For me, quite a bit, because the FAA had just started contract training with independent companies. Otherwise the FAA did their own. They also knew I was a flight instructor. I had a lot of training on the floor, with live traffic, and they wanted me as one of their members when they started this group off.

But I told them, "I've still got kids in school. I can't. There's no way I'd even think about it." I had not planned to retire until I was at least fifty or the kids were through school.

Then I started visiting financial advisors and taking a closer look at my situation. I ran tons of calculations and different scenarios and went through a lot of paper and calculators and figured out the FAA pension. It's complicated because we can retire at a young age. There's stuff like age-reduction factor, and there's a lot of different factors involved that you have to go through ...and Social Security.

We draw something called a Social Security supplement because we're forced to retire [early]. A lot of calculations said that with my pension and with working part time, I could bring back pretty much the base pay of what I was bringing home. That's what led to the final decision. It wasn't just a whim. Like I've said, I'm a little bit controlling.

Many school teachers have these same options. They can accelerate their pension payments for a period of time prior to taking Social Security. Let's say you're 60 and want to retire. This acceleration process gives you more money out of your pension plan for specified amount of time, in effect acting as the Social Security payment you will eventually receive, before it actually goes into effect

It's a bridge. Not a complete bridge. Often people use it to cover the cost of health insurance until reaching Medicare age.

Beware though that age reduction factors vary from pension plan to pension plan. They are not all equal. And it is completely legal for a company plan to say, "this is a defined benefit and cannot kick in before sixty-five."

(Scott Wardell) Is there any part of retirement that really hit you as a surprise? Something you hadn't thought about?

(John) A couple things. One of them, no longer was I going to add to my 401(k). Once you retire, you don't have the ability to add to your 401(k). Also, we've now got long-term care insurance. So instead of adding to the Roth, I'm paying for the LTC. I'm playing with that.

Like a lot of people I didn't expect the stock market to go down so far when I wasn't adding to my 401(k). When it went down, I wasn't adding to it. That kind of took me aside, because I was thinking I was in an era when everything was going up. Suddenly, we had to think, "Wow, this could happen again."

Another thing that hit me was when they cut my part-time hours from thirty-two to twenty-seven. That made me open my eyes to the fact that I've never worked in the private sector before. I was always in a job that was guaranteed. Working for the government (generally) meant I wouldn't get laid off and that I'd keep getting raises every year. Now I'm in a job where I don't get raises.

They can manipulate my hours in the private sector. And they have. Things like that made me open my eyes. I should have known, and I guess I did. But now it's real.

(Scott Wardell) Any regrets at all?

(John) No. Some of the controllers still on the floor and are ready to retire come up and talk to us at Raytheon. The first question they ask is, "Do you regret anything?" And the first answer is "no." Absolutely not. Life's too short.

(Scott Wardell) How are most of these soon-to-retire people getting their advice? Through word of mouth or an advisor?

(John) Both. I always suggest that they make sure they go to an advisor, but they're getting both. First and foremost I think they're getting it from retirees. They want to know what we're doing and what we've had success with. We learn from each other. I think I was able to draw a few people to advisors because of what I've been doing.

Summary

John's story is a classic example of someone with the savings gene. He didn't wait for a wake-up call – some cataclysmic debt experience – he was on track from the get-go.

His story reminds me of a couple I know who told me that on one of their first dates they compared their Quicken spreadsheets, and based on that decided they were compatible.

Pretty romantic, huh? But some people are like that. The point is that John, a middle-class guy with not much likelihood of ever earning a lot more, had unbelievable order to his plan. He always knew what was going out, and was saving from the very beginning. It's a tired maxim I suppose. But it isn't so much what you make that matters, it's what you save.

On my scale of "The Five Ss" mentioned earlier, I think John, and I know him pretty well, would have slotted himself in as just above "Struggling" but not quite "Stable" as he began his career with the FAA.

His mentality has always been about, "Don't feel too safe."

Playing amateur psychologist a bit, I've often been struck that

John's job as an air traffic controller, is the sort of occupation where you have to maintain a very high awareness of everything that could go wrong, and how catastrophic a single mistake could be. You see this sort of thinking in the way he handled his finances.

He brought his job's worst-case scenario vigilance to his financial planning. That may not be the sort of gnawing picture of doom that the average person cares to lug around with him day after day. But the point of this chapter is that John is an example of someone who made his system work for him and created a remarkably secure retirement reality for himself and his family.

Also, John tested his retirement plan on knowledgeable people. He sought out other recently retired air traffic controllers and a series of financial planners. John wanted to run his plan up the ladder, to me, for another opinion. And even then he went home and ran his own numbers. It was a kind of compulsion.

Obviously, John's a special kind of character. Maybe two percent of my clients have his level of attention to detail. That's not a big number. But his diligence with the assets he had is a valuable example for anyone who cares enough to follow it.

Questions to consider:

1. If you have retirement accounts managed by your company, have you assessed if they could be better handled elsewhere?

2. Do you have a complete understanding of an elderly parent's financial situation?

3. What is your plan if that parent requires a significant amount of time and resources from you?

4. What would happen to your retirement income if your assets decreased in value by 45%?

Notes

1. Generally speaking when assessing your Life Insurance needs, consider a combination of term and permanent life. This way you can get (if you qualify) a larger amount of Term for the temporary need (mortgage, college costs, debt, etc.) and have a smaller portion to help support retirement income for surviving spouse and protect the estate.

Chapter 5

Trust But Verify

If you follow the news lately, you know there are some nefarious and/or incompetent characters in the money-handling business. These money "advisors" have conducted schemes that have left many in ruins.

A good financial advisor is not just someone who dots every "i" and crosses every "t" in your plan, but he/she is also both careful and patient about explaining exactly how all the pieces of your plan work together. In retirement planning, preventing confusion is at least as important as avoiding disappointment. Confusion – especially after retirement commences – is a serious wrench in the spokes of enjoying what you planned to be doing.

The story of Bob and Jackie, an engaging couple in their late seventies, focuses more on their preparations for retirement rather than what happened after they got there. One perspective on this chapter is the importance of being absolutely certain that everything you've bought is in fact what you had in your plan. It calls to mind the old saying, "Trust, but verify."

Bob and Jackie had been working with the same advisor for a number of years, and frankly, were well prepared for retirement. They had saved diligently. They had managed money well. They had managed their expenses exceptionally well.

Several years ago they came to me for a "second look," a review of their basic retirement architecture and their underlying investments. Something that caught my eye pretty quickly was a managed money account—an account designed for assets that get traded in mutual funds, stocks, and bonds. What was curious was that it looked like Bob and Jackie had an annuity set up inside a managed account. This is highly unusual because there is no productive reason for setting up an account this way. Because of this curious arrangement, an assortment of fees and riders had pushed the annual cost of this annuity up to a little over 3%, plus a 1% fee to the agent. So Bob and Jackie were unknowingly paying a fat 4% a year for someone to manage their money.

Snapshot

- **Age:** 75 and 78.
- **Marital Status:** Married. One surviving adult son.
- **Primary careers:** Architect (government employed), health care provider (severely disabled child).
- **Asset description:** Good government pension, solid investment portfolio.
- **Specific dilemma:** Long-term care situation possibly misrepresented/mishandled. Unnecessarily costly advisor fee structure.
- **Financial stability level:** Surplus.

Bob grew up in Kansas a few miles southwest of Topeka. Bob's father was a city clerk there but had lost his job after an election. The family moved to St. Paul, Minnesota during WWII where Bob's father got a job in an ammunition plant. Bob said, "He didn't have a college education, but he was a pretty savvy guy. Or at least that's what the government thought."

The family eventually moved to Portland, Oregon where Bob's father got a job as an accountant for a millwork business. Bob described his father as "...one of those guys who never took out a loan in his life. If you wanted something, you saved to buy it. I saw that. In fact, he never owned a home."

"They took over my mom's parents' home after grandpa died, and then from 1940 until dad died in 1969, they only rented." Bob learned about money and business at an early age, but not necessarily from his father. "From the fifth grade on, I had some kind of job, making my own money," Bob said. "The funniest was as a ninth grader. I was really just a janitor at a men's clothing store. But one Saturday they were short-handed for some big sale and they told me to fill in on the sales floor. What did I know about clothes? I was a kid. But I sold a guy a robin's egg blue suit that I wouldn't have worn if you paid me. But, you know, the customer is always right."

When Bob's older sister decided to go to college at the art institute in Kansas City, the whole family moved back to Kansas to be closer to her. Eventually Bob went to the University of Kansas and got an architectural degree. After graduating from architecture school, he went to Minnesota with a friend. "I didn't want to go to Kansas City, because they still had the stockyards downtown. Lord, the smell. And I knew I'd never be able to make a living out where my parents were at that time in Liberal, Kansas."

Because he had a commitment to the Air Force because of joining ROTC while in school Bob landed a job with a firm that was doing work on military bases. "So I got out of some of my active service requirement there and got a good start on my career."

Jackie was basically a farm girl from Santa Barbara County in southern California. Her dad raised pure-bred Angus cattle and worked for the same person for thirty-eight years. Jackie said, "We did our share of chores and I guess the savings account started when I was nine with the profit off a 4-H project."

Jackie got involved with 4-H when the owner of the business her dad worked for set up a program to raise an animal. "The arrangement was that instead of buying it [the cattle] from him, we raised it and he took half the profits when kids like me sold it. But that required us to keep records of the feed costs and things. It was good budget and accounting training."

Jackie recalled one of the early teachings from her father. "I do remember asking Dad around the eighth grade or something if I could have an allowance and him telling me, 'Well, fine. How much can you pay for your room and food?'"

Jackie spent five months on a farm youth exchange in Luxembourg before graduating from high school and going to nursing school in Los Angeles. She graduated in the top of her class, then, as Jackie said, "... on a kind of lark I met up with my roommate in St. Paul, Minnesota. She was from Wisconsin."

Bob and Jackie met when Bob's roommate was dating a nursing student he had met in California. "One day after Thanksgiving this guy, Bob, said, 'You ought to meet Shirley's roommate. She's a real sharp gal.'

"So we had a party and all of his girlfriend's roommates came over. And you know, as soon as she [Jackie] walked through the door, I thought, 'That Bob. He knows what he's talking about.' Jackie and I got engaged the following March, and married over the Labor Day weekend in 1961.

"Originally we told everyone the wedding was going to be around Thanksgiving but then we decided 'Why wait?' So I called my dad and said, 'Dad, Jackie and I are getting married in September instead of Thanksgiving,' and there was this pause on the other end of the line, before Dad says, 'Anything you want to tell me, son?'

"It went right over my head at that moment."

One drizzly autumn afternoon I had Bob and Jackie over to my office for a talk about their finances and decisions they – and others made for them – along the way.

(Scott Wardell) As you were settling in together as newlyweds, how were you arranging your finances?

(Bob) Well, Jackie was making more money as a nurse than I was as a fledgling architect. She didn't have a car. I did. She was saving some, but most of my extra cash was going to car payments.

(Scott Wardell) Was there a pension with your nursing job, Jackie?

(Jackie) No.

(Scott Wardell) And how about insurance? Had either of you bought any in those early years?

(Bob) I actually bought a $10,000 benefactor life policy while I was still in college. I don't remember how much the premiums were, but heck, I was young. It was pretty cheap. A fraternity brother sold me the policy and said, "You won't be sorry." Then when we got married I added another $10,000 to that.

(Jackie) And I bought one when I was seventeen.

Seventeen?

(Jackie) Yeah. An agent showed up at the house and my parents and I were all involved. It was with Lutheran Brotherhood. I paid the premiums.

I love this. While Bob's father was in the accounting end of business, it turns out Jackie's parents were the ones actively teaching her something about money. What they said to her was, "This is something that is good for you, and you'll pay the premium on it."

Life insurance for children is often a great idea, but it's better if the kids are involved in the process. It is an excellent teaching device. Obviously you're buying the policy at a moment in the child's life when the premiums are generally still very inexpensive. For many whole-life plans, that rate is locked in for the life of the policy.

However, a common mistake parents make is thinking this low-cost plan is a life insurance policy AND savings for a home AND a retirement plan all rolled into one. Put simply, life insurance is unlikely to do all those things. Cheap, childhood policies like this should be treated like a great value on insurance. It's money to cover parents in the event of a terrible tragedy and/or provide a basic coverage for a young adult through the years leading up to full-time employment. Additional savings and investments should be dealt with in other ways.

Jackie's parents might have considered looking for savings or investment solutions along with the insurance contract to diversify the range of growth. I don't, however, mean to diminish the importance of the life lesson that Jackie's parents emphasized by taking out this policy at a young age.

(Scott Wardell) Any other investments at that time?

(Bob) Well the father of this gal, Shirley, Jackie's roommate that I mentioned, was a banker over in Glenwood City, Wisconsin. He recommended we forget about moving back to Kansas and look at buying property around here in Minnesota. He was our first financial advisor, you might say. So in 1962, we started looking for property we might put a house on.

We found one [in suburban Minneapolis] that was perfect. It was close enough to where both of us were working that we could live with one car.

(Scott Wardell) So you had saved enough to cover the cost of buying this property?

(Bob) The guy who owned the land was an economics professor. Handlebar moustache. Real debonair character. When we said we were interested, he told us he had just turned it over to a real estate agent, but that if we were serious he'd pull it back, saving us about $1000 and sell it to us for $5000 ... which Jackie had in her savings.

(Jackie) What you're forgetting to say is that when we got married, we agreed we'd live on your salary and save mine.

(Bob) Oh yeah. I did forget that, didn't I?

(Scott Wardell) Yes, you did. But then you still had to build on this land.

(Bob) Right. But this same guy, the professor, told us he dabbled in investments and that he'd lend us $20,000 at 5.5% interest and ... this says something about the kind of guy he was ... he'd introduce us to three different bankers he knew and that if we could get a better deal from them he'd go along with their rate.

It turned out his was the best offer. But we hadn't planned on building right away. This was 1962 and I was still studying for my final exams. We were pretty much taking the conservative approach we'd learned from our parents. I think they thought we were crazy taking out a loan that big at our age.

I was making $600 a month about then. But about 1965, I was complaining about not getting enough administrative experience with this small four-person office I was working at. So one day Jackie tosses this want ad at me for an administrative job in the state architect's office. "Quit grousing and go check it out," she said.

(Scott Wardell) Did you have children at this point?

(Bob) Brent, our son, was born in 1964. Before that though, we had lost twin boys, back on January 1963.

I got the government job, which was a significant boost in pay. Probably 30%, plus a pension and progressive raises. It was mandatory state retirement.

(Scott Wardell) And Jackie, you were an RN at this point. Is that right?

(Jackie) Yes, but after Brent was born, I became a full-time mother. Our second child was born with serious handicaps, so it became imperative I stay home.

(Scott Wardell) Was your state job, Bob, offering any other retirement programs?

(Bob) Yes. In the mid-70s, it began offering a deferred-income program.

(Scott Wardell) This is a 457 plan?

A 457 is essentially the government version of a 401(k). It is designed for employees of public entities. Public school teachers, for example, usually have the option of a 403(b) or a 457. Parochial teachers generally have just the 403(b). Public employees have 457s and may not have any other option for self-savings, obviously in addition to their pension.

A 457 is a place in tax code that allows employees to put money in for matching by their employer, in this case the government. A 401(k) match has tax advantages to the employer that has no meaning to a non-profit or government agency.

(Bob) My superiors at the time said, "Bob, this is something you ought to get in to." So I started putting $20 in per pay period, and, if Jackie and I were doing OK, when I got a raise, all of that went in there too. I started at $20 a month, and pretty soon was putting in $50 a pay period, or $100 a month and it grew pretty well.

When the market dropped, the guys around me said, "Now is the time to buy more shares, when prices are low." But I never reached the maximum until close to the end.

(Scott Wardell) Outside of plans through your job, are there other investments you were managing at this time?

(Bob) No. Other than kids' college savings accounts, no.

(Scott Wardell) And in terms of advice, you were running pretty much on general knowledge and tips you were picking up? There was no personal professional advisor at this time, which was by now the mid-80s?

(Bob) No. There was no advisor. Not until I retired in 2000. By then I had accumulated $488,000 in that deferred-income thing.

(Scott Wardell) And Jackie had you gone back to work?

(Jackie) No. But because of [our son's] special needs, I volunteered at schools and they eventually asked me to be a substitute special ed teacher. When my disabled son moved out of the house and I had more time, I started a small business offering respite care for people taking care of family in-home. But I was dealing with my own taxes, and there was no pension or anything like that.

(Scott Wardell) So what eventually motivated you to hire an advisor?

(Bob) Well, this was about 2000 and I just thought it was time to make sure we were getting the most out of that deferred-income money. It looked to me like it was pretty static. But it was 2003 before a friend called and asked if I wanted to go to this presentation by an advisor at a nearby golf club. I went, and this fellow gave a kind of one-stop shopping speech and we signed up to get more information.

(Scott Wardell) You both still had your life insurance policies from way back?

(Bob) No. I had cancelled those two when interest rates were high. They were making 3% and I told the agent, "Interest rates are 10% and you're paying 3%. This is ridiculous." So I took the cash value and rolled them into an … account paying 3 1/2%. I did that on my own, maybe based on talking to guys at work about life insurance. But I also bought a $100,000 term insurance just in case I kicked the bucket, Jackie would have a nice chunk of money.

This was in the early '80s. That's when I took out the term insurance.

(Scott Wardell) We're getting to the real issue at hand now. So you did business with this guy you met at the country club. You hired him as your first financial advisor?

(Bob) Yeah. We set up an appointment, and it was almost like we were committed when we got there. The wheels turn pretty quickly. But we both thought it sounded pretty good.

(Scott Wardell) Were you both confident you understood what he was saying?

(Bob) Yes. We began with a conversation about IRAs and we talked about our level of comfort, which I think was "moderately aggressive." It wasn't "conservative," but it got us into that 8% to 9% range we wanted. We had my government pension [to back us up].

But it wasn't long after we set things up with this fellow that he and his partner went in opposite directions. They split up. They were knocking heads. It was kind of a messy deal.

And also about then he told us he was getting out of the plan we had set up with [another company] and was moving us to [yet another company], because of some "limitations" or something [the first company] was placing on their plan. I wasn't real clear what that was all about.

(Scott Wardell) But you stuck with your guy, and didn't go with the partner he was at war with?

(Bob) Right. I stuck with my guy. The other guy was the numbers cruncher. Our guy was the people person. That's how that place was set up. This was 2003. It was the next year then that we finally got around to talking about long-term care. I was 68, Jackie was 65.

I had had a quadruple bypass in 2001 and Jackie was pretty convinced we needed a policy like that.

(Jackie) This fellow was telling us we weren't quite at the point where we could self-insure.

(Scott Wardell) This is where the story gets twisty, right?

(Bob) Yes. This guy recommended what we thought was a long-term care policy, but as we have since learned, it was a long-term care *rider* to a life insurance policy in the amount of $185,000 for each of us, with the balance we didn't use for long-term care going to our heirs.

(Scott Wardell) Had you talked to anyone else about long-term care to see how theirs' was set up?

(Bob) I hadn't paid much attention to insurance. And I don't think Jackie had either. But you'd see on the news that the state was recommending long-term care insurance and that it came with a tax [break], so it seemed like a good idea.

(Scott Wardell) But it was presented to you, by this advisor, that this was the normal way to do a long-term care policy?

(Bob) Yeah. But when the premium costs came out, I balked. Mine was $7,618 a year! I think it was higher than that originally, but our guy knocked it *down* to $7,600. It was $11,000 to start with. He recommended we do it. He said, "This is what I'd do."

(Scott Wardell) Right now, are you thinking that $11,000 premium was for a straightforward, normal long-term care policy, and that the reduction to $7,600 was because he turned it into a rider?

(Bob) I don't know. But when I complained about the $11,000 he said he had knocked it down to $7,600 and that at the $7,600 rate it would be paid up in ten years.

Jackie's policy was $4,735 a year. So we were paying almost $12,000 a year in long-term care premiums. It was stiff. But we took out the policies.

//

Here's a red flag moment for any consumer.

You'll notice there was no discussion between this guy and Bob and Jackie where he said something like, "Let me size the plan down," meaning less benefit and less cost.

Lots of things could have happened but we don't know for sure. It could be the agent could have pre-submitted Bob for long-term care and the home office told him, "No way we're insuring this guy," at which point the advisor went to Plan B and added a long-term care *rider* to the life insurance policy.

But our evidence so far is that this advisor had not done a tremendous amount of homework. Why do I say that? Because there would be no good reason why he wouldn't simply tell Bob he had been declined. Bob isn't stupid. He knows his condition and that being declined is a possibility.

\\\

(Scott Wardell) And you paid on these two "long-term care" policies at those rates for several years?

(Bob) Yes. Until at one of our annual meetings a few years back I complained that the cash value of my policy was dropping while Jackie's was going up. I said, "Something's wrong here." And the advisor assured me that everything was fine, and the whole thing would be paid up on schedule in ten years.

(Scott Wardell) Then you get the letter.

(Bob) Yes. Then I get the letter, just this past July, telling me that after about eight years of making premium payments the policy had lapsed and that I was responsible for keeping enough money in it to cover the costs.

Well, cripes!

//

Bob and Jackie met with me after a seminar I held with another advisor on the topic of retirement. The idea was to look at their retirement income and see if it was going to hold up.

I discovered that their income will sustain them quite well because they live a very frugal lifestyle. They were living within the guaranteed payment from their various sources. But our service is to stress test their retirement income by running the numbers up to see how far their retirement plan would hold them.

Part of this standard testing involves looking at the asset-allocation picture. For example, if they're getting a 4% or 6% return on some asset, it is factored into this model.

That's when Bob and Jackie brought in some additional papers. What jumped out at me was that they were being charged an annual investment management fee on an annuity contract. Annuities hold more opportunity for fees than many other products. This isn't to say I'm opposed to annuities, only that you need

to ask very specific questions when the topic comes up. Such as, "What is your fee on this?"[1]

Important discoveries like the additional fees mentioned above are what happen sometimes when you get other people involved, people who know how to read the statements.

Bob and Jackie's response to me when I told them about this fee structure was to say, "Well, is that unusual?" which is kind of what you expect from someone who isn't in the business.

My next step was to call the company–not the agent–and ask them to *detail* all the fees. I asked:

"What is the mortality and expense ratio on this annuity?"

"What are all the rider fees, on an annual basis?"

"And what are the underlying investment fees?"

If you're in a situation where you're doing this on your own, ask those questions and add them up. But often, after you ask directly, you'll find the insurance company still can't tell you ... precisely.

You probably won't hear them say, "The agent is charging you a fee on this." Instead you'll hear, "Well, there is this amount that gets extracted every year and goes to Such and Such Capital." So you dig out the statement from this capital management place and you see they're charging you a fee *in addition* to all these other fees.

Word of Caution: If you are paying fees above 2% on annuities, ask a lot of questions about "why"? If they move above 3%, make sure you're getting all the value from that contract to justify the fees.

It can be and often is bewildering. It takes some digging. The average person is generally not equipped, I'm sorry to say, to even tell a second advisor what to look for. I truly believe there'll be an emerging class of advisors who do nothing more than review the work of a primary advisor and offer a second opinion.

(Scott Wardell) So you called your guy and told him you wanted to have a talk?

(Bob) Uh huh. And he told me, "I'm kind of busy," and I told him, "Really? Well I'm kind of busy too."

(Jackie) We told him, "We want to meet this week, not next week."

(Bob) He started the meeting talking about, "Let's look at the big picture here, Bob" and telling us that we'd made $200,000 on the $488,000 from the deferred-income plan, with the minimum distributions we had to take out. Well hell, I knew what we'd made. The question I wanted answer to was, "What is going on with this insurance policy?" He was trying to deflect us, and I didn't care for that.

(Jackie) We never got an apology from him.

(Bob) Yeah, there was no apology.

(Scott Wardell) So what was his explanation for this long-term care "policy" lapsing?

(Bob) Well, he said I was in a high-risk pool. And I think I told him, "and *I'm paying* for the damn high risk." But somehow he said too many people had made claims on it, and the company had changed names and had a new board of directors and strange stuff like that.

Finally he told us that what we should do is cash out Jackie's policy, which had a value of $28,000 and buy another policy he had, with Mutual of Omaha that I think cost $50,000. He told us, "Within two years, it'll triple."

(Jackie) It was pie in the sky.

(Bob) He told us this would be a "1035 transfer."

///

A 1035 Transfer is a way to move from cash value from one insurance policy or annuity contract to another without having to pay Federal income taxes on the amount transferred.

\\

(Scott Wardell) But, just so we're clear, this guy had assured you when you first noticed the declining cash value of your policy that everything would be okay, even if you did nothing but continue to pay the premiums?

(Bob) That's right. I noticed it along about year five or six and he said, "Don't worry. It'll be paid up in ten years." In one of the meetings, when I reminded him of that, he did say, "I'm sorry about that."

(Jackie) I just did not understand how that worked.

///

I've lost track of the number of clients who have said to me over the years something to the effect of, "This is so over my head I don't even want to know..."All I can tell them is, "Well, that's fine if that's your choice, but I have a fiduciary responsibility here to explain this to you. So I *have to explain it to you*."

It's not unusual for people to place their trust in their advisors over digging into the technicalities of the plan on their own. I see it every day, and it leads to situations exactly like this. Always make sure, no matter how complicated a plan may seem, that you can walk away from any financial meeting with the ability to demonstrate an understanding of the products you're being offered or sold.

\\\

(Scott Wardell) In the meetings with your guy did you ever get to the point where you understood that you do not have a standard long-term care policy?

(Bob) No. I mean, I signed the policy. And this guy signed it as the agent. But do I look through all this gol-dang stuff when I've put my trust in my advisor and he's telling me what we've got?

//

Another anecdote I love in this story is Bob pointing out to this guy that he's been charging 3.8% in regular fees and another 1% over that ... and the guy agrees to drop the 1%. Not retroactively, but going forward. But he does so only after guilt-tripping Bob by asking, "How do you expect me to make any money on this deal?"

Bob and Jackie persisted and the advisor eventually also removed 1% more in fees of the annuity contract.

Point being, there's not a big question here about who was putting whom first in this relationship.

\\\

(Scott Wardell) So have you severed all relationships with him?

(Bob) No. Not yet.

(Jackie) We'd like to.

//

One problem here is that Bob and Jackie had an annuity contract with two more years of surrender charges remaining. I told them there was no way it was worth it to take those charges, several thousand dollars, just to get rid of this account. It was too expensive.

And complicated. Because if they just wanted to get away from this particular agent, they'd have to go out and find someone who is licensed with that particular product.

The irony of course is that if you go to another advisor to handle this, that person isn't getting paid while all this is going on and the original advisor–the one you want to get away from–might still be collecting some level of commission (trailer).

\\\

(Scott Wardell) When you first signed on with this guy, did you consider "auditioning" anyone else?

(Bob) I talked to a neighbor who was working with a state investment board, and he gave me a couple names. But I never made contact. Once we met with this fellow, it just seemed like the easy way to go. And you know, I think people are kind of reluctant to recommend financial advisors.

In fairness to the guy we went with, I have to say that when the stock market crashed, he got us out before it really dropped and saved us a lot of money (prevented losses). And he didn't charge us. He moved us into bonds. Now, with the market back up, he's getting us out of some of those bonds, and charging again.

(Scott Wardell) So what are you inclined to do now?

(Bob) I was told that the first thing to do is to lay it out for the insurance company. But I'm thinking of sending it to the state Attorney General, our U.S. Senator, and maybe the Governor, too. In the letter to the company, I'm asking for my premiums in full.

//

As shady as a lot of this sounds, I still believe most companies want to do the best thing by their clients. So the first thing to do in a situation like this is appeal to the company.

Do I think the company will immediately take action to correct your situation? No. But it is both a matter of good faith on your part as the consumer, and a perhaps a better long-term position before elevating the matter to a legal complaint status.

Bob will have a hard time getting his seven years of premiums back, simply because the company will argue that it stood prepared to meet its obligations had he died during that period. He *was* covered.

Bob's argument, based on his view of the matter, will remain: "Yes. But your agent completely misrepresented what I was paying for." The process of sorting out reality might take a while or may never be resolved.

So your first call is to the company's customer relations department.

\\

(Scott Wardell) Before your experience with this advisor, was there ever any other serious investment?

(Bob) Well, I try to forget about one we got into back in the mid-1980s. My mother was still alive then and she had some money that wasn't earning much, and a guy I know suggested we talk to this woman who was selling these promissory notes that were guaranteeing 15%.

They were with a couple outfits out in Denver. Well, it looked pretty good. So we took $10,000 of Mom's money and kicked in $20,000 of our own . . .to buy these promissory notes and wouldn't you know the two joints out West both defaulted. All that money was down the drain.

The gal we bought them through encouraged us to hire an attorney, and for $600 I think he wrote one letter.

(Jackie) It's embarrassing we didn't learn our lesson then.

(Bob) Both of those guys were convicted and ordered to pay restitution. I'm still getting $5 a month from that one.

//

So again, the bottom line strategy is to make noise, create a ruckus, and if the company doesn't respond, take it up the ladder. The state might well want to find out if there is a pattern of this kind of behavior going on.

I don't think Bob was saying that he distrusts everyone. Rather, he was saying he doesn't feel confident recommending an advisor to somebody else *because so much is at stake.* Bob would feel vested if he made a recommendation, and if his friend had a bad experience, he would feel a responsibility.

\\

(Scott Wardell) Just out of curiosity, in retirement, have either of you continued with part-time work, developed paying hobbies, or anything that generates an income stream?

(Bob) Well, (he laughs), right now there's more loss than income, but we live next to woods with lots of birds. We liked the idea of feeding birds, not squirrels. So I took up the challenge of designing a squirrel-proof bird feeder.

(Scott Wardell) I'll take five.

(Bob) You can't afford 'em.

(Scott Wardell) And Jackie, did you continue with your respite care work?

(Jackie) No. I retired from that after my last client passed away. I did some hospice care volunteering, but I gave that up after our youngest son died of leukemia.

(Bob) We had arranged our will so that our oldest son would have had the resources to care for his brother if he had outlived us.

(Jackie) He [our disabled son] was with us for twenty-two years, but state insurance took care of that when he moved into the group home.

(Scott Wardell) As I say, no matter how much you like whomever you're working with, or how good it all sounds, "Trust, but verify."

(Bob) Right. We trusted, but didn't verify.

Summary

One of my mentors in this business told me that to be a truly good financial advisor, "You have to have the head of a capitalist and the heart of a social worker."

As I re-visit this story, I'm struck that while the advisor Bob and Jackie were working with had the head of a capitalist; he may have missed the part about really, deeply serving his clients.

No one who has the clients' interests foremost in mind takes the cavalier attitude that, "Hey, in ten years it'll be fine."

I suspect – because I've met them – that there are lots of people who believe illustrations shown to them by an advisor, but don't understand what could happen if markets change, and the impact it could have on their situation. I don't know what assumption this advisor was under that these costs were going to be sustained. But my guess is that he had to project that policy to earn 8% per year just to survive. And that would be just barely. And then the market crashed.

So here is Bob, who was following this, and asking, "Why is this going down?" He was asking because he was comparing his policy to Jackie's, which was going up. Bob was paying attention and he told this to his advisor. This is "back-asswards" as they say on the farm. You want your advisor alerting you to this and offering effective solutions.

To put a finer point on it: The loss of value would have been absolutely evident in a normal annual review.

The technical point, not to be forgotten in this story, is that there are long-term care policies that Bob and Jackie could have bought subject to their insurability. Moreover, there are such policies that have a seven- or ten-year pay, an option designed for people who prefer to pay more premium now to have it paid off faster. But that isn't what was going on here.

What Bob and Jackie found themselves in was a situation where they had the costs of the life insurance itself, *plus* the costs of the long-term rider. In other words, a policy laden with costs that was then hammered with poor overall returns. And their advisor was *still* saying, "Don't worry, it'll be paid off in ten years."

Bob knew something wasn't right. It just didn't add up. Up to this point, he had a good overall experience with the advisor. So it took him a while before he decided he needed a second opinion. In this case it might have saved Bob a lot of stress … and gotten this whole situation straightened out before the situation was really unstable.

See the epilogue for questions every client should ask when auditioning an advisor.

Questions to Consider:

1. Do you know what you are paying your financial advisor?

2. If you've purchased long-term care insurance, is it a policy independent of any other policy you own? If you are uncertain, have you asked your advisor for clarification?

3. Have you considered taking your entire portfolio to another advisor and having another set of eyes?

Notes

1. On variable annuities in particular, make sure to read the required prospectus provided by the issuing company outlining all of the fees and charges.

Chapter 6

Chaos in the Exurbs

The Great Recession took a huge toll on many people. Some who got caught up in the sub-prime game knew better, others were confused by the lending system. Another subset of victims were decent, entirely normal Americans who misjudged and misplayed the easy credit of the bubble years and found themselves in very serious trouble.

Doug and Sheila are as pleasant and friendly a couple as you'll ever hope to meet. But they are very much a part of that last group. Namely, average middle-class Americans who had no real control of their budget, spending habits, and planning discipline, even as they both approached retirement. Career public school teachers, each had a pension, but even that guaranteed income was imperiled by the disaster they found themselves in when I first met them.

By their early sixties, the two reduced their material belongings to an aged Ford Escort that they stored in a friend's garage and whatever fit into four suitcases. Seeking to rebuild their finances, they headed abroad to teach in wealthy but culturally conservative Kuwait.

Anxious to get their story into this book, I interviewed them on one of their semi-annual trips home.

Snapshot

- **Age:** 61 and 63.
- **Marital status:** Married, two adult children.
- **Primary career:** Both public school teachers.
- **Asset description:** Two pensions, but no home and few investments. Must continue working.
- **Specific dilemma:** Serious money mismanagement throughout their working lives. Two bankruptcies. Impulsive, money-losing investments. Extreme credit issues related to unchecked lifestyle spending. Currently retired after teaching in Kuwait.
- **Financial stability level:** Struggling.

Both Doug and Sheila grew up on small Minnesota farms, which is an environment that often masks a lot of financial vulnerabilities. Food isn't usually a problem, and most of your neighbors are pretty much of the same economic class. As a kid, you're not all that aware of what you don't have.

"My parents were never spenders," Sheila told me. "They never talked to me about money, about how to manage it. Dad was a farmer for a long time. After he sold the farm, he bought gas stations. He had three at one time and ended up with one, all in small Minnesota towns. One time with friends from high school, a classmate looked at me and said, 'You know, we probably all grew up in poverty, but none of us ever knew it.' If you judged us simply by the numbers – household income –she was probably right. But it didn't feel that way."

Part of the charm of Doug and Sheila is that they were literally neighbors as children, with Doug's family working land barely seven miles away. They never met as kids, but shared the same provide-for-yourself ethic that everyone around had. "Mom made everything out of the garden," says Doug. "We raised cattle. We had plenty of meat. The only thing we ever bought in town was flour and spices. Otherwise our family took care of everything."

What they also shared, unfortunately, was a pretty low level of financial literacy. Neither set of parents talked money in front of the kids, at least to the point of offering education. "Dad was pretty controlling," is Doug's description of the line of command. "He handled all the finances. Mom worked as hard as he did. But she handled the house and the garden. We were a very conservative Lutheran family. We worked hard but never really got a paycheck. The first time I got paid for a job I think it was in junior high: $1 an hour for pumping gas. We definitely had a work ethic. We weren't slackers."

The most Doug's father ever gave him for college was $500. Everything else he earned from construction work in summers and between semesters. Sheila's first job was on an American Indian reservation, an environment where she was exposed to some grim realities about poverty and addiction.

"It was an eye-opening experience. I learned as much as the kids did. I had students who were older than I was. I had a student who was convicted of stabbing someone. The tribal council told him, 'Here's your choice. Go in the army or go back to school.' It was a tough year for me. I was Little Miss Peace Love and Beads. Seriously, I thought everybody wanted to be saved. But there, no one wanted to be saved. At the end of that year, I got a job in a small public school."

Both managed to leave their under-graduate years without significant debt and both soon had adult jobs with the opportunities to begin serious retirement planning. If only they had. Other than their built-in teacher's retirement plans, which as you'll see have been a godsend, actual financial planning and management was as taboo as discussions about money were around their childhood dinner tables. Life simply began the process of acquiring and accumulating with nowhere near enough attention paid to the consequences of imbalanced cash flow and expensive debt.

(Scott Wardell) So from very early on, in your twenties you both had steady jobs. Were you aware then that you had to save money for the future? Sheila?

(Sheila) I had teachers' retirement. But, frankly, I never thought about it. Retiring was so far down the road. But from the start, something was being deducted every pay period.

(Scott Wardell) Was there ever a staff or faculty meeting to explain your investment choices?

(Sheila) No, never.

(Scott Wardell) And you, Doug?

(Doug) We were married and for a year and a half while I was still finishing up, I was bouncing around helping my dad on the farm. He was getting old and he had arthritis real bad. I was the youngest, so it was kind of like I had to stay there. I was the last one.

My first job was working with the school recreation department as a summer assistant. We built a house when Sheila was pregnant with our first child. I'd been applying for teaching jobs, but in the early Eighties, they were laying off teachers like mad. I remember applying for every job in a fifty-mile radius from where we lived and I didn't even get an interview.

I had been working part-time for the railroad and an opportunity came up that meant moving into Minneapolis. My parents sold the farm and actually bought the house we had built. Sheila got a job with a suburban school district here in the Twin Cities, while I kept on working for the railroad, making pretty good money.

But I absolutely hated it. I was sitting in a little cube with my back to another guy without any people interaction, nothing. Financially we were doing okay, but I hated it.

I was in my thirties when I got hired as a physical education instructor by the same school district where Sheila worked. She started in '84 and I started in '86.

(Scott Wardell) How were the finances at this point, with both of you working as teachers?

(Doug) That was when our financial issues first hit. I took a heck of a pay cut. But what I was doing, with the railroad, wasn't something I wanted to be doing for the rest of my life. School was a career. I'd always wanted to be a teacher, but we took a huge cut in pay to do it. We decided though we had to make up for it by both getting our Masters.

Sheila got hers in '87 and I finished in '88. That meant we'd made up money-wise to where we had been when I was at the railroad. But with both of us in Masters programs, we loaded up a pile of debt.

//

My thinking here is that Doug and Sheila really needed to spread out this graduate degree business and the debt they took on. Public school teachers typically have what are called "lane changes," salary increases based on tenure and advanced degrees. Getting their Masters was clearly the right move, but if Doug had said, "Sheila, you're a couple years ahead of me. You go get it first, we'll handle that debt, then I'll go," they would have been less overwhelmed by the bills that came in.

> Even with his lower income, Doug could have taken a class or two and gradually increased his income. A lot of what you see in their story is, "Too much, too fast." I understand Doug's urgency, because he was older as he started his teaching career, but they could have timed it out.

(Scott Wardell) Did you have a financial advisor at this point?

(Doug) No. We met people who wanted to be our financial planner, basically to sell us whole life insurance. But no. [An Insurance Company at the time] went out and recruited coaches and people who were high profile around the school district. So pretty soon you had the football coach and he showed up at your house with two young teachers. We bought more dang whole life insurance policies just to get them out of the door!

We bought all these little policies and ended up with this big bill (in premiums). After a few years we cashed it in at a huge loss[1]. But like I say, we didn't understand how it worked. But there was nobody at that time.

> Doug and Sheila had accumulated several term insurance contracts that looked cheap, and whole life that had promised them everything. The end result was a cash flow imbalance that impeded a lot of other things they needed to do. People need to understand what their life insurance architecture looks like. If you have no real idea what your insurance is doing, you are going to be easy prey for the sales guy who'll tell you it'll shine your shoes and be a delicious whip topping on your favorite dessert. Don't *pretend* you understand. Actually understand. Or at least ask someone who does.
>
> I had two other clients who were spending $40,000 a year in premiums and couldn't figure out how they were going to send their fifteen-year-old to college. Crazy stuff. But they had no idea what they were doing.

(Scott Wardell) So most of your debt in your thirties is loans from getting your Master's degrees?

(Doug) Not all. But that was where it started. We bought a house in suburban Minneapolis in 1981, lived in it till '84, then bought a house a little further out. We were in that one for eleven years, then moved again to a bigger house, lived there for another eleven years, until 2006 when we sold it.

A big part of our problem was credit that was so easy. Too easy. Everybody was more than happy to give us money to do this, money to do that. A lot of the time we were probably robbing Peter to pay Paul. We'd get one loan to pay off two others.

What jumps out at me is pretty obvious, namely, "Too damned much house." Realtors are trained to get you to buy as much house as you can afford. But that is often to the detriment of almost everything else you can do financially.

I advise people to report only two-thirds of their income when talking to a realtor. Don't report it all because they might sell you right up to the limits of what you can afford. They'll get you to smell the new carpet and buy to the max rather than match the property to your needs.

(Doug) And credit cards! Well you know how it was. They were a dime a dozen. They'd throw these cards at you, and you'd max them out. We had cash flow, so we were paying our bills, but all we were doing was paying the minimum.

We always had this idea that we were going to be able to pay everything off at the end. But we were thinking, oh, we can get a different card with a higher limit, then pay everything.

There's a kind of two-part scolding here: One to Doug and Sheila, obviously for not knowing how money works, for being kind of clueless about cash flow; and two to the whole great American credit industry that was willing to keep giving them money despite their very tight financial situation.

(Scott Wardell) Soon you were facing bankruptcy, right? And this was in the '90s that most people remember as a fat and happy time?

(Sheila) Yeah. In the early '90s we filed for bankruptcy for the first time. It wiped out about $47,000 worth of debt.

(Scott Wardell) Who advised you through bankruptcy?

(Doug) Ha! It was the guy on TV! It really was! We went to him. He was a lot younger then!

(Scott Wardell) Did the TV guy give good advice?

(Doug) Not knowing what to do and how to do it, he was okay. We got rid of all that debt and we ended up in place where we could kind of start over. Chapter 7 wiped out our debt. We had gone into our second house, the larger house at that time. So we got rid of all this short-term debt. But as far as bankruptcy's impact on our credit and how that was going to devastate us down the road...

My advice to people facing the serious problem of bankruptcy is to seek out a bona fide expert. There's no question Doug and Sheila needed professional help.

A comprehensive look at managing their debt might ... *might* ... have been the answer. Doug and Sheila found out the TV guy's game was strictly about getting his clients into a bankruptcy arrangement–pronto. Quick turnover. What they needed was some counsel about how "Oh, by the way, this is going to really hurt your credit over the next three to five years (or more).

I would suggest at least two sets of professional eyes on something as serious as bankruptcy.

(Scott Wardell) Let me guess, the bankruptcy attorney didn't explain that to you so well, right?

(Sheila) No. You know what he did? He sat down, looked at this, looked at that, looked and this again, looked up and said, "Yup, you can do this. No problem." There wasn't one word about the long-term consequences. Granted, we should have known. It's not like we were young. But we didn't know. He said, "Yeah, let's do it," and we did.

(Scott Wardell) Looking way back, does it seem like Chapter 7 bankruptcy was the best thing to do?

(Doug) I think at that time we just felt that our backs were against the wall. The kids were ten and twelve. Young.

(Scott Wardell) Were you thinking you had to clean this mess up because college was coming down the road?

(Doug) Exactly. And I can't speak for Sheila, but for me, it was just so personally devastating. My dad died in '88. He was so controlling as a financial person. His attitude was, "You don't buy this. You save money, then you can buy it. You don't borrow. You don't get loans. You don't do any of that stuff."

That was the whole mentality. For me to have to go through this ... I was so ashamed. Dad had died by then. But still ... Dad wasn't the easiest person to talk to. Let's put it this way: As a farmer in Minnesota, he was the only Republican in a world of Democrats. He was very conservative. That's just how he lived his life. So for me to go through bankruptcy was really hard emotionally. I thought, gosh, how much more embarrassing can it get than that?

(Scott Wardell) But you both have steady jobs. It's the mid-'90s. The economy in general is pretty good. You have Teachers' Retirement (TRA). There was hope, right?

(Doug) Yes. Generally speaking, we were making a good income. Because we had (Teachers' Retirement) TRA, the pension money was being put away. We had the deferred comp. As far as long-term planning goes, we kind of let our jobs take care of that. It was automatic. But we kept accumulating short- term debt.

(Sheila) It was very dumb. We were very dumb.

(Scott Wardell) And what are you spending it on? You bought new homes. But other than that, just stuff?

(Doug) I couldn't even tell you what we bought.

(Scott Wardell) We're not talking Vegas, here?

(Doug) No. No. But we'd go on vacation, and we bought a timeshare. We had that debt. You get stuff like that. And our kids were getting older. They had stuff that they needed. They never get any cheaper, you know! Then we started looking at college. We bought a second house in the same city. We refinished the basement there. We fixed up the backyard.

(Scott Wardell) Two houses at the same time?

(Doug) Yeah, for a while. We sold one and moved into the new one.

We bought the new one in '95. We didn't have any trouble getting a loan. If you could blink, take nourishment, and sign your name, you got credit.

(Scott Wardell) Even with the bankruptcy filing?

(Doug) We bought the second house before bankruptcy impacted our credit. But the recovery was amazing. After about three years of being a bad risk, it was like we were golden again. Chapter 7 had wiped out the debt. There was nothing there. We didn't owe anybody anything. It seemed to us it was really easy to borrow money. Our income was going up. We had more cash flow. But when you talk about living paycheck to paycheck, that's what we did. We were just managing to stay ahead. All the basic stuff, like cable and cell phones and things like that added up to a lot of money every month without us noticing much.

///

As a consumer, you have to stay alert to monthly fee creep. A little here for cable, then premium cable. A little here for new cell phones, then smart phones with baffling but expensive data plans. Another check for the health club all your friends have joined. The total amount of recurring expenses leaving your checkbook is subtle but substantial. Like millions of others, Doug and Sheila let this "creep" get its hands around their financial throats.

It may be a while, and I say "thank God," before the United States returns to the kind of recklessly easy credit of the '90s and early 2000s. I keep telling people that every single system out there has learned from the banking industry the tricks of, "How can we get customers to create recurring revenue for us?" Do you know what ATT's dividend is on its stock? 5%! That's roughly double Standard & Poor's 500 average. And

do you think that has anything to do with them being masters of the recurring revenue system? Of course it does. It's essential.

(Scott Wardell) But your spending after the bankruptcy, this was primarily the mortgage and what you thought of as essential bills, the stuff of life?

(Sheila) Well, we took vacations. But we're not into hot cars. The mistake that kind of tipped the tea kettle over for us was we made those two investments.

(Scott Wardell) Uh oh.

(Sheila) Yeah. It was one of these things where you refinance your house and pull out equity, because houses were just shooting up in value. So we refinanced, pulled out an extra $5000 - $10,000 for this investment where we were going to make a ton of money.

Do I even have to say that this is wrong and inadvisable on almost every level? As a professional advisor, I could not and would not agree to such a move. But ... people will make their own decisions. If you find yourself in this situation, please be certain you-have a locked-in, automated, virtually impregnable system to pay off your loan to yourself. Why? Because *no one* has the discipline to write the check every month, as they all say they do.

And by "system" I mean what I often refer to as "self-garnished wages," an automatic re-payment plan over which you have very little control. Deductions from your paycheck. That kind of thing.

(Scott Wardell) OK, I'll bite. What was the investment?

(Sheila) It was something to do with an auto security and all that kind of stuff. It was a security system for cars. Like where you put the chip in the dog.

(Scott Wardell) Who put you on to that one?

(Sheila) Well, it came out of Florida. A guy talked about it, and it sounded like a good deal. You were buying stock for $1 a share or something like that. We ended up investing about $12,000. It was going to be our ticket to make a ton of money and pay everything off.

///

Of all of Doug and Sheila's problems, this ranks very highly. They also invested in a timeshare that they could ill-afford. When you have substantial high interest-rate debt and your savings goals are behind target, you should seriously consider avoiding high-risk programs … entirely.

There's a term in the industry, "accredited investor." Accredited investors are people who have at least $1 million in assets outside of their home. Those people are usually doing something right. But even they will stop and think, "How much am I going to put into something that looks risky?"

What Doug and Sheila got into here was "an unregistered investment." Quite often these, "You have got to invest today to get in on the ground floor" deals turn out badly, as they did with Doug and Sheila.

Often there is an emotional reaction to these kinds of investments. As in, "Oh my God, I am so lucky to have heard about this!" But what people should stop and say to themselves is, "If this were real, then the people with big money – accredited investors – would have smothered this 'opportunity' by now."

I believe in "portfolio drivers" and risk investment. For example, the bio-medical field today is full of seemingly fascinating opportunities. But there's a lot of research and homework that needs to be done before getting into something like that, especially if you are not accredited.

\\

(Scott Wardell) And what happened?

(Doug) They basically went belly up. We didn't have an advisor or anything. We were still out there trying to figure this stuff out on our own. We lost everything. We made nothing. It was ignorance. It was stupidity. I think we were just naïve.

(Scott Wardell) So now we're into about the mid-2000s. What was your situation?

(Doug) Well, we'd refinanced our house a couple of times. The mortgage was almost $400,000. And we were thinking we're getting to the end of our careers, or close to it. The kids were in college or through college.

(Scott Wardell) Did you pay the full bill for college?

(Doug) We helped with a lot of things. We've given our kids a lot of money. It wasn't just college stuff. We helped out initially with loans and things like that.

(Scott Wardell) Did you take on school loans yourself?

(Doug) Not with our daughter. But we did with our son. Our son went to a small private school. We signed on for some loans for him to kind of get him through. The federal loans he signed on for. We got a couple of private loans through Wells Fargo.

///

The "college talk" needs to come at least five years before junior heads off to school. Savings needs to start long before that. When your kid is somewhere around fourteen, you should have a reasonable idea of what you can afford and tell him or her what they are going to have to contribute.

If you decide to take out a private loan in your name for your kid's education – because you can get a private loan – you need to have the conversation with that kid along the lines of, "I'm taking this loan out for you, but you are going to have to pay it back." Those words need to be spoken ... clearly ... if you are someone who is looking at any possibility of a precarious retirement.

The other element, in the context of keeping up with the Joneses, is making a clear-eyed assessment of where you can get the best education for the least money. There is a lot of research and soul-searching to be done at this point of life. Talk with an advisor or other professionals on all the ways to handle college costs, and get a good understanding of how to file the FAFSA form.

People get awfully hung up on the pedigree of "the right school," and as a result, they often over-pay for something they could get much, much cheaper somewhere else.

I will also say that if you are at the point where you're considering private loans, you're most likely at the point where you're buying too much school. The fact that you have to go to bank is a sign that you're stretching.

(Doug) But now we were getting to the mid-2000's and we were in trouble. We had got a ton of debt, and all of a sudden we couldn't pay some of our bills. I can't even remember what the credit card was. It had a $15,000 credit limit. But that was what we did the backyard with. But we have a nice patio. But with all the remodeling, everything just started piling up.

Which meant we started picking and choosing which bill we were not going to pay. It just started steamrolling on us. Still, for our twenty-fifth wedding anniversary, we were able to go to Hawaii. I think we probably financed that somehow.

A couple thoughts on credit card debt, without belaboring the obvious: The best rule I know is one my dad told me when I was a kid. "Never buy a depreciable asset with borrowed money." That includes cars, although almost everyone violates that rule at least once. But in this case, the invention that Doug and Sheila didn't have when they started running up the debt is a debit card. A debit card guarantees you're not going to spend more than you have. For those who aren't disciplined enough to pay off a credit card every month – and know they're not disciplined enough – do yourself a big-time favor and trash the credit cards. Go directly to debit cards. Its old-school advice, but it works.

Too many open cards are bad for your credit score, even if you're not carrying a balance. If you have more than four, I say you've got too many.

People are easily confused by the credit scoring system. That's because it is a very strange, heavily-gamed system. There's no question about it. But it's what we've got. Fight it if you want, but it won't do you a lot of good.

The bottom line though is that the system is trying to assess your ability to pay. And missing credit cards payments is very hard on your credit rating. Defaulting of course is worse. But accumulating debt very quickly is tantamount to the road to ruin.

(Scott Wardell) And about now, in the mid-2000s, was when you met the couple working in China and decided that traveling abroad was something you wanted to do when you retired, right?

(Doug) Yes. It was 2005. We were very deep in debt. We had to sell the house. We had kept on refinancing, which meant the payment kept going up. We put the house on the market at $500,000. We found a buyer and closed in late '06, about a month before we would have gone into foreclosure.

(Scott Wardell) And you were doing this to be able to travel in retirement?

(Doug) We didn't know all the financial ramifications of what we'd be able to do. We just knew our kids were on their own and that if we could sell the house, lease a townhouse, we'd be able to clear away debt and be able to do some things. The sale did clear off a lot of stuff. We basically walked out even. But by then we'd had an issue with the IRS and with the state. We were behind on our taxes. The house was kind of our bank. Whenever we needed money, that's where we went.

(Scott Wardell) A lot of people went through the house-as-ATM phase.

(Doug) Seriously. We maxed out every nickel that house was worth. So when we sold it, we got rid of some of that. But we still had a lot of baggage. So in '06, we filed for bankruptcy a second time. But this time we couldn't do a Chapter 7. We had to go Chapter 13 because our incomes were so high.

(Scott Wardell) This all happened at the same time, in '06. You sold the house, leased a townhouse, and filed for bankruptcy. Was this a coordinated plan on your part?

(Doug) No. If we were that smart, we'd never have gotten into trouble in the first place.

(Scott Wardell) So what was left over, in terms of debt, after you sold the house. The tax bill?

(Doug) The credit card bill was still out there. We still had good income. Two of them. So we did a [Chapter]13. That basically tied everything in a big bow. We got a bankruptcy payment. The 13 took care of all the debt, everything that we had accumulated to that point, including the credit cards. But now we had this monthly payment. So we were paying for that.

///

The experience here with Doug and Sheila is so much a matter of choices. "Do I do this? Or do I do this?" Do I take the short-term gratification, or do I take the longer-term view?

Almost every one of my wealthy clients has figured out a way to avoid taking on expense layers and adding new income layers. If you're not wealthy, ask yourself, "Do we need the cable TV? Do we need the health club we never go to?"

There's all this stuff we think we need ... that we don't. You're just fine without it. Although if you drop the health club membership, consider taking up jogging or long walks.

\\\

(Scott Wardell) So the Chapter 13 filing at least put all your debts in one manageable box. Did it cover everything?

(Doug) Well ... we didn't talk about the fact that we had bought a lake cabin, did we? Honest to Pete, we wanted to live the dream! One of the things we did in our first house [. . .] was to put in a pool. It was like going to the lake but staying home. The kids were real little at that time, and we thought if we had a pool in the backyard, we could go to the lake everyday! It cost $7,000. Above ground with a deck around it. It was a blast. That was probably the smartest thing we ever did. We used it every day. The kids learned to swim. Everyone wanted to come to our house because we had the pool. The kids' friends and ours all liked to come over because we had all these amenities. That was the kind of mentality we were in.

(Scott Wardell) But then you later buy a lake home?

(Doug) Before our kids went to college. We wanted a place back where we grew up in western Minnesota. We couldn't get credit through the normal channels, but a friend of mine from high school was an officer in a small bank. We arranged the loan. This was '03. We had it for three years. It was another $1,000 a month payment. We sold it in '06.

///

> People love lake homes/second homes. Some even rationalize them as an investment. But what I often see is people who look at their indebtedness and say, "Pretty good. No big problems." Then they look at the loan- to-equity ratio on their primary home. If it's down to say 50%, they tell themselves they're ready to take on another $1000 a month for a second, vacation home.
>
> Unfortunately, the part that gets overlooked is saving for college and retirement. If the extra $1,000 slows the latter down, they should – but don't – ask themselves, "How do I feel about retiring at 75, instead of 65?"
>
> Ten more years of working has a nasty way of cutting into the relaxing time at the lake. If you're in a predicament like we see here, I really urge you to consider staying at a resort for a couple weeks every August instead of taking on another mortgage.

\\\

(Scott Wardell) Remind me, you sell the main house just ahead of foreclosure, and what happens? Do you get a lease on a townhouse?

(Doug) Well, sort of. We leased – to buy – the townhouse through a friend who was a contractor. It wasn't selling and he needed somebody in it. Our credit at this time was just crap.

(Sheila) He took a chance on us. He really did. And he didn't have to. But even during the transaction part of it his closing agent told him, "Are you kidding me? You're going to sell to these two?"

(Doug) But we were still both working our tails off! We had good cash flow, but huge debt. Our credit was shot. Our friend said, "We can sell it to you on a contract for deed. That way you can have the benefits of ownership. You can get the homestead credit, and I get it off my books."

(Scott Wardell) So you were actually buying.

(Doug) On paper it was buying. We were leasing a $450,000 townhome for $1,000 down. Our mistakes were our own. But we also had friends who believed in us. And this was a situation where a friend knew we were good people.

(Scott Wardell) But still you're not seeking any kind of professional guidance. With all that's going on, why not?

(Sheila) Shame. That's what I think it was.

(Doug) Probably even arrogance on my part. I got us into this situation, I thought, so I'm going to get us out. But the way we got us out was to keep borrowing.

///

I cannot tell you how often I run into exactly this piece of psychology. Doug is more candid about it than most men I work with. Men often say, "I got us into this, I'm going get us out." It's the financial play-out of the "men never stop to ask for directions" joke.

The financial industry has a role in this. Because a lot of time we talk over peoples' heads just to prove how smart we are. The consequence is the client thinking, "I'm not going to go talk to that guy anymore. He'll make me feel stupid."

But there are alternatives. In Minneapolis, and in

most big cities, there are places you can go for a very low-cost consultation. Lutheran Social Services will charge you $50 to talk to a debt counselor. These are not bloodsuckers out there bayoneting the wounded, but this is real help. It's a very good idea for $50.

Sadly, the pride issue is very common and gets in the way of people getting help.

(Scott Wardell) When did you start thinking about teaching overseas as a way to get things under control?

(Doug) In '09. That's when we got serious about this overseas thing. This was from the couple we met in Hawaii ten years earlier. We decided we needed to look into that.

(Scott Wardell) What sort of research did you do on overseas teaching?

(Doug) Well, here's the thing. I wanted to do it with the Department of Defense [DoD]. Because of the government benefits and all that. Basically you're on a U.S. military base, and you're teaching military kids. You have the military insurance and everything else. But by the time we came along, getting a DoD teaching job was like getting appointed to the Naval Academy [. . .] those jobs are hard to get because they were really sought after.

(Scott Wardell) You were both closing in on the ends of your teaching careers in Minnesota, right?

(Sheila) Doug had a couple years left to teach. I was done. But if he could get a leave from teaching and if we could get a job overseas and continue to pay into our retirement here and all that, it looked like it might be the best way to go. We were trying to think outside the box because by that point our box was pretty small. We were very naïve. We had made so many poor decisions. But at that point we really had to look at retirement. I realized, "I'm going to be sixty-years-old." It was scary.

(Doug) Teaching and living abroad was something I'd wanted

179

to do, based on the conversation we had with that couple in Hawaii. We'd never traveled or been anywhere outside the States. I mean, we didn't suffer. We'd had a Caribbean cruise and that type of thing in our younger years. But we'd never been out of North America. The travel part was really enticing. We wanted to be able to explore. But we weren't going to be able to sit here in retirement and afford a trip to Europe for three weeks on my paycheck or her retirement.

(Scott Wardell) Had you tampered with your retirement funds in any way through all your financial difficulties?

(Doug) Well, our daughter got married in '05 and we hadn't put any money away for a wedding. So we took it from my deferred compensation plan. That's how we paid for the wedding. We didn't touch Sheila's, but I borrowed $15,000 out of mine. I took the financial hit, the penalty. But we had to pay for a wedding.

That was the first real dent in our long-term retirement plan. It hit my side pretty hard. We didn't pick up a loan for the wedding. We got it paid for. But it put a dent in our retirement.

///

The conversation that didn't happen here is, "Honey, we can't pay for this wedding," or at least not $15,000. We can contribute maybe $5,000. But Doug and Sheila didn't say, "I'm sorry. I can't afford this."

Shame is not a good reason to avoid having an honest conversation with your financial advisor when

making big financial decisions like paying for a wedding. Precisely discussing decisions like paying for weddings helps people in Doug and Sheila's situation discuss how to form the proper architecture to potentially: 1) find a way to save enough to fund the event or at least, 2) find a way to slow down the accumulation of debt as much as possible.

Borrowing for weddings, borrowing for vacations, borrowing for vacation homes, borrowing for schools— stop, stop stop. It has to stop somewhere. Controlling or not, Doug's dad was mostly right about debt.

(Scott Wardell) But you were getting more serious about working overseas?

(Doug) Yes. Sheila decided to work an extra year. But we knew she was going to retire in June 2010. So in the fall of '09, we thought it was time to start going after this overseas thing. Here again, we got started late in the game. We should have been doing this a year earlier.

(Scott Wardell) But you were still working at the school district in Minneapolis?

(Doug) Right. Sheila was retiring. But me, I had to go to HR and my principal and say I might not be back next year. And ... I needed a letter of recommendation.

(Scott Wardell) You needed a letter of recommendation before applying at the overseas hiring fair in Iowa, is that right?

(Doug) That's right. Sheila, she could have gone anywhere in the world. English teachers are highly sought after. It's trickier with me. The thing is though, married couples are highly sought after, because in most of the positions, everything, your living expenses, are included. Two can live as cheaply as one. They don't have to provide separate apartments for her and another one for me. If they hire us together, it's financially advantageous to the school.

(Scott Wardell) But you had to find someone that needed two positions.

(Doug) Exactly. So we kept looking. A lot had English, but nothing in my area, physical education or health. Eventually, I started getting emails from this school in Kuwait. The man said he was going to be in Waterloo [Iowa] and he'd like us to stop in and see him.

(Sheila) But I said there's no way I'm going to Kuwait! I'm not even going to the interview! I even told my principal that!

//

This idea of teaching overseas is actually one of the better decisions Doug and Sheila have made, maybe because they let it percolate for fourteen years. The stuff they moved on impulsively – the Florida investment, the time-share – is rarely, very rarely, a good idea.

They did a lot more research on teaching overseas too. Where they made good decisions, they had done more homework.

\\\

(Scott Wardell) What was your problem with Kuwait? The culture?

(Sheila) Yeah. It's in the Middle East! It's such a mess over there! But, you know, I ate my words. And it ended up being very good. They had a spot for both of us.

(Scott Wardell) Still, you had misgivings?

(Sheila) Absolutely... Normal people don't go to Kuwait. They just don't. We tossed and turned all night long trying to decide. But once we laid out the financial part, it became easier.

(Scott Wardell) How so?

(Sheila) Well, in places like Germany, where we wanted to go, paid more than what we would make in Kuwait, but they didn't include a thing. You had to get your own housing, your own furniture. You didn't have any insurance. But each job posting came with a "savings index." It told us how much we could save.

The savings index in Germany was like 5%. The Middle East schools all had the highest savings index. You might not have gotten paid as much, but you could save more. Saudi Arabia has the highest savings index.

In Kuwait everything's included. It's not going to cost us a dime for anything other than travel, entertainment, and transportation. So we signed the contracts.

(Scott Wardell) And Doug, how have you handled your leave of absence from your school in Minnesota?

(Doug) I discussed it with our union people. I knew exactly what was going to happen. I knew the leave would be approved, and basically, the timing couldn't have been better. I was four years from retirement. But within five years of retirement, if you take a leave of absence, the school district is more than happy to get rid of you for a while. You're at the top of the pay scale. At the same time, the district will continue to pay their half of my Teachers Retirement Account. So, for me, rather than having to pay $8,000 a year to get to retirement, now I pay half of that. I only have to pay about $4,000; the district keeps kicking in their half.

That was huge. For me to be able to retire at sixty-two and not get penalized for it.

(Scott Wardell) And how did your expenses look as you packed up and headed over to Kuwait?

(Sheila) Well the payment on that townhouse was high. About $2,400 a month. But we were able to get out of the lease. Our lease was up August 1st and we left August 10th. We did it because it was something we had to do. Because of all of our mistakes.

(Scott Wardell) You both have health insurance through the schools, right?

(Doug) She does. I don't because I'm on leave. But she still has her health insurance here. We're covered over there.

//

Fortunately, Doug and Sheila had good medical plans through their schools. Their situation would have been immeasurably more difficult had either of them suffered a serious medical problem and they didn't have the coverage they did through the school.

To their credit, they were also very conscious about how decisions they made would affect that coverage. They paid close attention to the health insurance factor.

\\\

(Scott Wardell) So what are you able now to put away? I mean save, in the time you're in Kuwait?

(Doug) We haven't saved a lot yet. We sold Sheila's car. We wiped out that payment. We've paid off both the State and the IRS. So those debts are gone. We kind of took last year [overseas] and did some traveling. But we were able to wipe out debt. Right now we have cleaned out almost everything. All that we own today is a 1997 Ford Escort with 447,000 miles on it! That's it. That's the only thing that has our name on it.

//

My overview of Doug and Sheila's situation as they decided on this Kuwait idea was basically to warn them, "You can't go backwards." The rule was simple. No more debt and you have to save everything beyond your expenses.

I also told them that, "By the time you get back, you have to have, at the very least, a down payment on a new place to live here in the States. And that has to be in a protected, highly-liquid account. A short-term CD, perhaps. In their case they needed $40,000. To their credit, they did make a good effort saving. This "pay yourself first" mentality forces the rest of their budget and keeps them on track.

Their biggest risk to the plan was and is their credit

card usage. To date though, they've been very good about it.

(Doug) We don't own a house. That's gone. Our son took our furniture. Other than the clothes on our back and what's in our suitcase we don't have a whole lot. But we don't have any debt to go with it. So now, one year into this Kuwait adventure, we're even.

Sheila retired and has three pots of money. She's drawing her retirement, and we've been putting that away.

(Scott Wardell) What's your life plan now?

(Doug) Our plan for right now is that we probably will go back for one more year and finish our contract in Kuwait. We haven't decided yet. But I think we're leaning toward doing a third year. It would be a big benefit.

You get paid more, and there are bonuses for finishing your contract and bonuses for re-signing.

(Scott Wardell) So you think that after these two years, you'll be on a pretty solid footing? Two pensions, no debt, and some savings? What happens when you move back to the States?

(Sheila) We should be able to save my whole retirement check. That is a significant amount of money. When we come back, I'm not going to work. Doug has one more year.

(Doug) I have to finish off one year under the terms of my leave of absence.

//

What I suspect is they'll have to work the third year in Kuwait, and then do substitute teaching well into retirement to really make this thing go. But they won't be so burdened by debt, because they finally got smart about cleaning that out.

The last time I saw them, they had managed not to take on any more credit card debt. I believe, and I hope, that they've had that scared out of them.

\\\

(Scott Wardell) You two are down to a pretty minimal lifestyle right now. How does it feel?

(Doug) I have to tell you, it was a hard decision. But getting rid of everything felt good. It felt good to go through the closet and get rid of clothes. It was like we could breathe again. When we got on the plane last August, we had four suitcases, two carry-ons. That's it. It's really freeing to be rid of all that stuff, the material stuff.

Our goal this year was to get rid of debt. We went into this without a lot. But our credit, boy, I don't think we could get a Kohl's card cause we were so over the top. But now, with the Chapter 13 being paid off early, all our debt dropped off our credit report at the end of 2012.

If you're asking about longer-term plans after we come back for good, we'd like to probably buy something here, on a little smaller scale. We have to have some place to live when we come back permanently. But we want to go to Arizona for a couple months every winter. We have to decide how much do we really want that.

(Scott Wardell) What kept you from seeking professional help for so long?

(Doug) It's the frame of mind that says, "It's debt. You don't really have anything to bring to the table." When we first talked to you, Scott, it was like all we have is Sheila's retirement. We don't have any money to give you to invest.

It was the embarrassment. And our experiences in the past. Too many times you talk to an "advisor" and all they want to do is sell you insurance.

(Scott Wardell) But here's a tougher question, how do you avoid getting back into the debt cycle again? It seems to be something you'd want to avoid, especially now into your mid to late sixties.

(Doug) Well, we don't have any credit cards. The hardest thing we had to learn when we went into Chapter 13 was to pay as we go. That's also how we got into tax trouble. We jacked up our withholdings, the number of dependents so we'd have more cash flow.

People say you learn by your mistakes. It would be nice if we didn't have to learn it fifteen or twenty times.

Summary

I call Doug and Sheila the Classic Personal Financial Recovery Plan. You know all that talk you get from financial experts about putting away $2,500 a year from age twenty-five on? Well guess what? It almost never works out so smoothly. Instead of looking at a retirement statement of a million bucks, I find plenty of people who are facing sixty or sixty-five and dealing with a financial train wreck, from which they have to recover ... somehow.

Obviously, without their forced savings through Teachers Retirement, Doug and Sheila's situation would have been even worse. But if you look at them and ask, as I did, "How did these really fine people make almost every conceivable financial mistake?" the answer is that they never defined their relationship with money. They never got real with each other by sitting down and walking through their day-to-day finances and creating a realistic budget. Their personal finances remained an abstraction through most of their working lives.

I had a professor of calculus, calculus I tell you, who came to see me. This particular guy owed 125% of the value of his house – *before* the crash. He had borrowed $45,000 a piece on two new SUVs and was carrying $60,000 in credit card debt.

You know what his explanation was? That the people who loaned him the money knew something more about his finances than he did, so he must be good for it. That, friends, is what I call "transference of responsibility," something you do when you have no relationship with money.

Doug and Sheila took the attitude that the lenders they dealt with knew more than they did, and therefore they must be good for all the loans they kept getting. Nonsense. You cannot transfer responsibility for something as critical as your financial well-being.

If you have any sense at all that you're getting in over your head, I strongly recommend a monthly meeting with your spouse to discuss cash flow and how to reduce expenses. If that doesn't solve your problem, seek professional help. I don't mean to push financial advisors on everyone, but the services people like me provide are not just about moving investment income around. A good advisor has resources to guide you through a debt reduction program and a number of other critical financial/life decisions.

Do not let shame keep you from seeking help. Do not fall victim to pride by declaring, "I got us into this, I'll get us out." Do *not* do that. If you're in that situation, that's all the proof you need to seek out professional help. Get it.

Another pitfall of ego getting in the way of financial decisions is being the super parents who pick up the check for everything their children want. This kind of pride seriously distorts logical thinking. One of the best role models any parent can be is an example of financial prudence. There's no shame in being middle class and there's absolutely no shame in navigating your way through life without debt you can't manage.

Something else to stay away from is the "singular deals" like those that Doug and Sheila fell into, specifically the guy-from-Florida investment and the time-share. What is too good to be true almost always is. Run from "singular deals," deals involving one specific thing brought to you by a sales person. Do *not* do it. If you believe that there are much smarter people than you out there playing with investments, then also believe that they would have long ago snapped up these super-sweet singular "deals." I hate to break it to you, but you probably aren't anyone's idea of an investor of first choice.

There are valuable lessons to be drawn from the Great Recession. Many people had no choice but to take a hard look at how to reduce debt and expenses and pare things back to a level of reality. That is a clarifying experience everyone, no matter what their level of wealth, should seek out and nurture even as the economy recovers buoyancy.

But if you are as close to retirement as Doug and Sheila were, and facing even half of their challenges, I can't emphasize the following strongly enough:

Both on your own and with a professional, project your future in stark, easy-to-understand terms. By that I mean, assemble your income and expense numbers and chart precisely the cost to you – in terms of how many years more you will have to work full-time or part-time – of providing yourself with things, easily expendable luxuries and affectations, you really can live without.

The tactical device I recommend to couples in this situation is for each to look at their discretionary expenses – cable TV, the gym membership they never use, that $80 lunch– and take out 30% of your expenses. Not his, or hers, but *yours*.

Also, don't be fooled by your co-workers who check their stocks twice a day. There are a ton of people who focus or obsess about their investments, but have no idea where the money is going when it comes to cash flow. These are the folks who dip into their retirement savings and their 401(k) IRA to pay for college and weddings at the cost of a 35% penalty.

What? 35%!? Yep. If you cash in any part of your retirement plan, except a Roth, you will pay a 10% non-deductible penalty before 59 1/2, and state and federal income tax. For many people, that's a 35% cost to get their hands on their own money.

A lot of people think cash-flow management is for newlyweds, or singles just getting out of college. That is true. But it's also for every stage of your financial life. A person who knows how much is coming in each month and how much is going out in each category is very likely to be financially independent one day. Add to that the strategic model of save, share, spend, you'll find people who understand what money is and how it actually provides happiness.

Questions to Consider:

1. Do you have a basic household budget in writing? Why not?

2. Who would you turn to first if you felt bankruptcy was the only way out of your financial problems?

3. Have you had an honest conversation with your children about how much college and wedding expense you can handle?

4. If you are in range of age 60 and have no choice but to continue working, what will you do, and for how long?

Notes

1. Whole life policies typically do not build cash value quickly in the early years. Therefore, surrendering whole life policies after the policy owner has held them for a short while (such as Doug's three to five year period) often results in getting back substantially less than the owner has paid in premiums.

Chapter 7

So What Do I Do Now?

Being in the business of financial advice, I generally like to project the attitude that *everybody* needs me. It's better for cash flow, if you know what I mean. Occasionally though, I do run into some truly adept people who may not need my financial advice so much as some life-planning advice. Jim Jensen is one of those.

A terrifically talented, almost supernaturally disciplined guy now in his early fifties, Jim has pretty much run his own financial ship for his entire adult life; a life he spent earning everything he has ever made. The family he grew up in was distinctly middle-class. He's had a couple advisors, one a high school buddy back early in his working career, but he largely planned his own course.

Even when people have done as well with money as Jim has, playing your own financial advisor can be problematic. Jim has done well, but I will never stop arguing that two sets of eyes are better than one. Always. More to the point, if you're as bright as Jim, you owe it to yourself to be rigorous about a second opinion on your financial strategy.

Jim has been a guest on my radio program. But until he came to my office one morning, I had never heard several of the details of his life story. He has a few idiosyncratic touches: He is a remarkably meticulous thinker, a man for whom well-considered decision-making is not only essential, it is professional.

Snapshot

- **Age:** 54
- **Marital status:** Married, no children.
- **Primary career:** Actuary and VP of operations in the financial industry.
- **Asset description:** Meticulous planning with solid insights into investments. A few million plus.
- **Specific dilemma:** More than adequate finances, but no plan for what to do upon retirement.
- **Financial stability level:** Surplus.

Jim grew up in a very modest suburb of Minneapolis, a place of nearly identical post-war bungalows, big shade trees and quiet streets. His favorite story about his father was the time they were finishing their week-long vacation at Jim's aunt's lake cabin. A skinny seven year-old, he was pestering his dad for one last spin around the lake in his aunt's boat.

As Jim recalls, his dad said, "How much gas have we got left?" Jim said, "Not much."

OK," Jim's dad replied. "Run and get the can. We'll go to town and get her some gas." As Jim headed off to get it, his dad called after him to get the spare can from her shed, too.

"But Dad," Jim remembers retorting, "we're not going to be here that long. How much gas do we need?"

Jim's father replied evenly: "We're really lucky that people have us here, and as long as we do a little bit more than they expect, they'll always want to have us back." And this was a family member's cabin, a place where it may have been easy to assume such courtesy wasn't necessary.

As it turned out, Jim and his older brother Joe were math prodigies. With Jim there was that incentive that exists with every younger brother to work 20% harder to keep up. Jim's skills were strong enough that when his parents decided to pull him out of Catholic school for a better math program in public schools, he tested a year ahead of his actual age. His dad, however, insisted Jim not jump a grade, worried that as a "little guy" he'd be forever playing catch-up to kids a full year older.

Jim has a funny story about being the only employee paid with a check at a restaurant he worked at in high school. The boss figured out he was the only one who knew what to do with it. Oddly, Mom and Dad weren't exactly math experts.

"I don't mean to denigrate my parents. But I don't think they really understood a lot of (financial) things. Dad [who ran a women's hair salon] didn't know there was such a thing as Social Security. At one point I remember he said, 'I think I'll retire at about sixty-five.' And Mom [who worked in a department store] got this worried look. 'Well, how can we afford that?'"

He said, 'Well, I talked to some people down at work, and they think I would qualify for Social Security.' They had no idea. But they saved their money."

Jim's mom and dad had put away enough to get the boys into college, with the help of a few loans, which were being handed out at the time at 4% interest simultaneous with standard rates hitting 18%. Some of Jim's savvier pals advised him to put his repayments on "slow pay," but, typical of Jim, he insisted on a rapid repayment ... on the grounds that "other kids need this money."

(Scott Wardell) Your career in finance took off pretty much right out of college, is that right?

(Jim) Yes. My brother heard about an actuary exam. He said, "I'm going to do this. You should look into it too." I took the first exam, and like I said, I've always been good at math, kind of a curve-buster. But this was against people who bust curves even better than me. And they were far better prepared.

I underestimated what it took to get through the first exam. I didn't pass. But I got a decent score, and that gave me some hope. My brother didn't pass the first time either. Or the second. He passed it the third time. I passed the second time.

I found an ad for an actuarial statistician. I actually didn't know what that was. But it said "actuarial," and I thought, "Well, it's a start." I went out, interviewed, and they hired me. They paid me nothing of course. Maybe $8,000 to $9,000 a year, which wasn't much even in 1978.

But I thought, "I'm just trying to get into the business." Heck, I was still living at home. I didn't need that much money. The deal was that when I passed my first exam, I'd get a raise to like $12,000.

(Scott Wardell) Every good story is entitled to one twist of coincidence. Yours, Jim, involves a rusty lawn mower.

(Jim) Yeah. It's interesting how I got into Investors' Diversified Services (IDS). There was a friend of mine who worked at the same small company before I worked at IDS. We'd eat lunch together. One day she said, "Could we stop by my parents' house?" I said, "sure." So we pulled up. She went inside and I saw this guy outside trying to start the lawn mower. He couldn't get it started. I assumed it was her dad.

For some reason Joe and I had lots of go-karts when we were kids. I know small gas engines pretty well. It was a nice May day, and I thought, "I'm going to get out and help this guy" you know, rather than sit there and do nothing. So I walked over and told him, "It sounds like you've got compression. You think it's gas or spark?"

He could tell I knew something. He said, "Well, how can I tell?"

I said, "Let's pull the plug and see if it's sparking or not." It wasn't. I said, "It could be your condenser. It's an old mower. Maybe you've got rust on the magnets on your flywheel." So I pulled the cover off. It was all rusty. I cleaned it all up, checked the spark, put the plug in, and said, "Now try it." It started.

If you help a guy fix his mower, you rock! So we kind of became friends at that moment. Anyway, it *was* her father who was *also* chief actuary down at IDS. I honestly did not know that at the time. A while later he set me up with an interview at IDS. I got the job and stayed there for twenty and a half years.

(Scott Wardell) Did IDS have an employee benefit plan? What were the options? Do you remember?

(Jim) There was my retirement plan. I think it started as a defined benefit (pension), then switched over to a defined contribution (401(k)). There was a [contribution allocation] that I set up, conservatively. Again, my upbringing was one where there was not a lot of money. To be honest, I went into math and then on to be an actuary because I thought it was my only chance to get into the big time, financially.

(Scott Wardell) How much were you contributing?

(Jim) There was a certain amount that you put in that they matched. I always put in the max. I think they'd match you on the first 2.5% But you could put in up to 5%. So I did another three voluntarily. I always did that.

///

There is almost nothing that beats the value of a company retirement plan that matches employee contributions. It baffles me why everyone doesn't grab the opportunity to max out employer contribution when they can. I'm sorry to be harsh, but the way I was raised makes me say it is gross financial ignorance to do otherwise. Still … I've had people tell me they passed this up because, "I didn't understand it," or "I didn't get the memo," or "I didn't have a contribution to match."

Well, Jim got the memo, read it, signed up, and has been accruing the benefits ever since. Still, one error I see here on Jim's part, and in others I've met, is investing too conservatively. Jim took the conservative route because as a young guy of twenty-three – even a young smart guy of twenty-three – Jim feared what he didn't understand. The market was new to him so he invested conservatively.

When you're young and retirement is still far in the future, the ability to take more risk exists, which, potentially, may result in better growth.

Jim was contributing every month, he would have mitigated some of the risk by dollar cost averaging.

By that I mean, if Jim buys the same stock or mutual

fund at regular intervals and with a fixed amount, say $500 every three months, he is said to be using the dollar cost averaging method. If the market price of the selected stock or mutual fund declines, Jim will have bought a greater number of shares than if he had purchased them all at the same time.

On the other hand, when the market price increases, Jim will be buying fewer shares. Over a period of time, this strategy usually results in Jim buying the selected stock or mutual fund at an average *cost per share* less than the average *price per share*.

(Scott Wardell) How was your lifestyle at this point?

(Jim) I started with IDS on June 11, 1979. My wife and I got married six weeks before that. She was working as a dietetic technician at a hospital. We did not have a lot of money. We lived in a one-bedroom apartment. We had one car. I'd drive her to work in the morning, then I'd catch the bus to my office downtown. When she was done working, she would drive downtown and pick me up. We lived within our means. My parents did. Her parents did. So it was what we did.

(Scott Wardell) Did the two of you have a dialogue about finances?

(Jim) Well, the only thing we really wanted to do at the time was get into a house. We wanted our own place. That was important to us. So the first year we were married, we never [spent] one of Sandy's checks. We saved them all. We had to have the down payment. I didn't want to go to my parents or her parents for the money.

We saved every dime she made that first year. It wasn't a lot of dimes. But it added up to $10,000 - $12,000. That became our down payment. We lived off my money, and by the summer of 1980, we bought our first house. Parents always try to talk you out of that. They always do. It's so much money. But it really wasn't. It was $59,000 to $60,000. Something like that.

//

I have to say that in my 30-plus years in this business, after working with hundreds of clients of all income ranges, those who said, "I'm going to pay for this myself" fared best over the long run with their financial decisions. They quickly developed an advantage over those who ran back to Mom and Dad at every need or misstep.

The success of achieving your first big long-term goal – saving for a down payment on a house, a car, more education – typically lays the groundwork of discipline, research, and planning required to be successful in long-term finances.

I tell younger people, "By all means, seek advice. But avoid taking an easy check from Mom and Dad. Educate yourself. Make your own decisions and develop the confidence to learn from mistakes."

Also, I have heard countless stories of couples who have lived on one check and invested the other. It takes great discipline to make that work, but it's a model young couples in particular should consider since it may have a significant impact on their financial freedom.

\\\

(Scott Wardell) With the down payment on the house accomplished, how did you change your long-term planning focus?

(Jim) At the time we probably didn't have as much focus on saving as we should have had. Sandy quit working after we bought the house. I was doing better. I passed another [actuary] exam, and was making more money. The focus at that point was my getting through the whole series of actuarial exams. There are eleven levels to become a fellow in the Society of Actuaries. When you were half done, you became an associate. When you were done, you became a fellow.

(Scott Wardell) So were you getting a bump in pay with each of these exams?

(Jim) Yes. I did the math, and like most companies, we had

five levels of performance at work: "Doesn't work," "Meets expectations," "Exceeds many," "Exceeds most expectations," and "Far exceeds."

I did the quick math and figured if I hit "Exceeds many" at the top, I was going to get a 4% raise. If I made "Far exceeds," I'd get a 5% raise. At the time I was making maybe $30,000 a year. If I passed both exams, I'd get a $1,500 [raise] per exam. That's $3,000. Well, I'm pretty good at math. $3,000 of $30,000 is 10%.

It took me ten years to reach Fellow status. One of ten who start the exam process finishes it.

(Scott Wardell) Did you have a regular savings plan at this time?

(Jim) As you moved up to different levels at IDS, you got into restricted stock programs, and ultimately, stock option programs. So there was all the money in the world that you actually needed. Each year we got a nice bonus, and we always saved the bonus.

Would I say we had a regular savings plan along the way? No. Other than putting into my 401(k)s and things that were funded by the company. But we stocked my annual bonus away in a basic savings account.

///

What you decide to do with a sizable bonus or an extra-large paycheck is the next progression in the "financial imprinting" process. Those of you disciplined enough not to blow a windfall on a new Mercedes or a month on the Riviera and save at least half, or use it all to pay down debt, create a much clearer path for success. Again though, I differ with Jim's decision to move so much of these bonuses to low-interest, overly-safe accounts, such as a basic savings account. His core value of saving and maintaining low debt is absolutely commendable. But my criticism is that he was in a position to generate more potential growth than he got in those years. At the very least, I would have recommended moving a percentage of his bonus into a "growth" bucket.

\\

(Scott Wardell) With this steady movement up the ladder, you were improving your standing in the company. The future, retirement, and all that must have been on your mind. Was there someone you were turning to for guidance?

(Jim) Eventually. I handled it myself for quite a while. It was only when I started working with an advisor to help me figure out what I was going to do with all this stuff that I started moving into diversified investments and all the other things that I've gotten into over time. In hindsight, I should have found an advisor much earlier. I should have. I should have had somebody who helped me be more structured about savings at that time.

Really, I was just working with a friend of mine from high school. I would not say he was pushy. I probably needed a little more push.

///

For most people, the choice of a financial advisor is a combination of word-of-mouth and personal chemistry. He or she seems "trustworthy" and "likable." That's human nature. No one trusts their money to someone they neither like nor trust. And usually, this criteria works out well enough.

However, an effective financial advisor will be both persistent and empathetic about the most important steps needed to prepare you for financial success. That person will also – and this is important – argue *against you* when they see you about to do something counter

productive. A good friend, you'd hope, would do the same.

You may not like hearing someone else tell you what to do with your money, but you are not getting full value from your advisor if you don't cultivate a relationship that permits them to confront you candidly when they believe you're doing something stupid.

\\\

(Jim) My wife and I always knew we'd be together forever. It'll be thirty-two years this April. We never had kids, so that's a lot of money we didn't spend on things other people do. The point is, I really wasn't too worried about the money aspect. I was shocked by it, actually. My goal was to make $5 an hour like my dad. I kind of had that $5 an hour mentality. Then suddenly I looked at my paycheck, the stock options, the restricted stock, and I said, "My god, that's actually a lot of money."

(Scott Wardell) One of your career milestones was that you were asked to administer an IDS life insurance program. Kind of a big deal. I remember you saying that being drawn into that program was an education for you on the essential value of life insurance coverage; until then, you really hadn't looked at all the facets of it. Tell us how.

(Jim) It was an education because I was building life insurance [products for IDS] at the time. But I thought it was about spreads and cost of policies and all that. Abstract numbers, decimal points and percentages. But that's not the way to look at it. What [life insurance] really is about is what people are trying to do with it. Are they trying to transfer money? Are they trying to fund education? Do they want to minimize premiums? Do they want to put a lot of money in?

Once we understood what they were trying to do, we built very different insurance programs.

(Scott Wardell) What were you doing, personally, at this time with your own insurance?

(Jim) Interestingly, all I did was use group term through

work. In hindsight, I think it was a good move given where I ended up. We don't have kids that I will transfer money to. I'm not doing capital transfer [on a tax savings note]. I could have built a lot of assets up inside a life insurance program and avoided taxes each year, which would have been nice, I guess.

///

Jim did the right thing signing up for this term policy at work. Term life through your employer is typically one of the easiest and cheapest ways to get coverage. However, in my opinion, it is rarely enough. Your situation could be very different, but for the average person, term insurance in my experience is effective for a portion of what most people need.

Jim's wife Sandy would have been in a world of hurt had Jim died. He was far and away their source of income. I tell clients to think about how term and permanent insurance might work together.

In my humble opinion, my industry has done itself a disservice by getting so dogmatic about its term vs. permanent bias. I am prepared to argue that most people need both. Alone, I believe neither does everything you need in most cases.

That said, the cost and timing can get tricky. If you need to buy term because you can't afford permanent insurance, then I strongly recommend you consider buying a guaranteed convertible policy, a policy that allows you to convert at least a part of your term policy if you reach a point where you can afford permanent insurance. If you find yourself lost in any of this jargon, for God's sake ask.

\\\

(Scott Wardell) And were you personally into any annuity products at this time?

(Jim) No. [I was working on the design of] life insurance, disability programs, and long-term care programs, although I have not bought long-term care (LTC).

(Scott Wardell) Why not?

(Jim) Because in my mind, based on my calculations, if you have less than about $300,000 in assets, you really don't need it. In a catastrophe you'll quickly eliminate your assets and other means will pick it up (medical assistance). If you have between $300,000 and $700,000, that's where you might need protection. More than $700,000 and you'll have enough money to handle the situation ... unless you're really looking to transfer money to somebody else. So I'm in the category that I don't think I need long-term care [LTC].

///

I don't necessarily agree with Jim's point of view on LTC. I have seen where people who are close to affording being self-insured still buy the coverage because of an anticipation of how it will change how care is provided. You see, many spouses are inclined to provide care for each other when a policy is not established to provide care and the need is apparent. Hence, point 3 below: Providing a respite for the caregiver.

If you buy LTC, and I generally recommend buying LTC, make sure that the long-term care policy you buy has the most vital features, like zero-days elimination on home health care. Also, most policies have an inflation rider. You should consider this feature and ask your advisor if it matches with your State's "partnership rule."

Second, after age sixty, periodically reevaluate your needs. Look to see how the LTC market has changed. Check to see if there are new government benefits that have come into effect. Obamacare will continue to have effects on the insurance market beyond what was legislated. It is a good idea to check on developments every five years. Also, if you are still working, check to see if your employer is offering such coverage. Again, sixty is a good time to discuss whether you need to add more coverage.

I never tire of this argument.

Many people back away from even investigating

LTC because they've heard it is so expensive. Long Term Care policies can be designed to be extremely expensive or moderate in price.

In my opinion and experience, people buy long-term care insurance for three reasons:

1. To protect their spouse from the loss of cash flow and assets. Long-term care can be *extremely draining* if you have to pay for it out-of-pocket. If you're not aware of the enormity of those costs – as they are today – you absolutely must educate yourself on this issue. The expense can be breathtaking. Adequate insurance to cover this kind of care – in-home nursing care, rehabilitation and so on is absolutely vital to protect quality of life for the spouse needing care and the healthy spouse – must be very high up on your "to do" list. Read closely over Chapter 9 on Ed Delmoro for the importance of long-term care. I don't want to think about the number of families who have been impoverished by trying to handle thousands of dollars a month out of savings and checking accounts.

2. To protect their estate in order to pass more on to their heirs. Jim has no children, so this is less of an issue. But even the childless might prefer to do something with their life's assets – donations to a foundation, a charity, a scholarship – other than watch it all disappear to nursing home expenses.

3. To provide respite for the caregiver, usually the healthier spouse. I've seen this reason overlooked a lot. But ironically, it may be the most important. The fact is most people who need care prefer to receive it in their home.

I suspect many of you reading this book have had a family experience dealing with a disabled or elderly relative. Even when there is plenty of money – the caregiver's quality of life often deteriorates dramatically if the responsibility for tending to the enfeebled spouse falls entirely on the caregiver. In effect, they become prisoners to their responsibilities. They often are exhausted by the task and feel enormous stress. For me, the concern is more on the dilemmas above the Medicaid/county safety net. I won't be mistaken for Warren Buffet, but in my late fifties I have enough gain on my assets, if the worst ever happened and I or my wife were badly incapacitated, it would just mean I wouldn't have as much to leave to my heirs. In addition to our children, which is not a concern for Jim, my wife and I have picked charities that have been there for people we know or that we truly believe in. We'd prefer to help them instead of watching everything we've worked for evaporate to provide something we can get via insurance.

Jim has an Actuarial Fellow's take on long-term care. He's run the numbers in a very objective way.

People really need to change their approach to assessing their long-term care needs. Too many people end up with a hodgepodge of insurance policies that they pick up at various points in their lives, very few if any of which are specifically dedicated to long-term care.

(Scott Wardell) How were you and your wife discussing these different options?

(Jim) I think because I'm the actuary, she doesn't engage in it as much. I have to show her how much money we have, because she questions whether we have enough. It's good to talk about it and I want her to know and be confident in what we're doing. I don't want her to ever worry about anything.

(Scott Wardell) So, do you feel like you've had thorough conversations about financial decisions?

(Jim) I would say no. When I tried to retire, I think that's when I realized how little we had talked about something as big as retirement. We've talked about it since—a lot more about what we're going to do and how we're going to spend our time and different roles we're going to play—but up until that point, not at all.

(Scott Wardell) Is that lack of discussion a cause for concern?

(Jim) No, not really. I knew the numbers were there, and after all, retirement's only about the numbers, right!? [He laughs.] My numbers were nice, and I didn't have to worry her about that. I thought it was the right thing to do. If we were in trouble, it would have been different.

Every marriage operates in its own way, but I generally advise regular, candid discussions about financial planning, regardless of how uninterested one spouse might be. A lot of people don't know how to "initiate" conversations about money, which is why it is so important that both partners attend the meetings with their financial advisor. The review meetings with an advisor may actually provide the format you need to have this conversation.

(Scott Wardell) Despite your successful career, you still found yourself caught in one of those seemingly inevitable latter-part-of-the-career company shuffles. Tell us about that.

(Jim) Oddly, I was starting to think it was about time to move on to some other opportunity. I was forty-seven when my then boss and I had a one-on-one on a Friday afternoon at 3:00.

We talked about this and that for maybe fifty-five minutes before she said, "Oh, I've got something else I want to talk to you about." You know you're in trouble when it starts that way. "The winds of change are blowing," she said. My group was going to be blended with another group.

I said, "I think that's a good idea." She said, "We may not need you to go with us." That part caught me off-guard. I said, "Oh my. How strong are these winds blowing?" She said, "It's about 50-50." "That's a pretty stiff wind," I told her.

So I went home and I took the weekend to think about it. Sunday I got a call from HR from the head of [the new group] asking me how I felt about the decision. Fait accompli. The winds of change had already blown into town.

Monday I was there when my boss came into her office. I said, "So this is a done deal!?"

She said, "Yeah."

The deal that was put together was, "We'd love to have you stay through the transition, and if, in fact, you don't find anything within the next year."

(Scott Wardell) Instead you accepted a position with another part of IDS, supervising a fifth as many people, and staying on until age fifty.

(Jim) I think it's hard to go that long in a company, because every day, every hour, there are little dings in the armor. They add up over time. At some point you just lose perspective, and the dings are what you are. Things happen. People leave. Good friends are told to leave. Decisions are made that don't make any sense. But along the way, I figured out you have to step back from it and think about what *you* do and who *you* are.

It may seem odd, but I always thought it was an honor to work in financial services. Most of the problems in the world are because people don't have enough money. Without money, you can't eat, parents have issues, kids can't go to good schools. A lot of issues are financially based and I honestly believe that what we did [as a company] ... we made a difference for people.

(Scott Wardell) Are you pleased with how you dealt with being moved out and forced into an earlier-than-expected retirement?

(Jim) One thing I'll tell you is I rarely make mistakes twice. When I screw up the first time, I usually pay attention and try to figure out why: "What did I do wrong there? Because I'm not going to do that again."

A couple years earlier Doug, a friend of mine, told me one day over a beer, "You know what? You're either going to be in control, or you're going to be controlled." At the time it kind of went over my head. I think that's because it's hard to teach people something when they have no emotional connection.

///

> **Jim's final drama with IDS, [at that time American Express Financial Advisors] came when, in the wake of the 2008 meltdown, Jim felt the company required nearly impossible budget cutting.**

\\

(Jim) The solution given to us by Finance was, "Get rid of your four programmers." Well, we were an information area, and a very specific set of programming skills were needed. Skills you can't just go out and get a contractor to do.

So I went to my boss, thinking it was time to be in control. It was time to do the right thing. I said, "We're talking about doing something really stupid here. It's going to hurt this group and it's going to hurt the company, and I don't want that to happen. We've got two leaders, myself here in Minneapolis and another down in Phoenix. I actually think we can run this area better with one leader, not two, and I think we need him more than me. So, rather than get rid of four programmers, I think it's time for me to go. It's been a great run. I've loved this company. But it's time to go."

There was no real personal jeopardy. I knew that I had more than enough money.

(Scott Wardell) When exactly was this in 2008?

(Jim) It was December 2008. All hell had broken loose. The stock options I had expired ... worthless. I had options at 26, the day I left the stock price was 63. It quickly went down to 12. At 12 they were worthless. And it never got back above the 26 while I held them. They actually expired on March 1, 2009, and March 10th was the low point in the recession. My timing on that was the worst it could have been.

In hindsight, it would have been smart to exercise half of them the day I left. Not that I would have been able to do anything else with my life, but I probably would have found more things to give money away to.

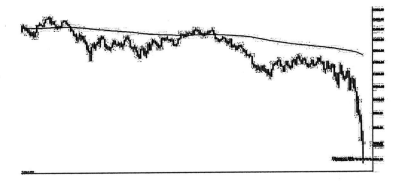

Jim was in the enviable position of not only having enough money to retire, but also enough to take a "big hit" like the crash of '08.

How did he manage that? By following the golden basics.

• He saved through his entire working career. He avoided debt.

• He matched his retirement assets against a realistic cash flow model.

(Scott Wardell) And no one advised you through any of that? The departure? The stock options? Anything?

(Jim) No.

(Scott Wardell) Are you saying you felt so prepared, even with all this, your cage didn't rattle?

(Jim) No. It hurt. Not for us, personally so much. But there are things I would have contributed money to. I'd really love to have another million dollars that I could use and give away. It would be nice. After tax, that's about what those options would have been worth. But, it is what it is.

(Scott Wardell) So you're just a little past fifty. Where are you in terms of career fatigue at this point?

(Jim) At that point, I loved what I did. I had great people I worked with. I could have kept going for another ten or twelve years. Change is hard and after twenty and a half years, you're kind of in the mode that, "This is what I do." And there's a belief, too, that that's all you can do. But that's not true.

(Scott Wardell) It was the Monday after you retired that your story takes a twist, right?

(Jim) Right. We had my retirement party, which was just a gas at a bar downtown. A lot of great friends from over the years came back, and a lot of my friends from work and colleagues came down. But then I went home. It was the weekend. On Monday morning I got up at 5:00; I got up at 5:00 every day. I looked at the clock, and I thought, "Huh! I don't have to go to work today. I can go back to sleep." And I slept till 8:00. I thought the same thing on Tuesday. Wednesday, I woke up at 5:00 and I thought, "Nobody cares if I get up today."

I swear to God, only then did I think to myself, "My grandfather died at ninety-nine, and my grandmother at ninety-seven. I lost my father last September at ninety-six. My mother is going to be ninety-five in July. I've got a lot of

days to wake up and think nobody cares if I get up today"
And I'm only 52!

It really was an, "Oh my God" moment. "What am I
going to do?" The responsibility of doing a job and being
responsible every day weighs heavy on you. But it's also
warming and comforting and it makes you feel valued. But
the day that weight is gone ... it's terrible. It was for me. I'm
not saying it would be for everybody. But for me the work
was the joy in it, not the money. The money kind of went
in the bank, and I didn't have to think about it that much. I
thought about what I did.

*(Scott Wardell) You've pretty well established that you're a remarkable
worker. But as you retired, albeit not exactly on your schedule, are you
really telling us you hadn't given any thought to what you might do in
your sixties, seventies, and eighties?*

(Jim) NOTHING! Not a bit! It hit me like a brick. It was
almost a panic. It was not almost a panic; *it was a panic.* I
guarantee I didn't go back to sleep the morning it hit me and
I had tough time sleeping that night.

(Scott Wardell) You talked about walking around your house like a stranger. It was the old story that you're invading the space of the person, your wife, who's been keeping the home fires burning, who has a specific sense of the way space is used during the day in and around the house.

(Jim) Yeah. I mean, Sandy had a string of twenty-six years of non- FICA earnings. She was on a pretty good run there. She got out of bed every morning, God bless her, ironed a shirt for me, and made me coffee. Then she'd stand in the office in our home and wave goodbye to me as I backed out the driveway to work. An amazing person. Then I'd come home at 6:00 every night.

All of a sudden I was on her turf. I was on her computer. And worse, I really didn't have any specific purpose.

(Scott Wardell) You hadn't thought of the big gear shift, the new relaxation mode...

(Jim) I had not. I don't know. I had no idea. Sandy and I never really talked about what we were going to do. Travel? Hobbies? Not really. We'd had race horses and had fun doing that. We had a boat out on the lake. We liked to do things we could engage other people in. But I was a total stranger in my house. I had a friend of mine tell me that, "You're going to be an invader in your house. Because that's Sandy's turf, it's not yours."

//

Jim is the type of successful professional who very much lived in the present, fully involved in his work. Much of his career was involved in "figuring it out," assessing problems in the here and now and creating solutions. The irony is that he never looked at his post-professional years as a problem that needed "figuring"... until it hit him like a half-ton of bricks.

If this reminds you of yourself, stop and daydream a bit. Imagine yourself at age sixty-five, seventy, eighty. What do you see yourself doing? Do you have a realistic plan for getting there? Does it require relocating? Developing a new skill? Networking with a new group of people?

How will you make that happen?
Write it down. Then talk to someone you trust—
your spouse, your financial advisor.

〰〰〰〰〰〰〰〰〰〰〰〰〰〰〰〰〰〰〰〰〰〰〰

(Scott Wardell) So you were "Jim the Problem Solver." Now you were home where you're not really needed, and there was a problem with that. What did you do?

(Jim) I just tried to get through Christmas! I ate cookies and tried not to watch Oprah. God, it was just awful! Daytime TV is awful! Worse, it was winter and all my friends were working. What was I going to do, go ice fishing? I wanted to do something with some value. So I stepped back and said, "Okay, I'm not working. I've had a lot of times when things haven't worked. Why isn't this working? Why do I feel so terrible? What am I feeling?" And I realized that I missed being valued, missed being needed. I missed making a contribution to something important.

(Scott Wardell) Jim's first move was to accept a part-time job with a business colleague.

(Jim) Once I stepped back, I realized I needed to do something that made me feel valued. Mentoring gave me that feeling. About then I was also asked to join the board of directors for the History Theater. So I got back into mentoring. Now at least I had some points in my week. I really looked forward to having breakfast with one of my mentees. And even though I pick up a new one each year, I keep up with a lot of them. I still meet with five of them on a regular basis.

(Scott Wardell) So you did take stock of what mattered most and what you enjoyed most? Blessed with resources sufficient to get into something new and fully involving, you, a theater buff among other interests, bought into a financially struggling but well-known dinner theater.

(Jim) Yes. A dinner theater. With a good name, but definitely in financial trouble. I liked the thought of 200,000 people a year shutting off their technology, coming to the theater with friends and family, where they talked, laughed, traded stories, and had a wonderful meal. Then ... the lights go down and live theater dominates their every thought.

I think that's valuable. That, and the 300 people who work there and contribute to it. It was all going to go away if somebody didn't step up and buy it.

(Scott Wardell) I gather you never saw yourself playing golf as your major retirement activity?

(Jim) No. That would kill me. I've got to do something more important than hit a golf ball.

(Scott Wardell) So is it fair to say that your vision of retirement is doing something more intellectually engaging than spending what you've accrued over the years?

(Jim) Definitely. 24/7 recreation would be the worst thing in the world for me. I haven't done this yet, but out of my investment portfolio I'm going to pay myself every two weeks. Because getting a check every two weeks is kind of society's way of validating that what you're doing makes sense. So I'm going to pay myself for the things I do. That's kind of silly, I know. But it's one way that I will validate myself.

(Scott Wardell) I did use the word "idiosyncratic" when describing you, Jim. Tell us why you always carry 91 cents in change everywhere you go.

(Jim) Well, it serves many purposes. I have three quarters, a dime, a nickel, and a penny. So, 91 cents in my right pocket every day. First of all, it reminds me that I'm in control. There are a lot of things I don't control. But I can control what goes in my right pocket every day. So that's the first thing it tells me. The second thing is it is the right amount of change. Because when you go to buy something, it's amazing, it's the right combination. I can get all the way up to 91 cents, but I can also do a lot of things along the way. If someone tells me something is $3.31 I've got that! Or $3.36. I've got that! I can do it! It's a fun deal. It's a lot of fun.

///

When Jim said to me years ago, "I bet you know how much change you have in your pocket right now, don't you, Scott?" I was caught a bit off guard. Of course I didn't know. How many of us do?

Eventually I took this quirk as a metaphor for knowing where you are, which Jim, the meticulous guy that he is, always has. In financial terms you translate this to knowing how well your expenses are in balance with your income.

Here's a quick quiz: Without looking it up ...

1. How much do you have in a cash reserve right this moment, to cover an emergency?
2. Approximately how much income does your family have coming in each month, and how well does it match up with your expenses?

3. How much are you currently saving each month?
4. How much debt do you have on your mortgage? Your credit cards? Student loans? Cars? Point being ... know where you're at.

\\\

(Scott Wardell) So, direct question, Jim. Have you been satisfied with the financial advisors you've worked with over the years?

(Jim) I would say no. Again, I have more money than I need, so you can't argue with success I guess. But if I could do it all over again, I would have interviewed maybe five different people and tried to pick somebody with the right approach.

///

Jim's point about "interviewing" a handful of possible advisors is well taken. The obvious problem is that most people aren't as adroit as Jim is with numbers, so they aren't asking as good a set of questions.

(See the epilogue for: "Questions for Interviewing A Financial Advisor")

But don't be daunted by that. Most advisors will happily give a prospective client an hour of free time. Set up an appointment. Bring in your most recent tax and investment records and ask them for a quick analysis of what you might be able to do better.

Take notes. Thank them and set up an appointment with the next advisor on your list. Compare notes.

While you're talking to these people, pay close attention to how many questions they ask of you and if they are really listening to you or essentially making an extended pitch of some kind.

Many professional advisors develop well-intentioned biases as they go on, following rules that have worked for them, but can have the effect of making them less objective than they should be. For example, are they going to recommend an annuity or life insurance regardless of the problem? Or, do they refuse to use annuities when the situation calls for it? (You're testing to see if they have a "one size fits all" approach to financial planning.)

By the time you've made three stops, you should have a fairly good feel for the best "fit" for you. Ask for references of other clients. Call two or three of those people, and ask them about their satisfaction with response time and their general satisfaction.

Most people of course wouldn't know how to interview five different advisors.

Picking the right advisor often comes down to someone who matches your requirements of style, competency and service.

Again, as we've seen with Jim, you have to dream a bit. You need to have thought about what it is you want to do when you quit working, when you're sixty-five ... when you're eighty. You need to have done that much basic work to give the advisor a fair chance of creating a plan that meets your needs ... and dreams.

(Scott Wardell) Have you ever taken an aggressive investment strategy?

(Jim) In some parts of my portfolio, yes. I've got all kinds of bonds and mutual funds, and domestic and international, and small cap and large cap and mid-cap, and now the theater.

You know, Scott, it's interesting. I've been both an owner and an investor, but I really like being an owner. As an investor, I put money in, but I don't really care about it other than, "Do I get more money out?" I prefer to own the things that I truly care about. Like my home, like my future. Like the dinner theater. I care about that stuff. Therefore I own that stuff. I don't invest in that stuff. That's just how I think about it.

I've told my advisor that if I lose every dime I put into the theater, but we allow that place to continue for ten years and 300 people continue to have jobs, and another two million people do something enjoyable... I'm OK with that. I don't have any intention of losing money. But if I do, I don't care. I'll die happy. It doesn't matter.

Summary

Jim's story has relevance to stories here despite the lack of crisis in his financial situation. He was in a position where he could make mistakes and they didn't hurt him. What he didn't work out as well was what his days were going to be like after all his careful investing.

Presumably, people retire to enjoy the parts of life they haven't had the time to be fully engaged with while they were working. But even that takes preparation. In Jim's case, he had the money to go on vacation when he wanted. So he always went somewhere. What he didn't do was stay around the house and get the feel of what those kinds of days were going to be like.

So while you're still working, ask, "What am I going to do with myself ... really?"

If you can answer that question, the job of a financial advisor becomes a bit more focused. The interaction I want with my clients is not just talking sense about their money. It is also about drawing them out on the subject of what it is that they want to do with their dreams and desires.

When we meet for the first time, I don't make excuses; I pry. I want them to talk to me about the things they want – a condo in Arizona, a pontoon boat, a trip to Europe, an inheritance for their children, or money for their favorite charity. If they can't tell me, I encourage them to go home and think about it. I won't necessarily decline them as clients, but I'll be frank that I'll be more effective for them if I know how they see their lives five, ten, twenty years down the line.

People in Jim's situation, with adequate income and in good standing with their company and nearing retirement might want to think about taking a leave of absence. Do it just to test the waters and get a real feel for what life after the job is going to be like.

Obviously this is a wonderful luxury in a tough economy where Jim is the exception rather than the rule. But a leave of absence is a concept worth exploring for people on less income with some work flexibility, and, more to the point, it is a concept that does wonders to clarify your retirement planning thinking.

What you're testing is not your financial wherewithal so much as your emotional stability. And I find a lot of companies surprisingly open to adjusting senior employees' work schedules prior to actually parting ways with them entirely.

A lot of people are well-advised to see if their employer is open to reducing their hours, from forty to thirty, or whatever keeps their insurance benefits in effect. Why? Because many professional people, like Jim, are bored by retirement. They enjoyed the work, if not all the bureaucratic time-sucking. The happy middle is an agreement that continues the work without eating up as much time.

Obviously, Jim doesn't have to work again. But a lot of people are accepting that they will have to work part-time after they retire. Most, though, have never actually done anything other than their career work. Think of some way to make a "test run" if you will. Spend a season working at a garden center or doing whatever you've thought you might enjoy doing. See how it feels. Does the reality match the fantasy? Is there a Plan B and C if that first idea isn't what you expected it to be?

Ask a retiree who has done it, and very often you'll find that a lot of that part-time work has been heavily romanticized. If you realize the fantasy isn't what you want when you're already pretty deep into that fantasy, you're in a tough predicament. A predicament that could have been avoided.

Also, if a financial advisor is only talking to you about your money, chances are the conversation is really about commission. What should be going on, and what you should absolutely expect from a good advisor is to be drawn out in an extended conversation about you. What do you want? How are you prepared to make that happen? Have you thought about downsides?

An effective test of an advisor's commitment and value to you is if he or she is drawing you out on your dreams and desires, if they are searching for how well you've considered the pros and cons of those dreams. Frankly, I think of sorting through the dreams as the fun part and can't imagine how an advisor can do a decent job for someone if they don't understand, a) What the client wants, and b) How well the client has thought through their dreams.

Demand to be drawn out by a good advisor.

Questions to Consider:

1. Have you and your spouse taken the time to imagine what you want and can do when you're 65, 75 and 85? Why not?

2. If you're still working full-time and you're getting the feeling that your job is jeopardy, are you in a position to negotiate a leave of absence or a reduced work schedule?

3. Have you developed any interests outside your career that might be emotionally and financially rewarding enough to pursue, if not full-time, 20 hours a week in retirement?

Chapter 8

Mr. Indispensable

Sometimes you do everything right. You work hard. You live sensibly. You save, and you prepare for a comfortable retirement–and then, as the saying goes–"stuff" happens.

Meet Kathy. She's retirement age and lives in a small southern Minnesota farming town. Her husband Doug, born and raised there, was a plant manager for a local manufacturing company,. He managed all the family finances. He handled pretty much everything, in fact. Until he suddenly fell ill, at the moment of retirement, and died.

The essence of Kathy's story is about coming to grips not just with her husband's passing, but making critical decisions about finances, and getting the correct information about her options in a moment fraught with emotion. Hers is also a story of their remarkable resourcefulness together over the years and how people of quite modest income can assure themselves a pleasant retirement ... if they make a few essential decisions early on.

I visited with her in quiet tidy home Doug built with his own hands.

Snapshot

- **Age:** 62
- **Marital status:** Widowed.
- **Primary career:** Beauty shop employee and bookkeeper.
- **Asset description:** Moderate savings plus insurance policies.
- **Specific dilemma:** Husband was money-handler for family. His untimely death at the moment of his retirement, left her floundering for best way to stabilize finances until Social Security and Medicare kick in.
- **Financial stability level:** Stable but shaken from husband's death.

The first thing you need to know, and I sensed when I first met Kathy and Doug many years ago, was that Doug was a pretty intense guy. One of 15 children and no great family wealth, Doug was obviously someone who had been in a few scrapes along the way and learned how to deal with life first-hand. Like a lot of men of his age and economic class in small towns, Doug learned how to work with his hands and took pride in what he could build. The relationship of a Do It Yourself ethic to saving money was very direct. Much of the time there was no other way.

At the heart of Kathy and Doug's financial story is the fact that they lived essentially their entire lives together ... without a mortgage payment. Doug, with help from his small army of brothers, built every house they lived in, selling a couple along the way for modest but significant profits to trade-up.

Very few of us are going to be able to pull that off. But he did, to the point of obsession sometimes, because it was his most available option. He also self-managed the family finances, with mixed consequences, as we'll see.

Kathy too came from a family of modest means. "Mom and Dad struggled," she remembers. "When they first got married they lived in a trailer that probably wasn't as big as my camper. With two kids. But they were never into big debt. You saved until you had enough money to get what you wanted to. When Mom and Dad bought the house, the people who sold them the house left them the couch and a lamp. Mom had a few pieces of furniture from the trailer. But that's all they had when they moved in. It's hard to believe."

Neither Doug nor her wanted that kind of life. Kathy worked part- time jobs – at a beauty salon, as a bookkeeper – and tended the home. But Doug's untimely illness as he was retiring forced her to step into the breach and make several critical decisions to protect her retirement years.

(Scott Wardell) Kathy, I wanted to bring you into this book because I think people will be interested in what happens when things are sailing along just fine and all of a sudden things blow up due to the loss of income from a spouse. What I want readers to understand is this:

How do you reassemble the pieces into something that is meaningful and that works? There are a lot of people who don't get those pieces reassembled.

Maybe you can talk to us about the key things you had to focus on when Doug passed away? And how you recovered, personally and financially, from that?

(Kathy) And you think I'm going to know the answers?

(Scott Wardell) I hope so. Let's start by talking about the upside. You two did a lot of stuff well to get ready for retirement. Without the work you did early on it would really be pretty messed up right now.

(Kathy) Right.

(Scott Wardell) So let's start with you and Doug. You were both working and saving.

(Kathy) Right, we both had retirement plans in place with our employers. Mine wasn't much. But it was a little. We both had life insurance policies from when the kids were small, knowing if something happened to either one of us, we would need a few important financial things in place. Although we had always talked about changing those policies.

I remember saying to him, "If you happen to die first, I'm going to need more." But I was actually thinking that I would be the one to go first.

(Scott Wardell) What kinds of life insurance were they? Do you remember when you bought them?

They were Whole Life. Many years ago Doug bought them. I've had [a little life] insurance [plan] from the time I was a small child. My parents bought it for me.

///

It has been my experience that people have a hard time getting their heads around what I have called "insurance architecture." It really isn't that difficult.

The approximate model – very approximate, I should say – is this: Some combination of permanent and term depending on your needs, your cash flow, and your debt. What Kathy's folks did was buy her a Whole Life insurance policy as a child, good for her entire life. That was both nice and smart of them.

As Kathy's story unfolds, we'll see that her late husband Doug was tempted from time to time to drop insurance altogether. Thankfully, he didn't. Because upon Doug's death, she very much needed the money from his life insurance to act as a bridge for funding her health insurance.

The critical rationale behind a well-designed

insurance architecture issue is this: Even if the kids have been to college and the house is paid off, the cost of health care is incredibly high until you reach age sixty-five and qualify for Medicare. That cost alone could cripple your retirement plans. You need some kind of guaranteed income – a bridge – to help cover health care costs alone.

Almost everyone has some dependence on a spouse for income. Even if the majority of your assets are in IRAs and you're not entirely dependent on your spouse, the combination of two Social Security incomes is significant. In Kathy's case, her husband Doug was getting $2200 a month. She will get $800. She thought when he died that she would only get $800 on her own earnings.

(Scott Wardell) So Mom and Dad bought a $10,000 policy, and you think, "That's cool. But now I'm an adult, I need $100,000." Too many people don't know they can often just add additional insurance onto that same policy.

(Kathy) Mine started as a $1000 policy. That was sixty years ago. After we got married I think we pushed it up to $25,000. And then we pushed it up to $50,000. So that's where it was when Doug died.

(Scott Wardell) Doug worked at the same manufacturing firm his whole career, right?

(Kathy) Right. He wound up as the plant manager. He began as a general laborer.

(Scott Wardell) The company had both a pension and a 401(k), is that right?

(Kathy) They had both, yes. A couple of times the business had been sold. So those things changed, but the original pension stayed and a new one started. We were fortunate because Doug was a salaried employee. Thankfully, he did buy additional life insurance through work.

As I said, the remarkable feature in this story is Kathy and Doug's lack of debt. Had Doug died with maybe still a portion of the mortgage to pay, credit cards, whatever, it would have been a disaster given how little insurance they were carrying.

The "layering" of income they set up for retirement was this: Doug's pension, Kathy's much smaller pension, some IRAs, and two Social Security checks. When Doug died, Kathy, then age 59, lost part of his pension *and*, she believed, the entire value of his Social Security. But she had the cash value of life insurance to compensate for a while, to act as that bridge to get her through six years to Medicare and the significant reduction in costs that brings.

Every successful retirement that I've seen has some degree of layering. Pensions, IRAs, and Social Security. The weakest, obviously, are those depending entirely on Social Security, then Social Security with only IRAs.

But as I say, what Kathy and Doug had going for them was really minimal debt. They avoided acquiring layers of expense. At the time Doug died, Kathy's expense burden was really only the property taxes, maintenance of their home, and daily living expenses. The amount of money she needed to live on was remarkably minimal, maybe $32,000 a year.

Basic no-brainer: Drive your income layer up, and drive your expense layer down.

(Scott Wardell) So you had your parents' policy, plus the one policy you two bought on your own. You also had, as you later found out, Doug's work policy. In addition you each had pensions building and you were contributing to 401(k)s. Simultaneously, you were raising your kids. There must have been several times when cash flow was pretty tight?

(Kathy) There were a lot of times when the company was struggling and they were working thirty-two hours a week. At one point they'd cut Doug's pay down to 60% or something like that.

But we always knew that those policies and 401(k) s were important. We never went without them. We were fortunate because Doug worked really hard when we were first married. He built the houses we lived in, and because we built at the right time and sold them at the right time, we were at the point for the last twenty-five years we never had a house payment.

(Scott Wardell) That really is kind of amazing.

(Kathy) When we first got married, we bought property across the street from the concrete plant. We built that house, Doug and his thirteen brothers. They salvaged a lot of the material. They'd tear down farm buildings–like barns and things that people didn't want anymore. Doug felt good about that because it was dry wood. You know how the wood you buy is green and goes every which way? Doug never built anything with that. He got books–he read all about building and everything. He educated himself.

(Scott Wardell) Was your first house new construction?

(Kathy) Sort of. It was an older home that someone had put a new basement under. We demolished the house on top and started over. We used the existing basement. Our total cost for that was less than $10,000. Then probably five years later we sold it for $38,000.

Doug built three homes before this one we're in now. He was the main person involved with all of them, the general contractor. When he started one it was kind of crazy. He never did another thing until the house was done. He came home from work every day and instantly went to work on the house. He worked until he went to bed at night. He did that every day of the week until the house was done.

Needless to say, we didn't go anywhere. We didn't do *anything*. We didn't take time off to go to a movie or go out for dinner. That's how committed he was to the house projects. At least until we could live in it.

//

Doug knew he was not going to get ahead on what he was making working a blue-collar job in small-town Minnesota. He knew he'd have to work angles other than relying simply on income from employment.

During the go-go nineties and early 2000s the idea of applying your own sweat equity to big projects like renovating an entire house kind of went out of style. Money was easy. "Hire it. Flip it." But I think there's a fresh realization that our own labor is worth a lot more than we thought it was.

Buying and renovating foreclosures on the market is still a huge opportunity–if you're prepared to contain costs with your own sweat equity.

(Scott Wardell) Was that construction phase a hard time for you?

(Kathy) It was.

(Scott Wardell) It was like he was obsessed.

(Kathy) With our first house, the one with the basement, we wanted it to be a little bigger. But the cost of adding on was somewhat expensive. One day though Doug heard about somebody who had this whole side of a block he wanted to sell. He wanted $8000 for it. So we bought it–a half of a whole block–and sold off the other two lots.

(Scott Wardell) So you ended up getting your lot almost for free? I remember Doug liked to wheel and deal.

(Kathy) Right. He would find a little thing and imagine where, maybe not right now, but later, this could work out for us.

But it was tough at times. With the third house, we moved in in January and sold it in July and started all over again. Some lots came up for sale in the next block. Doug saw another opportunity. He loved it. He got help from his brothers, framing and roofing. But he loved the work.

(Scott Wardell) It's interesting. He was a long-term employee. But he had this entrepreneurial spirit. Every house you built was built to sell and make money?

(Kathy) Right. And we did. We were very fortunate because it was a few years ago. Houses in town increased in value. We sold the first house for $38,000 and bought another larger house but had minimal house payments, like maybe $100 a month.

It was so manageable. We sold the second house for more than double our costs and so on. To the point that with the last house we lived in before this one, like I said, we had no house payment at all. But we didn't sell that one at a good time.

It was 2008. But we got $125,000, which we were able to put into [our current house]. I had inherited a small amount of money, which we put into this one and again did not have a house payment.

Many people have something they're good at and can do on the side. I won't go so far as to say a successful retirement *depends* on developing talents like this, but it sure helps, both in terms of adding an income layer and building a new, enjoyable business and social network.

Think of all the people who work with computers. A side business building websites, or repairing computers run out of your basement a couple hours a day in your pajamas and with your dog at your feet is suddenly another layer of income ... one that you enjoy.

So many people say they are simply too busy with their careers to develop side work like this. But what I tell them is, "Look a little deeper." Over and over I've seen how hobbies that pay are a godsend for retirees. Woodworking, some kind of auto repair or restoration work, freelance writing – on your schedule. The added income, plus the new social network has an invigorating effect on people.

(Scott Wardell) Was there kind of a grand plan? Was the whole point of buying houses, fixing up, and selling them to build a retirement nest egg?

(Kathy) More or less. But the process expanded a bit. Doug went on to help my brother build two houses.

(Scott Wardell) The turnover of these houses sounds like it worked out pretty well for you, financially. Was that building/selling process the major source of your nest egg money? Or, as you look at it now were there investments that provided more income?

(Kathy) I can't say that we actually had a plan to keep doing it over and over again. We did stay in the house before this one for thirty years. The nest egg was really the money we saved by not having a mortgage. So I guess the answer is yes, it was the houses. As I say, I did eventually receive small inheritances from two uncles who passed away and didn't have family.

(Scott Wardell) Tell us where you were working at this time.

(Kathy) I was just working part-time, three days a week, as a cosmetologist. That's when the kids were small. Before we got married I worked up in Minneapolis. But after we got married I was back down here. I managed a place called First Fashion Flair.

Then I went to work for Steve, a local accountant. Later I worked as a payroll clerk for a construction company. I was there for ten years before I went to work at Luther Memorial

Home as a services director. I worked there for three years until they downsized that job.

///

Kathy continues to work on an irregular basis for the area's ambulance service. This too is a good move because the ambulance program money is put into a pension for them.

Is it a lot? No. But it is a layer. And it keeps her active doing something she enjoys because it is meaningful.

\\\

(Scott Wardell) Doug obviously had a pretty remarkable work ethic.

(Kathy) Yes. He loved to work. He never ever came in and sat, plopped down for the weekend, or even after dinner at night. He would *never* sit in his chair and do nothing. When he didn't have a house project he got into woodworking. He even built a shop out back.

We would go to craft shows and look at things and Doug would say, "I could make that." One time we actually saw some wreaths, heart wreaths like people would have in their kitchens. We came home, got out our tape measure and made enough wreaths, and sold enough, to pay for a trip to Florida. The money from wreaths flew us to Disney World.

We made lots of little wooden things. I would make the decorations and put them together, and we sold them at a local store here in town.

Eventually Doug got into building furniture. He did the shelving that you put over the top of your windows. People have those all over the place.

(Scott Wardell) He was making extra money by doing this. It was a hobby that paid.

(Kathy) That was Doug. Always with a goal in mind. He got very good at woodworking. We would sell things. Little teeter totters with kids on them, reindeer and stuff.

(Scott Wardell) Was he driven more by the project or the money?

(Kathy) It was equal. But really, he could not stand to sit still.

//

One exercise I read recently asked the question, "If I had to make $100 today, what would I do?" Would you sell something? Would you hire yourself out? To whom? Doing what?

This quickly leads to imagining what tools you might need to generate $100. A wood-splitter to sell firewood? An old pick-up truck to move and deliver stuff? A set of specialty tools to do computer repair or custom sewing?

\\

(Scott Wardell) Talk a little bit about managing the cash flow in the house. You had very little debt your whole life. Was there ever a temptation? Did credit cards ever creep up on you?

(Kathy) No. We did have credit cards, but we never spent more than what we could pay off in a month. We never had a balance on any of our cards. And we each had our own credit cards. We got to the point where for the last twenty-five years or so we had separate checking accounts. Doug would pay for all of the utilities and vehicle insurance. We did have car payments once in a while. But mostly we saved until we had cash to pay for a car.

//

I generally don't recommend the average married couple using separate checking accounts. If one of you has a business building homes, that's different. Not to play family counselor here, but one of the things that keeps marriages together is the economic piece. In my experience, when I see couples building two separate financial lives in their household, the reality of their finances becomes mysterious to each other. A somewhat better alternative is a careful allocation of expenses. One partner pays "X" bills. The other covers "Y"

On the other hand, Kathy and Doug did have bona

fide household and business expenses. So it makes a bit more sense. What will you see here is Doug, the family's primary expense manager, bringing Kathy in to managing part of the expenses. Namely, "You've got to manage these expenses." And it worked, because now she can ... and does.

(Scott Wardell) Tell us more about these separate checking accounts. Did you do that right from when you got married?

(Kathy) No. We had a joint checking account. But I would probably spend more than I should have. Because, well, I was always sewing, making the kids' clothes. I wouldn't always plan well for when we had insurance payments and stuff like that. So we'd have to take money out of our savings account.

Finally Doug said, "Let's try our own personal accounts."

I was responsible for the kids' clothes, the groceries, entertainment, and gifts. He did all the rest. If we went on a big vacation, like to Florida or Las Vegas, he always paid for that.

Neither of us was all that lavish. Doug was a hunter and fisherman. But he didn't always have to have brand new [equipment]. He was happy with something used, and he was not big on the clothes. I'd kid him, "I know you're working on the house, but please don't even go to Fleet Farm [the big box farm hardware store] with what you're wearing!"

It was the way he grew up. When you have fifteen kids in your family, used will do just fine. Neither one of us grew up in wealthy families. We didn't need the best. We bought something and used it until it wore out. *Then* we might buy new.

(Scott Wardell) So Doug was getting close to retirement. You were putting into the 401(k). Who was watching the investments?

(Kathy) Doug was watching the markets all the time. Sometimes he would call me at home before three o'clock in the afternoon, and say, "Go into my account and switch this much money from here to there." He had to do it before the market closed.

(Scott Wardell) Really? How regularly did he do this?

(Kathy) Several times a week, some times.

///

Doug was a classic type in this regard. I meet scores of people who think smart money operates a certain way. But they're usually wrong. They think they're going to make money playing with individual stocks, but they don't do much in-depth research on the company or stock.

Most failed investment strategies originate because people like a product. I had a client who was infatuated with Hasbro based on the success of the Transformers movies. But he ignored the fact that the movies, produced by a different company, were a very small part of Hasbro's business.

For a while, on the other hand, Apple cultists loved to tell me that they made a small fortune buying into a company they loved. I'm not saying it never works, only that it works very, very rarely.

Doug bought stocks based on product and he was always convinced a stock was going to go through the roof because it had such a great product somewhere in the company's portfolio. Mostly, he broke even.

People like Doug think they've found something Wall Street hasn't caught on to, which I'm sorry to say almost never happens. Doug did do *some* research. He knew if a company had great customer service, which I agree is often a positive indicator of a good investment. But that's maybe a quarter of the research he needed to do. Again, to repeat an important rule of thumb: Make sure your core retirement is in place before investing play money – and play, if you must. But don't do it with unrealistic hopes of hitting the jackpot.

\\

(Scott Wardell) Money was important to Doug.

(Kathy) Very much.

(Scott Wardell) What was driving the importance of money for him?

(Kathy) Security, mainly. Pretty basic. It wasn't like he wanted to do anything fantastic. He always told me that if I died first, he would probably move way up north by his brother. He said he'd be happy to have a one-room house, a bathroom, a bedroom, and just be up in the woods somewhere. And he *would* have been very happy. He didn't have a lot of wants, like a brand-new car or a big fancy truck every year. He was very content with the basics. I wanted more than he did.

(Scott Wardell) Did Doug have any specific dreams for retirement?

(Kathy) He never had a whole lot of traveling goals until about four years ago. We went on a cruise to Alaska. After that he thought, "Maybe that wasn't so bad, to be able to do that." But he never wanted to go out of the country. The year after our oldest daughter was married, my mom decided that I needed a treat, so we went to Europe for two weeks together. Doug never wanted to go there.

He couldn't wait until he could go out fishing and not have to worry about coming back to work the next day. He loved fishing, not having anything that demanded his time.

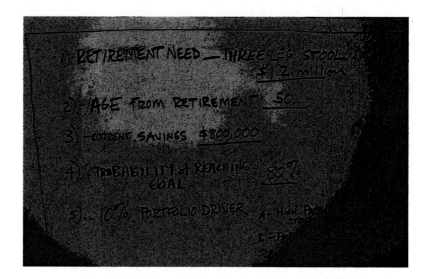

(Kathy) I thought maybe he would go nuts [not having a regular job]. Because, after a while it would get old, it seemed to me. But he loved, *loved* to fish.

(Scott Wardell) So what were you thinking about for retirement?

(Kathy) We were thinking it would be nice to go camping and other places with his brother. Everyone in Doug's family camps. Sometimes there get to be fifty or sixty of us camping together.

(Scott Wardell) Did you talk about when to retire?

(Kathy) We debated a little a few years ago. Times were really stressful at [Doug's job]. It just really went down. They did a lot of government work, and they supply a lot of tools for Sears. They were also selling in Europe. They have machines so fine you can see the hair on Abe Lincoln's head on a penny.

We were debating whether Doug would retire at sixty-two or sixty-five. I wanted to retire at sixty-two. But of course health insurance was a big issue. You can't just walk away from that.

(Scott Wardell) To be clear, Doug's health insurance from his company was covering both of you?

(Kathy) Correct.

(Scott Wardell) Had the company plan deteriorated so it was covering less and less?

(Kathy) There was an increase in our premium that we paid. I'm still feeling that now, because I'm still covered under COBRA. Doug was a salaried employee at the time of his death. So instead of eighteen months of COBRA coverage, I am getting thirty-six months.

I have a year left and then I have to go out and try to find health insurance until I am sixty-five.

I mention Health Savings Accounts (HSAs) elsewhere in this book. If your company offers one, give it serious consideration. Let's say you're forty-five and you want to retire at fifty-five. You can build up these HSA accounts so that you can withdraw from them tax-free to pay qualified health expenses. The downside is that you can only use it for qualified health expenses. But you can use it for a Medicare supplement, which almost everyone should consider.

If an HSA is not available to you through your employer or otherwise, consider funding a Roth IRA for the specific purpose of using a large portion of those dollars to cover the health insurance bridge from retirement to age sixty-five and Medicare.

A third strategy is not nearly as attractive. That is to build up a very large cash reserve and take out an extremely high-deductible health insurance plan. And by "very high" I mean a $5000-$10,000 deductible, which can be a serious hit if both you and your spouse need care.

In Doug's case, an adequate HSA account would have required a $300-$400 monthly contribution from the time he was in his mid-forties to adequately cover him from retirement at age 62 to Medicare. That was a bill he would have had a hard time making month after month.

Also, bear in mind, with a Roth IRA you cannot take a tax deduction for the contribution, but the investment comes out tax free if you are over 59-$\frac{1}{2}$[1]. With an HSA, on the other hand, you pay with "before tax" dollars and it can be withdrawn tax free for qualified medical expenses.

\\

(Scott Wardell) Now, in your situation, you'll have to bridge from sixty-two to sixty-three with your COBRA, then take the Open Market health insurance plan until you get to Medicare. If you are eligible for the state insurance exchange, you will at least have options you can choose from and you'll have comfort of knowing that you can't be turned down for a pre-existing condition.

(Kathy) Right.

(Scott Wardell) Remind me, the company Doug worked for offered Doug part-time work after retirement, right?

(Kathy) Yes. The company didn't have any prospects for replacing him. They were getting people coming in who really weren't knowledgeable about what was going on. So the president of the company asked Doug if maybe he would like to work part-time, which meant he could get health insurance, which of course was a big issue.

Working part-time, probably less than thirty hours a week was acceptable to him, because he'd be able to have his seasons off, for fishing and hunting time.

///

I had a client, a sixty-year-old woman, come in the other day and tell me she was quitting her job. She was fed up with her boss. But rather than pursue some other department, or going part-time or consulting, she just flat-out quit.

It wasn't that the guy was abusive. She just didn't like him, and walked out. So what happened? She spent six to nine months looking for work, blowing through all her cash reserves, and negatively affected her retirement plan.

DO NOT BURN YOUR BRIDGES!

Doug did not burn his bridges, which helped him negotiate part-time work.

I can't say that loud enough. Be rational. Make an effort, a Herculean effort even, to resolve conflict before simply telling the boss to, "Take this job and shove it."

In this story, Doug was a nearly ideal employee. A smart, skilled guy who dedicated himself to a small company. But even in today's corporate world, managers know that while they bring in new people, they can't necessarily bring in experience. What that means to someone approaching retirement is that it makes sense to go to the boss and ask, "What can I do here? Can I keep my current job as a part-time thing? Can I leave and be hired back as a consultant?"

And where, three or four years ago, an employee broaching this conversation might have to had to be prepared to give up benefits to negotiate such a deal, today, as the economy comes back, many big companies are so flush with cash that the benefit package can be less of a factor.

The key, as we see here with Doug, is being a valued employee. So if you're ten years away from retirement and you've got a so-so relationship with your boss ... suck it up.

Seriously.

(Scott Wardell) Kathy, tell us your story about signing up for Social Security. This got pretty chaotic.

(Kathy) We actually signed Doug up when he'd hit sixty-five. He had already been diagnosed with cancer. About the same time, we looked again at an insurance policy he had with his employer. It said that if he stayed working with the company, the premiums would be paid by them. But only if he was still working.

(Scott Wardell) So what happened with Social Security?

(Kathy) Well, the twist was that he had already signed up as though he was going to stop working. He had to unsign. We called and cancelled it.

(Scott Wardell) He was looking out for you at this point. He was resigned to the fact that he was going to die.

(Kathy) They told him there was no cure.

(Scott Wardell) So he said, "I'll just keep working, so that you get this life insurance." That's what made him cancel Social Security?

(Kathy) Right. He needed to be working and not drawing Social Security to get that. But afterwards, the insurance company called and said, "Because you're sixty-five, you need to be on disability, rather than working."

We explained to them that he had just a few more months to live, and they allowed him to keep working, sort of. His employer said he was working in order for him to get the benefit. And eventually they paid me by giving him a year's worth of vacation.

In other words they paid me all the way through the next November. They paid me his salary, which they were not obligated to do.

///

All of our stories, as you see, have at least one key piece of homework that the people involved didn't do. Kathy, for example, had no idea how she was going to make it, after losing Doug's Social Security. She had no awareness of the widow's pension for Social Security. I actually took her in to the Social Security office to set this up for her.

You see, she didn't have to wait until *her* retirement to collect her Social Security. If the surviving spouse is at least 60 years old, he/she is eligible for a percentage of the deceased spouse's benefit.

Although there is a discount for taking an early survivor benefit from social security, she will not be penalized on her own account if she chooses to switch to it at full retirement or at age 70.

\\

(Scott Wardell) A company giving away a year's salary is not a story you hear a lot these days.

(Kathy) The president of the company and Doug were very good friends. There was a time when his employer was doing very poorly, twenty-five years ago. It was down to just the four or five people. They were the whole company. At that point the president told Doug, "If you stick with me I will pay you four times your salary when you retire." It was like a bonus, way out in the future. The boss made good on his word. At least some of it. When he died Doug was the only one of that group left.

///

The story here is very unique. Doug's company was nigh onto extinct. Doug and other employees were down to barely half of their previous salaries, and the boss called in the few of them left and promised them he'd make it up to them if they could pull the company out of its death spiral. In Doug's case he was promised a lump sum of four times one year's salary, or about $190,000. But that intention was not in writing.

Based on Doug's handshake deal the company forecast owing Kathy something like $135,000, beyond the company insurance policy he forgot they were carrying. But ... the company has never fully rebounded from its low point. Kathy received a year's worth, and may never see the rest.

Whenever possible, get your handshake deals in writing.

\\

(Scott Wardell) So Social Security was cancelled and Doug died in April. Here you are then. Doug is gone but his salary is continued through the November after next. You had that. And you had life insurance proceeds coming. But you thought you had lost Doug's Social Security. That's when we got into the widow's pension. If Doug had not unsigned for Social Security, you would have had to wait several months to collect that, right?

(Kathy) Yes. I didn't know any of that. But I needed to be sixty-years-old. I was 59 and a half at the time he died. Doug has been gone three years now.

(Scott Wardell) Let's review your life insurance again.

(Kathy) Doug had $100,000 of personally-owned life insurance. Because he was a salaried employee, he had another $80,000 or $90,000 that he wasn't even aware of having. It was a company policy he didn't have to pay for, or wasn't aware he was paying for, I should say.

(Scott Wardell) What was he making at that time?

(Kathy) I don't know. Probably $45,000. The policy was probably two times salary.

(Scott Wardell) And that "surprise" money, the company policy you weren't aware of, was basically what you used to build this bridge to cover health insurance and other things until you reach sixty-five.

(Kathy) Right. We knew we had to do something so that money wasn't taxable. If we had waited until Doug died, and had taken the money from the policy he had at his employer, it would have been taxable to me. We had to really hurry. We did this like a week or so before Doug died. When he died, that money rolled over into his IRA.

(Scott Wardell) Then his IRA became yours. So you have the IRA and the sixty-year-old component, the "widow's pension" of the Social Security coming in, and his employer's pension. What percentage-to-survivor of the pension did you take?

(Kathy) 100%

(Scott Wardell) For the rest of your life?

(Kathy) Right.

Many people tell me that once the mortgage is paid, they don't need any life insurance. Life insurance, as it turns out, has many uses other than paying the mortgage. In this case, Kathy would have been in a financial crunch if the life insurance had not been part of the picture.

(Scott Wardell) So once the dust settles you have the layers you need. A Social Security widow's pension, the pension from Doug's employer, whatever you need to draw from the IRA mixed together with the life insurance to build the bridge to retirement. How do you think this would this have worked without the life insurance?

(Kathy) Insurance was a large part of the whole deal. A very large part. I have been very fortunate because I'm still not old enough to retire. I am not drawing a retirement income. I would have to work full-time.

I would not be able to do what I am passionate about, working with the ambulance service and spending time with my great nieces, being able to babysit them or work a couple of days a week. Without the insurance bridge I would not be able to do that. It would totally change the picture.

(Scott Wardell) So life insurance altogether, yours and the "surprise" company policy was about $190,000 or so?

(Kathy) Right. Enough to make a bridge.

///

Doug's work insurance policy was two times his annual salary, or something around $90,000, and the two of them had their own of policy worth $100,000. Not big money, but sufficient to provide that "bridge," covering the partial loss of his $2200 in Social Security until her retirement and Medicare at sixty-five.

It sounds like more than it was. Kathy's worst nightmare – age 59 and a half, her husband suddenly gone and no money to pay for expenses – would have come true if not for the life insurance money covering the cost of her daily living expenses and health insurance. As a consequence of not being in the full-time workforce for thirteen years, she'd very likely would have had to go back to work as unskilled laborer. Translation: Low wages, long hours. The only other option was drawing early and aggressively from retirement accounts, and later living solely on Social Security. That folks, is called falling off a cliff.

Let me reiterate the value of having an annual review of your financial situation ... with both spouses, regardless of who handles the check-writing. This sit-down with an advisor can reveal the risks of reducing coverage in certain areas.

An annual review can also set and assess targets for the growth portion of your plan and harvest what growth you have to put into your income "bucket" for present day expenses.

(Scott Wardell) You say you had talked about cancelling your private [$100,000] policy?

(Kathy) Yes. Doug had talked about it for about ten years. We thought maybe once the girls were through school and everything. He said, "We don't need all that anymore."

He was going to purchase term insurance. He hated it when premium time came. But he never canceled it. I always told him, "If something happened and you died before I did, I would have a harder time supporting myself than you would supporting yourself."

(Scott Wardell) But he was unaware of the policy the company had?

(Kathy) Right. He was not aware of it until a couple weeks before he died. We weren't aware of it. It was one of those things he had in a folder that he brought home, put in a bottom drawer, and forgot.

As important as it is to have a core financial plan, if you're doing this by yourself it's almost as important to have a file drawer with everything in one place. By that I mean, paperwork that specifically identifies the whereabouts of cash, investments, insurance, file numbers, passwords and so one.

Kathy and Doug were self-planners, and that almost always results in what you see here – papers and policies all over the place. It's a nightmare for the survivor, especially if the survivor wasn't the one filing the papers.

(Scott Wardell) On his W2 it probably showed a deduction for life insurance. But he didn't do his homework on that one, did he?

(Kathy) Apparently not.

(Scott Wardell) You had done quite well managing the risk part of your portfolio. You set up the investment and income distribution plan. You made a lot of the right decisions. So, after all this, what advice would you give people of roughly your income group?

(Kathy) Well, we did some things: We had our life insurance in place. We didn't go crazy spending money we didn't have. I guess that was smart on our part. I still think we should have prepared better for retirement. But really, it was like we looked up one day and, "Oh my god! We're sixty!"

Doug would always say to me, "We don't have a house payment. We should be putting 'X' amount of money away instead." But we didn't. There just wasn't that much extra.

There's a general rule of thumb here if you've been able to handle an additional payment to get rid of your mortgage early, that payment amount is what you should continue to save each month even after the mortgage is paid. $300, $500 a month, whatever. Kathy and Doug should have done that.

The personality factor is that Doug didn't like being controlled, and he resisted locking himself into an automatic payment plan that would have taken, say, two-thirds of what he wasn't paying on a mortgage and deposited it into a savings plan of some sort. But he didn't like having his money out of his control ... which, ironically, is exactly the reason to automate payments like that.

(Scott Wardell) At the end of his career, Doug was making $45,000 a year. It wasn't like you had a lot of cash flowing in. By the way, was that his part-time salary?

(Kathy) No. That's what they pay for full-time. It's a small town. He was a manager with a high school education, nothing more than that. He would say, "Our oldest daughter is making twice what I make." That actually made him pretty happy.

(Scott Wardell) Doug's dad worked at the same company before him. I'm curious, was he a constantly running engine, like Doug?

(Kathy) No. His engine ran in different areas than Doug's. He was constantly with his music. Constantly. He was always in the back family room at their house playing on his accordion or writing music. He also did a very extensive family history. He even published a thick book about all of his family's history.

I knew from the first time I met Doug that he was always looking for an opportunity, and he knew his brothers would always help him. They were kind of rowdy when they were young. They probably fought with other people more than they fought with each other, which was a lot.

Doug and his brothers made a name for themselves when they were growing up. They did lots of naughty things. They did not have a good name! My parents were not happy that I was dating him. Not happy at all.

But I was a little rebellious at that stage too. I don't know. I must have seen good things there. But once all the brothers got married, they bonded and helped each other a lot. If one of them had a project to build a garage or something, they all helped. They've always been close.

In the table of The Five Ss[2] (showing the progression of surviving to surplus), both Doug and Kathy grew up in family environments best described as "Surviving" and "Struggling." Fortunately, they both responded positively and adopted a lifestyle that regarded sweat equity, frugality, and minimal debt as a natural condition of life.

Doug would have howled at some guy coming to his door pitching a lawn service. You know, spraying for weeds and mowing. Ludicrous! Likewise, putting in a big garden was an absolutely normal act of spring.

Even for big city dwellers with incomes, mortgages and annual property tax bills far higher than Kathy and Doug's, there are layers of expense – fees, luxury "necessities" – that can easily be eliminated, with benefit to savings and investment contributions, and personal happiness.

We accept a lot expenses purely out of habit.

\\\

(Scott Wardell) You have all these stories of Doug's family. With all the helping, and salvaging of old houses and barns. That takes an unusual instinct, to see value in recycling, restoration, and doing things yourself.

(Kathy) People today aren't patient enough to wait for someone to do that. They'd rather just bring in a bulldozer and bury it or burn it. They don't want to wait.

By the way Scott, I'm still hosting Doug's brothers for coffee. Here. Every Saturday morning at seven. So if you want coffee, my kitchen is open.

(Scott Wardell) Thank you, Kathy. I find your story fascinating in many ways. Along with being so remarkably industrious, Doug and you were actually very smart about how you handled the money you had.

(Kathy) We lived a very simple life.

Summary

Tom Brokaw's book, *The Greatest Generation*, captures a lot of the characteristics of Kathy and Doug's story, even if they were not part of that age group.

One of the main facets is the amount of work they did for themselves. Most of us pick up the phone and say, "The faucet is broken. Come fix it." Or, "The back porch stairs need replacing. Who can build them for me?" With a previous generation, what you heard was, "I'm going to figure this out."

I was once fishing up on a beautiful lake in northern Minnesota. Across the water a ways I saw this guy with his motor torn apart. Parts everywhere. All I could think was, "You poor guy. You're on vacation, and your motor's not working."

I went over and talked to him and said, "Jeez, I feel so bad that you're struggling with your motor." He turned to me and said, "Struggling? I'm learning more about this motor than you can imagine!"

"But you're on vacation," I said. "That doesn't matter. I can't tell you how much fun I'm having!" The guy was as content as a person could be, learning to fix a problem.

Doug and Katy are fix-it-yourself people, and that approach

benefited them in many ways. Whether or not you can build a house or make wreaths for sale, understand the value of the principle as it applies to your finances.

Questions to consider:

1. Do you understand all the benefits of your job? Health insurance, pension arrangements and insurance coverage. If you're not sure, ask.

2. Right now, do you know where all your important financial papers are located? Does your spouse?

3. If you are planning to stop working full-time and you are not yet 65, do you know how you'll cover the cost of health insurance until you reach Medicare eligibility?

4. Do you have an intimate understanding of your personal cash flow or are you surprised by the changes in your bank balance month to month?

Notes

1. There are costs and penalties associated with taking out IRA funds before you reach age 59-1/2. Consider consulting a tax advisor before making a decision.

2. See table in Introduction.

Chapter 9

Old School

There is so much turbulence, uncertainty, and second-guessing in the average American's professional career and retirement planning today, it is easy to forget a time not so long ago when such things were much different. When Baby Boomers' parents were at mid-life, millions of them could reasonably expect to continue working for the same company the rest of their careers. Moreover, if they saved even modestly and were fortunate enough to have a pension plan on top of their Social Security, they were assured of, at worst, an adequate retirement. Those days seem like a long time ago, don't they?

I still work with people who lived that kind of predictable life. Without question one of my most memorable characters is Ed Delmoro. Ed is the classic, old-school business professional. He had a successful, straight-line career path with a financial planning model that was equal parts institutional cover (his company – a railroad – pension), his own wits and wiles–of which Ed has plenty–and the good fortune to almost never make the dumb move that rattled it.

Ed is one of the most engaging characters I've ever met. He's blessed with a good salesman's discerning eye for human nature, an informal, self-effacing demeanor, and a razor-edged sense of humor that he deploys to great effect.

In the context of The Five S's I mentioned in the introduction, Ed today is definitely in a "Secure" position, with even a modest "Surplus." Ed's life went through some significant changes after a family tragedy:

the debilitating illness that lead to the death of his lovely wife, Linda, at the same time Ed was entering retirement.

I sat down to talk with Ed on a very snowy winter day. Ed's home is spotless, orderly, and decorated with dozens of tasteful artifacts of the kind of life often held out as an example of an American Dream. We were surrounded by photos of children and grandchildren, vacations, awards, and souvenirs, all important markers of Ed's life achievements and social connections.

Ed motioned me back to his sunroom off the rear of the house. The heavy snow accumulated steadily on the glass roof as we talked about his working life and the choices he made along the way, choices that as I say, many today would envy and many regard kind of wistfully as something out of a Norman Rockwell painting.

Snapshot

- **Age:** 75
- **Marital status:** Widower, three adult daughters.
- **Primary career:** 30-year railroad marketing executive.
- **Asset description:** Substantial railroad pension. Good investments. No debt.
- **Specific dilemma:** Sudden illness and death of spouse at the time of retirement. Long-term care planning.
- **Financial stability level:** Secure.

Ed grew up in northeast Ohio, the son of a part-time farmer, part-time Firestone tire worker. Ed's grandfather retired after 42 years with the Erie Railroad. It was fair to say that railroad work was in their blood.

It was a case of allergies and a crush on a girl in high school that put Ed on his life track, however. As much as Ed enjoyed farm life, pollen wiped him out after half a day out in the fields. Annoyed by being called "lazy" for having to cut out of fieldwork, Ed picked up a job with a local department store and flourished in air-conditioning.

"I'd ride my bike about six miles to work," he says, "and feel miserable when I got there. But I'd be at work in the air conditioning and just feel great, then get on the bike and feel miserable. So I thought, 'I've learned two things about myself: I feel really good in air conditioning, and I like the atmosphere of the department store. I liked all the interaction with people.' So at that point I decided I wasn't going to make a career out of farming."

His job with the railroad delighted his grandfather who told him to "Keep working, because I've got to draw my retirement. That means *you* got to keep the money coming in." But he only got the job because he knew shorthand, a talent he picked by taking a high school course that put him next to a cute girl he had his eye on.

Ed proved himself a natural executive. He understood business; people enjoyed his company and respected his judgment.

For the better part of three decades there were only minor interruptions in a smooth career journey. The worst, of course, came near the end, with the railroad industry under tremendous competitive pressure and the inevitable surge of younger executives convinced that the secret to turning things around was flushing out the old crew. At that point, Ed had to take, what was for him, an uncomfortable and aggressive stand.

(Scott Wardell) Ed, your father worked for Firestone and your grandpa worked for a railroad. Together they ran a farm. They had to know a thing or two about budgets and planning. You obviously had an aptitude to do as well in business as you did. Tell me what kind of financial advice you got from your parents and grandparents?

(Ed Delmoro) Mostly it was things I observed. A lot of it came through my grandfather because he was with the railroad. He was an immigrant and spoke only a little English to start. Grandma stayed home and raised the children and chickens. I remember when Grandpa retired. He was pretty excited waiting for his first retirement check. Finally it came and he rushed in all excited, tore open the envelope, and showed it to Grandma.

"That's not your name on it," she said, pointing to the top line. "It says *Agnes Delmoro.*" He was stunned. But it was true. The way it was with the railroad then, the spouse also got a retirement. Oh, Grandpa was fuming. He was the one who had worked forty-two years! But she got the first check! His came the next day, but darn, she loved flaunting that.

All that got my interest. I watched that and got to thinking, "They're retiring. But Grandma gets a check, too. And on top of that they get a rail pass so they can travel all over the US free. Free trains rides and two checks every month.". With that example, I told myself. "Boy, you've got to look ahead to retirement."

//

Few things generally create a higher probability of retirement success than coupling Social Security with a pension. I tell my clients one basic thing: when you retire, cash flow is king. It is the primary ingredient in a financially successful retirement. In order to "keep the money coming in" you need to balance a growth strategy with an income distribution strategy. You have to get cash flow out of your retirement assets and keep an eye on growth.

Another concept is money mechanics. If you're talking about an automobile, all the moving pieces have to come together to get it down the road. Money mechanics are about, "What fuel do I need?" And, "How do I re-fuel when I need to?" How do these various pieces of growth and income meld together in a way that allows me to move forward, growing my net worth or creating new income?" Ed has most of these mechanics in good order.

Although an endangered species, pensions still exist at some large companies and among public employees, most commonly in public schools. Many people with large pensions luck out when they retire. By combining their pension with Social Security and some investments, they are often pleasantly surprised by the standard of living they can afford, especially if they've paid off or are close to paying off their homes.

This is why I stress the importance of creating "layers" of financial income support: Pension, Social Security, part-time work, etc.

\\

(Scott Wardell) Did your parents ever sit you down and say, "Listen Ed, this is what you need to do you. Put away x-dollars a month?"

(Ed) Mother would say that more than anyone else. But her

family was never able to save a nickel. And us, I'm growing up in the [post] Depression here, Mom and Dad couldn't put money away, either. We lived well enough. We had a nice home, and enough food. But there was never any money in the bank. It actually wasn't until after Dad retired that he made most of the money in his life.

//

Ed is not a guy at rest for long. You see where he got it in the following story of his dad and the apartment complexes.

\\\

(Scott Wardell) What happened there?

(Ed) Dad had a group of attorney buddies in town, and since Dad could [fix] anything, when these guys had pipes freeze or something, they'd call and he'd go over and fix them without asking for pay. That was just the way he was. Eventually they came over and asked if he would manage their apartment buildings.

At first he said, "Oh, I don't think I want to do that." But they told him he wouldn't have to physically do all the work. "But," they said, "you'll at least know when to call the plumber or electrician." So Dad did that for a good number of years. He retired at sixty-one and did that apartment stuff for twenty years.

//

For most people, Ed's dad represents the retirement future, and I don't mean a surprise 401(k). Many people are probably going to have to work part-time. So start researching the part-time/semi-retirement job that you are good at and would love to do no matter what!

Ken Dychtwald, in his book, *The Power Years*, talks about how retirement looks very different for the Baby Boomers than it did for the prior generation. Many will work during retirement in a part-time job very different than the job they had as a full-time career. The choice

you have to make is to spend your post-retirement working at something you truly enjoy.

(Ed) [The attorneys] really worked the system for him. Because he could only earn so much money under his retirement, he could be on the attorneys' payroll only six months of the year. So he'd drop off and Mom would come on their payroll for six months. What they didn't know was that [the attorneys] were paying them way more than that. They were also putting money into a 401(k).

(Scott Wardell) "What?! Out of the goodness of their hearts?"

(Ed) Yes. Out of the goodness of their hearts! So when Dad actually went to retire, the lawyers said, "Well, you better plan a big trip." Mom and Dad went on a six-month vacation. They got a camper and took off. Dad lived to be ninety-six, almost ninety-seven. Mom was ninety-two when she passed away.

So even when they actually retired, as late as they did, they still had a great retirement. They were in good health and had the money to do things. Dad always said he couldn't believe what good people [the lawyers] were."

(Scott Wardell) [I suspect once the lawyers had grandpa on the payroll they probably had him enrolled in their retirement plan] So where, if anywhere, Ed, did you get real adult-style financial advice?

(Ed) I don't think there was any one person, really. There was a guy, thirty years ago or more, who had been calling me every month for years. I never told him "Go away." I just said, "Not now." He is my age and he's retired now, too. Finally though, after all his calls, I went in, sat down, and we put it all together. We just struck it off. I remember him telling me that he was amazed at what I had done without any real guidance.

I was never really a student of [financial planning]. I didn't do a lot of studying and reading. I just paid attention to what others were doing and what I was hearing.

(Scott Wardell) And what were these "other people" doing?

(Ed) A lot of them were speculating in the stock market and were not real successful. So I was very cautious with that kind of thing. I just didn't understand it.

//

First Rule, (or darn near a First Rule): Don't invest in anything you don't understand. Ed practiced this well. Second Rule: Don't run away from what you don't understand. Successful retirement financial planning takes a lot of time to research, design, monitor, and adopt. You either have to be dedicated to doing this work or hire a qualified advisor who you trust. If you choose the latter, insist on getting information and advice you understand. Do not be afraid to ask obvious or "stupid" questions. Do not relegate sole responsibility to yourself and your family. Stay closely involved with your financial decisions.

\\\

So you stayed away from the stock market?

Yes. I was doing more with bonds. Pretty safe stuff, as you know. I was always very conservative. Then I got into a 401(k). I grabbed that immediately when it was offered and put in the full amount that I could.

//

Know if you have a 401(k) and strongly consider taking advantage of a matching program if it exists. There is generally no investment that can compete with matching funds. This is free money. Make certain you know how much you get on your match and when you are eligible, sign up immediately! Be aware though that there are likely "vesting schedules" on the company match, and that in today's economy more than a few people are losing that match by being laid-off before being vested.

I can't tell you how often people tell me, "I didn't think I was going to be at this job this long. So I didn't

start putting anything and signing up for the match until years had gone by."
Don't be one of those folks.

~~~~~~

(Ed) I remember before going to [my investment] guy thinking, "I'm probably young enough that I should take a portion of this and put it into high risk [investments] just to see what I can do with it." So I did that and had to have my hand slapped when I was getting near retirement. I was told to stop doing as much of that as I was, which I didn't think was much at all!

(Scott Wardell) Did the high-risk investments do well enough for you that you were compelled to do more?

(Ed) They did, yes. But then, as I say, we had the discussion about pulling back. I was in my mid-Fifties then, I think. So I did. I sat down and looked at everything and I agreed. The time had come to pull back. And right after that the first recession dipped, in the late Eighties, remember? It was another good lesson for me because while everyone I knew was losing money, I was actually making money because I was in stable bond funds.

(Scott Wardell) So what was your planning like when you were twenty-five, a few years into your professional career?

(Ed) When I was twenty-five, it was probably a savings account and savings bonds, both as part of payroll deduction. But, you know, I was still single at twenty-five, driving a fancy car, enjoying the bachelor life. But I was putting some money away.

(Scott Wardell) So when did it really change for you? When did you make a real effort to plan?

[Ed laughs] Probably not until I was married and had three children. We didn't have the money to do it! You know how that goes. That's what made me really take a look at it and change things, and say, "Okay, now how are we going to do this?"

(Scott Wardell) Tell me about Linda's financial acumen. She was the big numbers person, right?

(Ed) Yes, she was good with money. She was interested in the stock market. She belonged to an investment club. And here's something I'll bet you think is important: We always sat down. The finances were always a joint deal.

///

Ed's right. I believe there are three very significant risks to not sharing your financial management with your spouse.

1. **He or she may not know where the investments are, so if something happens to you (including death), sorting these things out can be a mess for the surviving spouse.**
2. **Financial planning is about goal setting. How can you have the audacity to set goals for the both of you?**
3. **Financial acumen is developed by educating yourself, at least in part, through conversations about finances. If you're left out of these conversations,**

you will have difficulty making the right kinds of decisions.

In most marriages, one spouse has a greater affinity for the finances. Don't assume you know everything just because you've been married to that person for thirty years. Not having a conversation about finances should not be optional for married folks!

(Ed) We had one checkbook. She didn't work outside the house. She had a job before we were married and when we had the first child. But she didn't work again for fifteen years. We were always together though on the investments and the household budget. She would find creative ways to say, "Hey, we can put this money away if we did this."

(Scott Wardell) Linda had a savings gene, then.

(Ed) She did. I had it too, but I can be distracted very easily! She confirmed a lot of what I was thinking, but didn't really take action on. But because of her, because of talking to her, *we* did.

When I think about my theory of money even now, it's like, "Live like there's no tomorrow, but remember there might be twenty years of them."

I have so many friends that are such misers, people who won't do anything with their retirement money. Then there's another crowd I know that are just spending like crazy. That bunch jokes, "I better not live too many more years or we're going to be out of money." I can't operate that way.

It's important to know where exactly you are with your finances at any given moment. This should not seem boring or obsessive. When I talk about "imprinting" it is, at its simplest, knowing that you have the money to pay the bill. Back in Ed's early years, people balanced their checkbooks in the grocery store check-out lane immediately after they wrote a check. Now they get a credit card statement, discover how much they spent, and say, "Oh, my God!"

(Scott Wardell) Are you saying you don't operate on impulse?

(Ed) Well, I'm not a spontaneous spender. A lot of thought goes into every purchase. Except [he cackles] for my yellow convertible. I saw it and I thought, *Oh, my god! What is that?! I'm buying it! Give me the keys!*

"Don't you want to know the price," the guy asked me.

"Ya, I do want to know." So I had to calm down and talk about it!

(Scott Wardell) What made you a good salesman?

(Ed) I just always saw opportunities. I knew when I worked at the department store that I was good at sales. When I got the job with the railroad there were salesmen in the office. I watched them, kind of thinking, "I can do that better" or at least equally as well.

(Ed) Railroad sales are very tough. You're calling on companies and trying to sell them shipping contracts a long time in the future. At the end of the day, it's not like selling pencils. You can't get back in your hotel room and say, "I've sold this many." You might not know for a month or a year or six years if you were successful. It really takes a certain type of person. You have to be a self-starter and be confident.

And it was straight salary, no bonuses. You had your territory, and a lot of the game was not losing business to your competitors–predators who were out there trying to poach your customers.

I'm a people watcher though, and when I see someone successful I try to learn from that. Likewise when I see someone who's not successful, I also try to analyze what I see. I ask myself, "What could that person have done differently?"

Ed is one of those people where the extrovert's brashness is tempered by deductive reasoning and patience. He admits "no one was more of a company man than me" and he has several stories about watching the action around the company for a good long while before playing his hand.

The most dramatic confrontation came after he had been with his company for thirty years. A merger swept in a wave of Young Turks with the attitude that no one older than thirty knew a thing about how to run a modern railroad. The company's sales system was gamed, as Ed saw it. Morale cratered.

But Ed, seething like most other company veterans, held his fire for a while before exploding on the boss for not recognizing what was going on. Rather than firing Ed on the spot for such direct criticism, the boss, once he settled down, realized Ed had been the model company man, doing what he could to resolve conflicts and make the new situation work. The end result was Ed's career-capping promotion to VP.

(Scott Wardell) You had essentially gone off on your boss, in a pretty extraordinary way, telling him he was blind to some very bad behavior and wasn't doing a good job. That was risky.

(Ed) The [boss] said that he knew I was not in his office representing just me. He knew I was there representing the [original employees at] the railroad. And after I left, he thought, 'Oh my God. Ed's the guy I've trusted with all my customers' and there I am in there telling [the boss] that he's been misled. I didn't rat on the other guys. I just said that he was misled, and that he'd better take a closer look at some documents and make sure that they were accurate. I never said that I knew what they had done. Heck, [Some of the new people] had even changed their own titles!

I guess my attitude comes from growing up on the farm where Right's Right and Wrong's Wrong. And sometimes you have tell someone, "You were wrong."

He [the boss] said that he understood I was always the peacemaker, always the diplomat. So when he saw me in that office, he said, "What have I done to bring this on?" But he wouldn't have thought that if I had been in his office every day complaining about things.

(Scott Wardell) Were you regularly thinking of retirement at this point?

(Ed) Linda [Ed's wife] was focused on retirement. I was too busy. I was still traveling a lot. She was the one who would say "We need to sit down and talk about this stuff."

People tell me I've had good luck. But it wasn't just luck. I've had a wonderful life. A lot of it was just being in the right place at the right time and recognizing it. I think a lot of people are in the right place at the right time, but they're distracted and they don't make good decisions.

///

Ed and Linda largely avoided a very common mistake made by people who are doing well in their careers. They did not add on layers of new expenses simply because they could. Possibly because he was a

265

good salesman, Ed knew that someone telling you that you can afford something is no reason to buy it.

Conversely, when things are going badly, people often compound financial disaster by doing things that are very hard to fix. For example, I've had clients who out of fear sold off their growth stock when the market was very low (2008) in exchange for safe, fixed investments, hence, locking in their losses. That sort thing is very hard to recover from. In a down or depressed market, selling low might be a sign of desperation.

(Scott Wardell) In addition to Linda, I remember you telling me about one boss who required the staff to make a conscious on-paper list of goals, both professional and personal.

(Ed) Yes. He was a far-sighted guy. I put down that my first goal was to do my job, whatever my job was in the corporation to the best of my ability, and not be focused on the next job until I got it. Personally, I wrote that I wanted to get back to my roots. I wanted to do my genealogy, and take the family to Italy. That may have been in the wrong order. But the last one I wrote was, "To ultimately be sitting at the desk where you're sitting, asking the salesmen to be writing down their goals and objectives."

The boss looked at me and said, "You want my job?"

"Yes, at the proper time." And he was the man who ultimately promoted me to vice president when he retired.

(Scott Wardell) When you were promoted to Vice-President, you were in your mid- Fifties. You had this advisor with [your investment firm] What was he telling you to do with the extra cash from your promotion?

(Ed) He had advice, but I didn't really follow it. Having married later than others, and having my career bloom later in life, it came right at a time when we had major expenses. Three daughters, orthodontic expenses, which weren't covered at that time, college and weddings. A lot of money was coming in. But boy was it going out. I remember Linda and I talking, "When this is all over, we've really got to start saving."

(Scott Wardell) Did you have any serious debt concerns, with all that money going out?

(Ed) We did not. We did not run up credit cards. That's one thing we never did. We managed to live within our means. If that meant staying home on Saturday night and having candlelight hamburgers instead of going out for steaks, we did that. Our expenses were focused on family. We were both that way. We never lived beyond our means. And we never thought of it as a sacrifice.

Like many Americans in the later years of their careers, internal company pressures threatened Ed and Linda's life plan by pushing him out the door before he was ready to leave. Fortunately, the Delmoros were in a situation that few others find themselves in today.

(Scott Wardell) A few years after your promotion to VP another push came to dump older executives like yourself. That had to have been unsettling.

(Ed) It was. But I was in a position, where even though the economy had changed, I knew that I could retire early and get full retirement without any discounts. Also because of the railroad retirement, my wife would get a pension, too. Linda could also get full retirement at age sixty. So I knew that we were going to be fine. But yes, they were trying to throw me out of there along with a lot of older executives.

The short story is that Ed stood his ground as the railroad's new owners did everything they could to marginalize him, stripping him of responsibilities, benefits, and perks. He fought back. Eventually all the salary and benefits were reinstated, (in no small part due to the sway of his long-time customers), at which point Ed promptly retired ... and, does it get any better? He was hired back as a consultant, for four more years.

(Scott Wardell) You've told me that Linda and you would trade off basic family money management chores.

(Ed) We would take turns. I would take a year of paying all the bills, then I'd hand them over to her for the next year. Because I was nine years older, I was afraid that if I did all that stuff, the day would come when I'd be gone and she wouldn't know what hit her. When someone else is actually physically paying the bills, you just don't pay attention. So we would alternate, and we had dialogue going.

When we moved here and bought this house, the rate was 18% for mortgages. But we were able to find this house at 8 1/2%. To get it we had to come up with about $60,000 cash. We assumed an FHA loan and did everything but rob the girls' piggy banks. One thing we did do was borrow on life insurance policies. That was the lowest interest at the time, 4.5% I think.

///

The one lesson I try to teach people coming out of The Great Recession is that the Crash of 2008 demonstrated the value of having some place to draw money in case every other source was drying up. For many, life insurance was the place to go.

It can make sense to borrow from life insurance when all other cash reserves are used up. But be careful here: Drawing from life insurance cash value may end up harming the death benefit and the growth of the cash value. But at least it is an option.

And, it won't hurt you as badly long-term. A better plan, obviously, is a traditional cash reserve.

In the late seventies, with interest rates at 18%, a 4.5% rate from his insurance policy was without question the better move. But you must ask yourself, if you're borrowing from insurance, "What am I giving up to get this money?" The answer is, "Quite a lot", in terms of security later in life. Most policies reduce the amount of the death benefit of the loan when borrowed against. As a result, beneficiaries will receive less.

Therefore ... if you have an income stream to repay yourself, you have to get very tough with yourself and repay the life insurance loan.

(Scott Wardell) Did the two of you agree on the life insurance repayment plan?

(Ed) I remember one day I came home and Linda had these policies on the table. She said, "We're in a position to start paying on these, and I think we should do it." She was the one who orchestrated the plan, and we did. It wasn't easy.

But we didn't like debt. We paid the policies back, and we (also) paid the house off.

(Scott Wardell) You also described a situation where you had insurance all over the place. Policies of all sorts.

(Ed) Yes. I had a big insurance policy through the railroad. But then but I had other policies I bought on my own. I always believed in insurance. Most of the people in my family didn't. As a boy I'd see an uncle die, and the others would murmur, "Well, he didn't have insurance." So at nineteen I bought a Penn Mutual policy. I still have it today.

(Scott Wardell) What kind of nineteen-year-old buys a life insurance policy?

(Ed) I'm very orderly. Look around my house. I think your life has to be in order. And I think I was born with an old soul. I've always been aware that there's an end to everything. Someday I'm going to die, and someone's going to have to bury me, and until then this policy will earn money. It's another way of investing. The Penn Mutual was a $3000 policy. That was a lot of money when I was nineteen. The average income in the US that year was $4000. So it was almost a full year's salary.

(Scott Wardell) When you finally retired tell us what you did with the life insurance policies?

(Ed) We looked at a couple of them and decided we really didn't need all of them anymore. We decided if either one of us dies, the other one is going to be okay. There were a couple policies that had [policy dividends], where if we quit paying the premiums, the policy paid the premiums and it kept growing. We kept those. Linda had one big one and there were two of mine. The others we just cashed in.

//

A core concept about life insurance is this: Most people should have a base insurance protection for the majority of their lives. This base includes covering the mortgage. If something happens, you want that paid off. Then there is your spouse, the kids (education), and anything you choose to leave as a legacy.

Remember when you're buying insurance, the main purpose is to avoid risk, so be very careful about any risks that you take on within the policy. Some policies have interest rate risk, some policies have market risk—make sure you understand what kind of risk is inside your policy.

Basically, *understand the reasons for what you are buying*, and the consequences of putting investment risk inside your life insurance's cash value. A life insurance and planning professional can help you understand where you and your family are at risk in the event of a death or a disability. Most financial professionals offer a free consultation to help you evaluate these risks. I encourage people to take advantage of that service.

Company pension plans require making an election on the pension payout.

If Ed had taken the first option available to him from his company, there would be no reduction to the spousal benefit regardless of who dies first. In the second option available to Ed, the employee gets a higher payout and the spouse gets nothing in the event that the employee dies first. In his last available option, Ed's wife would receive 50% of the benefit, which would mean a greater dollar amount paid to Ed than if he'd elected 100% to Linda. This last option becomes relevant to Ed's story, because Linda was adamant that Ed was going to outlive her.

\\

(Ed) Looking at the numbers [of longevity in the family], that was likely. My aunts and uncles all lived a long time. She said, "You'd better keep some of it, so if it's you who survives, you'll be okay." So C was the option we went with.

My thinking here is pretty simple. Don't try to be your own actuary. Are you really going to guess on which of you is going to live longer? I mean, think about it. In Ed's case, all of his relatives lasted into their nineties, so he was playing amateur underwriter. Granted, the way it played out, he was right. But you don't want to gamble with this.

Yes, he is doing his math. He's saying, "I've got great longevity in my family. Yours, eh, not so much. And, I'm already ten years older than you are. So this is how I think it's going to work out." The key word is, "think." It is somewhat logical and not at all scientific.

All the things that Ed and Linda talked about were the right things. That kind of conversation they were having about age and longevity should be used not just about pension payouts, but also as a conversation about Social Security payouts.

If all things are equal (age of the spouses), if both spouses are in good health, which they were when Ed was making this decision, you probably want to defer to a cash flow analysis, making certain that even with some reduction in expenses for the survivor, there's enough income to support the surviving spouse's lifestyle.

(Scott Wardell) And when did you buy long-term care insurance?

(Ed) Not until I was sixty-eight. A young man came to the door, actually. He sat down and went through it all. But he said, "You know at sixty-eight, unless you're in excellent health, you're going to pay very high premiums."

I said, "I am in excellent health."

"But," he said, "they look at everything, prescriptions–" and I told him, "I don't have any prescriptions, or past surgeries."

He got more and more interested, and of course Linda was nine years younger, in excellent health. So after we went for our physicals, he called and said, "I cannot believe it! You just passed everything and I have people way *way* younger than you that can't even qualify."

So, buying at 68, I paid about $3,000 a year [to cover both Ed and Linda].

///

Here's the thing. Most people and their agents approach long-term care as an "all or nothing" proposition: Either you buy it, with hefty premiums, or you don't. And, I hate to break it to you, but in most cases that doesn't work. Too many people look at the price and cash flow and decide not to get the coverage.

I'll say it again. The main considerations for long-term care insurance are the following:

1. To provide for your spouse financially if you need expensive care.
2. To protect at least some of your retirement assets for your heirs.
3. To provide respite for a caregiver.

Not to overuse the jargon, but here is how you "straddle" the risk, how you mitigate the "all or nothing" factor: While you are in your early fifties, consider taking out a small policy that covers perhaps one half to one third of the regional monthly costs of skilled nursing home care. This has the advantage of setting you up with lower premiums while you are young and healthy for that portion of coverage.

Then, a few years later, add another layer that adds substantially more coverage a month. If you are still healthy, you've saved a nice chunk of cash in additional premiums for the period you waited to get the additional coverage.

All of this strategy depends on how much of a long-term care cost you could pay out of pocket. Many people can be self-insured while others are self-insured out of wishful thinking only. They believe that their health will never fail, or only fail too suddenly to require a nursing home. Remember that the majority of claims today are for home health care, not for nursing home care.

\\

(Scott Wardell) What were you thinking when you finally bought long-term care insurance at age sixty-eight?

(Ed) It really was because of me being nine years older than Linda and seeing people my age suddenly having strokes and their spouse becoming a full-time caretaker. I saw people who had to sell their homes and move into facilities.

I thought, "I do *not* want Linda going through that." I wanted a safety net that promised, if she has to go through [being a caregiver] she doesn't have to deplete our nest egg taking care of me. I got it mainly for her [financial protection]. But we were both insured.

///

Ed and Linda had the long-term care policy for four years before Linda fell ill.

\\\

(Scott Wardell) What were the early symptoms of Linda's illness?

(Ed) Her legs were weak. We went to the podiatrist and they said it looked like rheumatism. Others said arthritis. But I was reading stuff on the Internet and I think I made a diagnosis before they did. I thought, "Oh my God, this looks like ALS." I didn't say it to her, but in my heart of hearts I was sick. In everything that unfolded, I was seeing it.

Finally, with no clear diagnosis, we went to [the Mayo Clinic]. I think the [long term care] premium came due, and I thought, this is what I have this policy for. So I called [the insurance company], and they said, "Why on earth did you wait so long?" They made the claim retroactive for three months. You can't go further back than that (on this particular plan).

///

Ed had been retired ten years at this point. Linda got sick in 2005 and died in 2007.

\\\

(Ed) At that point I had to be very careful with my thinking. I knew I was seeing her through to the end of her life. That's a weight on anyone's mind. But I had to also make sure that I wasn't suggesting to her, or myself really, that her dying would also be the end of my life. But I had to tell myself that it was going to be the end of my life as I knew it.

Along the way, I had a revelation. Life is like a book. When I got my first job, that was a new chapter. Different things are new chapters. When you get married, that is a new chapter. So I thought, "This, Linda's passing, is a chapter of life." I see it all around me. I see it in the obituary pages every day. But you don't relate to it until you're in it.

I remember thinking about this on our anniversary. I didn't know what to write on the card I bought her. So I wrote, "I love you, Linda," then, in parentheses, "Until death do we part." I thought that said more than I could say in any other way. She read it and said, "I am lucky to have you to take care of me." I told her how lucky I was, knowing that the same was waiting for me if I were first.

We had those two years. We had a pact where every day was going to be the best day that it could be. Some days she could get up and felt good. I could help her get ready, and go out and about. Other days it was just home in the family room, with the fire and I'd bring dinner in on a tray and we'd sit together on the couch and get a movie.

(Scott Wardell) The two of you talked openly about death, isn't that right?

(Ed) Yes. I remember her telling me, weeks before the doctors decided it was ALS, "I'm dying." I didn't know what to say. "Are you afraid?," I asked. And she said, "No, I'm not afraid." I told her that's the most important thing. Because I knew her faith, I said, "I'm not afraid either."

Did I like it? No. Do I wish it would be different? Yes. But death is something you can't change.

(Scott Wardell) What were your and Linda's plans for retirement?

(Ed) When I retired, we had a talk about what we were really going to do. Linda was still working at [a department store]. I said, "You know what, I know you love working. But I'm retired, and now is the time when we should be traveling and doing things. We're both in good health."

I remember she looked at me and said, "I can be out of there in a minute."

She had her ten years in at the store, which locked in her retirement. It wasn't a lot. But something. So she quit, and we just had a great time. If we wanted to go to Europe, we just got on the phone, found out when the best tickets were and went. We were free to do what we wanted. We didn't have money concerns. Life was beautiful. And luckily, because I retired early and she retired early, we had ten wonderful years of retirement. Together.

//

If death is imminent, avoid making these two mistakes.

1. **Not talking about it. With all the emotions in the air, it is very important to get the whole family involved in what has been planned–and written down.**

2. **Not knowing if the financial plan can be "managed" by the surviving spouse. Think of your investments like a car, if you need to. "Would I leave my wife with a straight stick if she can only drive an automatic?" Some spouses spend years trying to sort out their spouse's financial "plan." Linda's passing meant that Ed, healthy and gregarious, with a heritage of longevity in his family, had to begin reassessing how he was going to spend the years that stretched ahead.**

\\\

(Ed) You have to [get out]. I'd seen other people become so reclusive. This house was like a cocoon. It was very safe here. Everything was familiar, and I thought I cannot just stay in this house. I have got to get out.

(Scott Wardell) Linda and you lived in this town for thirty years, yet you told me once that it was only after she passed away that you really threw yourself into civic activities.

(Ed) When I retired, I thought, "We've lived here all these years and I still feel like a stranger." But I hadn't really begun doing any volunteer work.

(Scott Wardell) And now you're the Christmas light man! [Ed organized a large community campaign to dress up his suburban downtown with elaborate holiday lighting.] What were the strongest feelings as you began a new chapter of your life without Linda?

(Ed) Well, you feel like a displaced person. You're not sure of what you're supposed to be doing, and you have a lot of people judging you. Oh my God, the things you hear through the grapevine. Somebody didn't think I cried enough at the funeral. They didn't know that I spent two years behind the scenes crying. Nobody saw that. It's heartbreaking. It's like taking a beautiful blooming plant and just watching it atrophy. And there's not a thing you can do.

But I thought, "Okay, I've always been strong, and I've always known who I am. And I'm going to be who I am, and if somebody else doesn't like it, that's tough." I remember one night deciding that I was going to the Chianti Grill and having dinner. Linda and I loved the Chianti Grill. We met all our friends there.

I thought I was probably going to have to hold my breath when I went in. But I was fine. Everybody else was a mess! They were wiping their eyes. People I knew asked if they could sit with me. They slid into the booth and it became a great evening. It was awkward for me. I felt so conspicuous. But when I got home I thought, "That was the right thing to do." It was like breaking a barrier to go back to that place.

You know how it goes. If you throw yourself into something, the *more* involved you get. The result being that when Linda got sick and ultimately died, I could not believe the outpouring of the people here. That was when this really became my home, not Ohio.

(Ed) You have to get out there. You have to throw yourself into it. Quit worrying if the water's going to be cold. Just jump in. Once you're in, you'll be fine.

I wish retirement were a different word. But I decided to think of retirement as commencement. Like I was graduating from the work force. That meant I was done there, but I had all these new opportunities in front of me. I couldn't stand the mentality where retirement is a rocking chair.

I didn't want to act or look the stereotype of retirement. I did not want to be wearing my twenty-year-old suits that were outdated and maybe frayed. I want to keep step with the times.

A lot of it, like sales, is how you present yourself. It's important to feel good about yourself! When you do, you're perceived differently. People regard you differently if you look contemporary instead of frumpy. It doesn't have to be a Brooks Brothers jacket, but keep yourself looking like you're part of the modern world.

Not like something that stepped out of a time warp.

Summary

Long-term care insurance is a key here, as in other chapters. Ed decided he wanted to transfer that risk – that high likelihood and extraordinarily high cost – to an insurance policy. He was well set up to pay such costs out of pocket, but he did his homework and opted to protect his assets with the policy.

The number of people I hear say, "long-term care insurance is too expensive" is troubling.

I ask them, "How much do you think it will cost?" At that point I find that they have no idea and haven't considered the full reality facing either of them should one or both of them need care full or part-time. Even home care for one spouse can be expensive.

Plus, when I ask them to guess at the annual premiums, they often say something like, "$6000 a year," when they might be able to get a good policy for substantially less than that if they're around 62 and much less if they're still in their fifties.

Frankly, there is some crazy, emotional stuff attached to the idea of long-term care. Approximately 71% of the claims start with home health care[1]. Men are particularly bad in this regard. They tell me, "I'm never going to a nursing home" and that "If I get that bad, I've already arranged for my brother to take me out behind the barn and shoot me."

That's funny, but ridiculous. All they're doing is compartmentalizing the inevitable in a place where they don't have to deal with it.

Ed was the exact opposite. He was very much a guy who took care of his family ... his whole life. When it came to the likelihood of disability, he didn't let the stupid, macho stuff get in the way. He realized instead that long-term care insurance was yet another way that he had to take care of his family.

His three daughters cared for their mother as well as anyone could ask. But Ed's planning meant that neither he nor they had to turn their lives completely upside down caring for Linda, something she would have hated.

All that said, I concede the insurance industry's approach to long-term care is complicated. Agents often try to sell you a big policy as though you need all of it now. A different strategy may be worth considering. As I've said several times; buy according to your needs and your cash flow. A basic plan will generally not break your bank through your fifties. Once into your sixties analyze it again and see if it's possible to add another layer.

Your financial advisor might have a selection of companies to look at. Some are better if you're healthy as a horse. Others are better if you've got pre-existing conditions. You need to be a discerning shopper.

Likewise, an advisor will be able to tell you which companies have a bad habit of constantly raising rates and which almost never do. You can try to do this on your own, researching the rate-increase history of a company, but it is confounding, believe me. Point being, if your advisor is any good, your advisor should know.

For Ed, the long-term care facet of his story meant many significant changes in the care provided to Linda. One key difference was their ability to ad an elevator to get Linda up to the second floor.

Likewise it meant the difference between regular professional physical therapy and Ed trying to provide that same therapy and risking, as I've seen far too often, a healthy spouse getting worn down and sick themselves, not to mention involving the children and greatly disrupting the quality of their lives. Without long-term care, the stress compounds through the family.

If full care 24/7 is required, the costs may be in excess of $90,000 per year[2].

Questions to Consider:

1. Does your spouse have as complete an understanding of your finances as you do? Why not?

2. If you are resisting buying long-term care insurance, what exactly is your plan for paying for the worst case scenario of 24/7 in-home care?

3. The window of robust good health after retirement could be short. How have you planned to make the most of those years? What exactly do you want to do?

Notes

1. American Association for Long-Term Care Insurance, "Long-Term Care," AALTCI

2. See Thrivent.com for state by state averages. Figure shown is for Minnesota.

Epilogue

A Conversation with Doug Lennick

I'm a big believer in trusted sounding boards, in another set of eyes and ears on ideas that seem logical. Doug Lennick, president of the Lennick Aberman Group, now known as Think2Perform, is a former colleague of mine, an author in his own right and a much respected voice on the confluence of finances and human nature. Doug knows the emotional competence it takes to make good financial decisions.

As an epilogue to this book on middle-class retirement planning, Doug was gracious enough to sit down for a chat on some of the significant factors affecting successful financial planning.

(Scott Wardell) Doug, what's your attitude toward a so-called "average American," someone whose expertise is not in the financial industry, wading into the stock market today? I have clients who think they can navigate their way through all the programs, products, hype and research that's out there. It's more than a full-time job for me, and it's what I do for a living.

(Doug Lennick) Well, I can tell you my point of view, and that is that few people are well-advised to go it on their own. It is not easy to do. And there are a bunch of reasons that's so.

One is that it is not easy to reduce the impact of your own emotions on decision-making. Some people don't fully appreciate the role emotions play. A lot of it is literally a function of how the brain is wired. People often misunderstand that. The brain is wired to *survive*. It's wonderful in many ways. We are designed to make it through another day. We're wired with this instinct for survival.

But survival instincts are triggered by emotions we experience in reaction to external stimulus, like crisis and opportunity. You and I have talked before about emotional intelligence. Well, one of the things I always say about emotional intelligence is that it is real.

People often don't get what that really means. It literally means that emotions are a form of intelligence, and that they exist independent from cognitive thought. That is really hard to comprehend because we talk about emotions cognitively and rationally. So, people wonder, "How does that make sense?"

But emotions truly are independent of cognitive thought, by which I mean memory, association, pattern recognition, problem solving and other processes we are consciously aware of. Nevertheless, emotions are a big form of intelligence. *But emotional intelligence sacrifices accuracy for speed.* It's a survival mechanism. It's fast, but frequently wrong.

So when it comes to money, our emotional intelligence really can't tell the difference between a bear market and a bear in the woods. You see a bear and it's like 12 milliseconds and your fear response is activated.

That's with a live bear. But in a bear *market*, you're not in immediate physical danger so your emotional intelligence won't know. So, for many people going it alone, it is very hard to recognize the situation they are in. The data shows that really smart people do dumb things with their money because irrational decision-making trumps high-IQ every time.

(Scott Wardell) The one thing I do like about people who are going it alone is that they are at least paying attention. There is this emotional factor, but on the rational, cognitive end of things how often do you meet people who aren't paying attention at all? They don't like financial planning, so if and when you sit down with them, their attitude is "whatever." But to your point about the intelligent ones, they still need a partner. Someone who says, "Wait a minute. Why are you doing this?" I know I spend maybe 20% of my time going back and undoing [financial] mistakes people have made.

(Doug Lennick) That's true. But what's also true is there is too high a percentage of advisors who spend 40% of their time helping people *make* mistakes.

(Scott Wardell) Exactly.

(Doug Lennick) One of the reasons data continues to show that *investments* work better than *investors* is that too often financial institutions and financial professionals working within those institutions actually get people to act on their emotions.

(Scott Wardell) I know what you mean.

(Doug Lennick) Most of the TV shows about money are designed to play around with people's emotions. Jim Cramer, Suze Orman and the like. So the industry historically gets people to do what's emotionally easy for them to do. But the consequence is that unlike a normal retail situation where you need a new coat, you aren't drawn to the ad that urges you to buy today because the price will fall tomorrow. You would never do that in the case of a coat or any other basic consumer stuff. But within this emotionally-driven investment industry people like buying stocks that are high-priced.

(Scott Wardell) And our systems reinforce that. Both the media and the culture at large. I know I'll sit down with a client and we'll look at their end of the year 401(k) statement, and almost as soon as I say, "Well, this one did well. It's up 30%", their reaction is, "Great. Let's buy more of that." My advice is usually to do the exact opposite, to say, "We've done well here. Let's take our profit and …"

(Doug Lennick) Rebalance …

(Scott Wardell) Right. Rebalance. But the point I'm trying to get across here is that temptation without the financial acumen to temper it is constantly saying, "That's a good fund. Let's put more in there."

(Doug Lennick) Yes. And they'll say, "Let's just guarantee ourselves a loss on these other funds that haven't done as well and pour it all in over here." And that's why if you just look at what's happened in the new millennium you can see this emotional mentality at work. Look at real estate. People loved buying real estate as late as 2006 and 2007. They were buying right into the real estate bubble. There was this belief going around, among professionals as well as investors, that there were certain cities within certain states where real estate could not go down: California. Florida. Las Vegas.

Likewise, people kept buying stocks until 2008. Then when it crashed, they bailed out looking for safer places to be. It could be cash accounts. Fixed annuities were pretty popular.

But your reader I think needs to be really aware of what they need from their advisor. We're well advised to need advisors, but the key characteristic we need to be looking for in advisors is trustworthiness. And, this is important, "trusted" and "trustworthy" *are not synonyms.*

The financial industry is littered with stories of people who were "trusted" but not "trustworthy". The most iconic name being Bernie Madoff.

(Scott Wardell) One of the best questions for consumers, Doug, is "How do you vet advisors before choosing one?" As you're suggesting, back in 2006-2007 a large percentage of advisors were still telling clients to buy into real estate.

(Doug Lennick) Well, as you know, I wrote a book called, "Financial Intelligence," and one of the chapters was, "Calling in the Experts." A question asked in this research effort that my company helped coordinate was, "What are the competencies of an advisor that result in a superior portfolio return and experience for a client?" And by a factor of 2 to 1 the most important factor was "integrity."

But the question of exploring another person's integrity has a lot to do with someone's interviewing skills.

I encourage people to get an advisor, but to regard that advisor as a candidate to be the chief financial officer to their household, and the client to think of themselves as the CEO. In that way *you* should design your interview of [your advisor], and your background check of [your advisor] and all the other things you would do in terms of due diligence as though you were hiring a CFO. The goal being to assess just how much integrity [the advisor has] and [is the advisor] really client service-oriented?

(Scott Wardell) You have sample questions in that chapter, that clients should ask, if I remember.

(Doug Lennick) Yes, we do. Of course, people can lie. But if you are relatively astute, you'll have a sense of authenticity when they speak. For example, ask your potential advisor, "What kind of rate of return can I expect if I work with you?" Listen to what they say.

(Scott Wardell) And of course the BS number is ... any number (he laughs).

(Doug Lennick) Right. The *only* answer is, "It depends."

(Scott Wardell) Yeah. If they start promising you specifics and pulling out this client who has done well and this client who's had great returns, you should think about running for the door.

It's interesting, Doug, because we have a chapter in the book where a couple's experience with a "trusted advisor" really went south. Because of that and others I've come across, my thinking has changed. I used to tell people, "Pick an advisor and stick with him or her," only because of the complexities of having two advisors. But now I'm at a different spot on this.

It is so hard for an individual to know the questions to ask, but I believe now more than ever in the old adage, "Trust, but verify."

(Doug Lennick) But you can find out the questions.

(Scott Wardell) That's true.

(Doug Lennick) You have to look to the competencies that will matter. One of which we know is "teamwork." So, when you're talking to someone you're thinking of hiring to be your advisor ask them, "How effective are you at working with other professionals?" And if that person says, "I prefer to work alone," you know you need someone else.

The reality is, it's a team thing that produces the best results. So since we know that teamwork works, we also know that not being a team player works less well.

If you're a Lone Ranger, I don't want to work with you. I want to know that if I bring in my accountant, or my lawyer, that you'll be able to work with them on my behalf. Conversely, the client has a responsibility that if he has these different professionals, or another advisor working, that they all have information to the total picture of your affairs, otherwise they're all playing with half a deck.

Even if both advisors are working with separate accounts, it's important for each to know how the other is handling that portion of your portfolio, because an advisor will make much different decisions if he believes he's handling all of your assets, or has no idea how the rest is being managed.

(Scott Wardell) Yes, it comes out much differently.

(Doug Lennick) Much differently. As you know, I believe in what I call The Smart Money Philosophy, which basically says, "If I prepare for the truth, and the truth is uncertainty, I accept that I don't know how long I'll live, how good my health will be, what the price of oil will hit." I just don't know. And this is another sign of integrity. If you ask somebody, "What's going to happen?" and they say to you, "I can give you an educated guess," that's great. But if they say to you, "This is what's going to happen," walk out the door. Because they don't know.

So whenever some financial person says to me, "Let me tell you what's going to happen with the stock market", I stop them and say, "Before you give me that information, which I'm sure will be very useful, I have another more important question. Namely, 'When will I die?'"

(Scott Wardell) While we're at this, there is the matter of a client doing reference checks on advisors.

(Doug Lennick) Yes, absolutely. And it's actually easier now than it has ever been. You can start by just Googling someone (FINRA). There are stories of "trusted" advisors who, if you go on-line, you can find there are 12 complaints against them.

At the very least, by doing a reference check, you are increasing your odds of picking a "trust-worthy" advisor. And be candid about yourself. Ask this advisor how they handle a difficult client, which you might be if you get upset about something. Then find out from his references how he or she has performed in those situations.

(Scott Wardell) Self-awareness on the part of both the client and advisor is really an ideal situation. Be candid about what you do and don't know and how stubborn or impatient you can be.

(Doug Lennick) It's pretty near impossible for any one person to be good at everything – retirement planning, accumulation planning, education planning and so on – which is why teamwork is important. So if someone says they've got it all, there might be an integrity problem in there.

(Scott Wardell) What has been your experience, Doug, in getting clients to set realistic goals?

(Doug Lennick) I haven't found it difficult to get people to answer questions about goals. They may not have thought about it much...

(Scott Wardell) ... and do you agree that goal-setting something they should expect from an advisor?

(Doug Lennick) Oh, absolutely. "What do you want to accomplish?" is fundamental. And I'm kind of a believer in "why," "what" and "how?" And until the answer to the question "why" is compelling, the answers to the questions "what" and "how" don't matter much.

This is where values conversations come into play. You have to start thinking about "why". Often it's as simple as "I'm the primary income provider for my family. I love them, so I want to take care of them." So, OK, that's a good reason "why."

I think you've found what we've found, Scott, which is that values conversations are more powerful than goals conversations. For example, someone who values health is more likely to achieve weight loss goals than someone who simply wants to lose weight.

The value is almost always more powerful. We also know from studying how the brain works that if we stop to reflect on our values and their goals, the process of reflecting engages the cognitive part of the brain. Someone who reflects on their values will improve access to their ability to make a rational decision.

That's why I say to people, "There's nothing I can do to raise your IQ. But there's a lot I can do to raise access to the IQ you have."

The opportunity isn't to get smarter. The opportunity is to get more rational with the level of smarts you have.

(Scott Wardell) And most people have plenty of smarts to do well by themselves.

(Doug Lennick) That's right. It's not an IQ issue. It's a question of accessing IQ in the context of stress and competing difficult emotions. That's why otherwise smart people do stupid things. It's not because they aren't smart, but rather because under pressure their emotions obstruct access to their rational intelligence and they make mistakes.

Most people confuse themselves. They think they're self-aware because they look *back* at their behavior and become aware of what they did. The real opportunity is to be aware *in the moment.*

That's why the consumer needs an advisor who can help them do that, help them access the intelligence they have and not allow emotion to block access to their intelligence and what they know they should do.

(Scott Wardell) We are, as you say Doug, so wired to do the same thing again and again and again, that getting people to change something that is important to them is a very difficult thing to do.

So many problems revolve around the classic American thinking that, "I can get whatever I can finance" as opposed to "I can buy whatever I can cash flow." Getting people off the path of thinking they can afford whatever they can finance is not easy.

It gets tougher when people believe they are doing this for the good of their family, or at least their children. Often it is a matter of people giving their children things the children would be so much better off paying for themselves, in the context of developing personal responsibility.

(Doug Lennick) And when you talk about today's world, the responsible choice we – parents, adults – probably should be making is to work longer. We're not born with the birthright to be able to retire. Although it's wonderful we're experiencing longer life expectancies, that wasn't the case when Social Security was created in 1935.

At that time, a large portion of the people who paid in never received Social Security benefits, because they died before reaching 65. And those that did receive benefits lived only a few years longer. Today we're looking at a very large number of people who may live in retirement longer than they worked and paid into the system.

My own parents are a good example. When we moved to Minnesota in 1967 my dad was making something like $350 a month. Mom made maybe another $150. We were fine. We had a house and a car and regular meals. But when dad retired in the early '90s he would complain to me that it wasn't fair he was only getting $1600 a month in Social Security benefits.

Dad was kind of a staunch Republican and I'd kid him that he sure seemed to like this socialist system he was getting money from. He'd say, "What!? What!?" And I'd explain that he was getting money from me and everyone who was still working.

But my point is that people have to learn to be responsible. You mentioned before we started here that one of your stories is about a couple that learned to be frugal, and they are living a fine life. Well, I think people have to learn that they might have to work longer than they originally thought and that they may not retire in the classic sense. Instead they may find that while they may stop doing the work of their career, they may need to continue doing some other kind of work to bring in additional income.

Point being, being "responsible" doesn't mean everybody gets to retire without ever doing any kind of work again and doing whatever they want. That just might not be true, and the sooner people face that the sooner they'll accept that they may have to finance part of their own retirement.

I used to think of financial independence as having enough money to do what I want. But now I define it as having enough not to need government assistance, family hand-outs, or charity. That may or may not mean I have enough money not to work.

(Scott Wardell) Let me ask you this, Doug. Human nature being what it is, have you detected any significant change in your clients' thinking since the '08 crash, and, more importantly, how long do you think it'll be before all that is forgotten and the cycle repeats itself?

(Doug Lennick) There's been a huge shift. I think we've created a new generation that will resemble the generation created by the Great Depression. My dad was still saving $200 a month when he died at age 85, because he never got over the fear that he might lose everything.

But after dad's generation, we got the wish everyone wanted; the children got "more" and they got "better." It's like the couple you were talking about who took on so much debt to give their children everything they wanted. It produces the double-whammy of depleting the parents' resources and never giving the children enough responsibility to gain a financial sensibility of their own. The result is they always need their parents to "do" for them.

I think we'll see a permanent change among a certain segment of the population, that being those who will always be thinking, "That can happen again."

(Scott Wardell) Have you identified the demographic this applies to most?

(Doug Lennick) I think the younger they are the more permanent it'll be. Their brains will get wired by the experience. Most of what people do is because of what they did. You mentioned something like this earlier. We have cognitive and emotional habits, so the earlier you establish these habits the better off. People who develop savings habits when they're young will be better off.

Many people at the first sign of light (of a full recovery) will go back to their old behavior. But there are going to be those who will not trust the permanency of the light and instead will say, "I'm going to continue saving money."

We went through a 25-year period in the United States where the savings rate was negative. It turned positive with the '08 financial crisis. Currently it's about 4.5%.

This was a balance sheet-driven recession, driven by excessive borrowing on the part of the private sector. That bubble kept blowing up until it burst. That experience has influenced consumers to think, "We've got to start retiring debt and saving money."

We now of course have a situation where the private sector has paid down debt and the government is increasing its borrowing.

Was there an alternative to the stimulus borrowing? I don't know. I really don't know. I just wonder if at some point you have to accept some of the pain.

(Scott Wardell) And if the point of all this research and testing and planning is to end the "pursuit" of happiness and actually achieve it, how are Americans doing in that regard?

(Doug Lennick) Well, there all sorts of studies, but one I saw recently and struck me as credible said that as a culture the United States, with 310 million people or whatever it is now, was the 35th happiest country on the planet.

The happiest were Denmark, Singapore and a province of Mexico with a unique ethnic makeup. What this guy did was then ask, "What do these places have in common that lead to these high levels of happiness?" He found a handful of characteristics.

One was "values-based living." The second of which, relative to money, was "sufficiency." Which meant that the people had enough, but not excess. In the United States that sufficiency number comes to about $70,000 a year for a family of four, and families at that level were happier than billionaires.

(Scott Wardell) And I think the level of happiness then more or less stabilized to about $120,000 before actually declining.

(Doug Lennick) Right. So it isn't about the money. It's about sufficiency. But the biggest factor that blew the United States out of the happiness index was, "trust." The levels of trust are so low. In institutions, government, people, friends and so on.

(Scott Wardell) What do you attribute that to?

(Doug Lennick) I attribute that to people earning mistrust. (He laughs.) If people screw you enough you don't trust them after a while. Look at the financial services industry, and the crash of 2008. The Financial Crisis Inquiry Report, which was published in 2011 basically concluded, and I thought this was hilarious, that, "the financial crisis turns out not to be an act of Mother Nature, but rather real people making mistakes".

The point was no one took responsibility. The government said it wasn't responsible for writing the laws that permitted all this stuff. The lenders said they weren't responsible for giving people without decent credit all the money they wanted. The borrowers said they weren't responsible for borrowing more than they could pay back and the financial services companies that packaged all this stuff into derivatives that they said later they couldn't even define, said they weren't responsible.

My point is that the recent years are littered with people who gained "trust" without being "trustworthy." Too many people in the industry are looking for the opportunity to be "trusted", instead of earning the right to be called "trustworthy."

(Scott Wardell) And that requires doing the right thing for clients, first.

(Doug Lennick) Yes. That's proactivity. That's required in this new world after the crash. You have to do the right thing *pro*actively as opposed to *re*actively. I think a lot of financial advisors are reactively trustworthy but not proactively. They respond well after a problem is brought to them, but they're not as good as they should be at diagnosing a problem and resolving it before they're told there's a problem.

(Scott Wardell) It might help of course if our industry loosened up the jargon a little, wouldn't it? I mean, you hear "securitized" bandied about as though that makes your investment safer, when in fact, as we've seen, it makes it riskier.

(Doug Lennick) Yes. I like what you say in the book about "trust, but verify." It's okay to start out with a little trust [in your advisor], but check it out.

(Scott Wardell) For example, I doubt most people understand what a "fee-based advisor" actually means.

(Doug Lennick) That's very true. I read some research recently that "fee-based" is one of the more off-putting terms. And the reason is that fees aren't associated with advice anymore, they're now associated with assets. So "fee-based" and "advice-based" are not synonymous.

What you the client want is an "advice-based fee" as

opposed to "fee-based advice." And that is significantly different. "Fee-based advice" is fees attached to assets. So the more assets you give me, the bigger the fee I get, and I'll give you advice along the way. But the term "fee-based" is used more by the people who charge for the assets (management).

The reverse, "advice-based fee," is straightforward. The advisor doesn't care how many assets you have, he simply says, "If you want my advice, this is what it'll cost."

(Scott Wardell) I've always thought one of the most important tasks of advisors was making themselves and the plan completely understandable to the client.

(Doug Lennick) I couldn't agree more.

Doug Lennick's "10 Questions to Ask a Financial Advisor Candidate"

1. What are your most important values? (This can provide information on an advisor's general orientation to values. Beware of an advisor who hems and haws when you ask this question. An advisor who is in touch with his or her own values is also more likely to act in ways that support your values.)

2. What is the one thing your clients say most often about you? (Best responses are: "Honest," "Trustworthy," "Keep my promises," and "Do what's best for them in the long term." All of those speak to integrity.)

3. Can you tell me about a time when a client wanted to make a financial decision that you didn't think was in their best interest? (This can provide information on an advisor's integrity. That is, is he or she willing to stick up for his or her principles even if it may cause conflict or result in loss of business?)

4. Can you tell me about a situation in which you made a mistake dealing with a client? How did you handle that? (This can provide information about an advisor's integrity. For example, was he or she willing to admit the mistake

to the client? Also look for non-verbal behavior, such as squirming or looking away, which could indicate that you are not getting a truthful story.)

5. Tell me about your working relationship with your most difficult client. What do you do that's different from how you act in your relationship with your favorite client? (This can provide information about client service orientation. For example, the ability to provide good service even when clients are difficult, and doing what's best regardless of personal feelings.)

6. What services do you provide that I might not expect from another advisor? (This also can provide information on client service orientation.)

7. How do you make sure that your clients always know where they stand relative to their financial and life goals? (This can provide information about an advisor's concern for quality and order, especially if the advisor seems animated and provides examples of his or her personal involvement in providing information, rather than speaking only about what the firm does.)

8. Can you tell me about a situation where you worked with another professional inside or outside the company to meet your client's needs? Who did you work with and what was your relationship with him or her like? (This can provide information on the advisor's teamwork. How easy it is it for the advisor to recall such a situation, and how involved did he or she seem to be?)

9. How have you personally responded to market volatility, and how have you communicated your thoughts and feelings about market volatility to your clients? (This can provide information on an advisor's self confidence. A good advisor will have emotions like everyone else, but will express confidence in his or her ability to help you prepare for life eventualities.)

10. What kind of return can I expect if I asked you to manage my investments? (This can provide information on an advisor's integrity. No advisor can predict the future, so

beware of promises to produce a high rate of return. Also, look for responses that indicate the advisor does not think of himself or herself solely as a money manager, but also sees his or her role in helping you prepare for a variety of life events and helping you make decisions that support your values and goals.)

–From *Financial Intelligence: How to Make Smart, Values-Based Decisions About Your Money and Your Life*

Books by Doug Lennick

The Simple Genius (You) – How to Get What You Want and remain true to yourself (written by Doug Lennick and Roy Geer)

Financial Intelligence – How to Make Smart, Values-Based Decisions with Your Money and Your Life(written by Doug Lennick with Kathleen Jordan, Ph.D.)

Moral Intelligence 2.0 – Enhancing Business Performance and Leadership Success in Turbulent Times (written by Doug Lennick and Fred Kiel, Ph.D)

Moral Intelligence – Enhancing Business Performance and Leadership Success (written by Doug Lennick and Fred Kiel, Ph.D.)

CPSIA information can be obtained
at www.ICGtesting.com
Printed in the USA
FFOW01n0153010518
46402343-48171FF